A Journey through Norway

Unique places to dine and stay

Sources

Personal conversations with the hosts at 44 places.

Alsvik, Ola : *Historien om Lørenskog.* Lørenskog Kommune 1998.

Bendz, Marit : *Førde. Ein by vert født.* Kommunalteknikk 5/2000.

Berg, Carl Johan : *Hotel Continental: Familiejuvelen.* Hotell, Restaurant og Reiseliv 7/2000.

Berg, Cecilie Louise : *Smakfull suksess. Magma.* Interiør Magasinet 4/2000.

Bjaanes Hrasky, Øyunn : *Grand Hotel – en del av vår historie – i nåtid og fortid.* Velkommen til Grand Hotel.

Brekke, Nils Georg og Engevik, Anders Kåre : *Solstrand.* Solstrand 1996.

Brekke, Nils Georg, red. : *Kulturhistorisk vegbok. Hordaland.* Hordaland fylkeskommune 1993.

Brochmann, Caspar : *Mors Hus. Hotel Continental – En personlig affære gjennom 75 år.* Grøndahls Forlag AS, Oslo.

Egjar, Heidi : *Harahorn : Toppen av service.* Reise & Konferansemarkedet 6/1999.

Engen, Arnfinn : *Freda hus og gardstun i Gudbrandsdalen,* Lillehammer 1992.

Farbrot, Audun : *Continental frue.* Økonomisk Rapport 9/2000.

Fischer, Gerhard : *Utstein Kloster – Kongsgård – Kloster – Herregård.* Utstein Kloster, Stavanger 1965.

Gabrielsen, Tove : *Slik har de bodd. Røisheim.* Publikasjon ukjent 1969.

Gjestgivargarden Walaker Hotell 300 år, Solvorn 1990.

Granlund Sæther, Nina : *Holmen Gård. Norsk Husflid* 6/1996.

Harsson, Margit : *Kongevegen over Krokskogen.* Hole Historielag 1997.

Heitmann, Anne-Lise : *Solstrand Fjord Hotel.* Interiør Magasinet 2/1996.

Helstad, Joachim : *Rica Bygdøy Allé Hotel. Hotel i Særklasse.* Korka mai 2001.

Hopstock, Carsten og Tschudi Madsen, Stephan : *Rosendal Baroni og Bygning.* Universitetsforlaget, Oslo 1965.

Hosar, Kristian : *Strynefjellsvegen 100 år.* Statens vegvesen Oppland og Statens vegvesen Sogn og Fordane, Lillehammer 1994.

Huseby, Leif : *Grand Hotel – Trekk fra hotellets historie og utvikling gjennom 100 år, 1874 – 1974.*

Høydal, Hallgrim : *Ud fra den kvalme Byluft – Tuddal Høyfjellshotell 100 år.* Tuddal 1995.

Knagenhjelm, Wibeke: *Tradisjonsrike turisthotell i Sogn og Fjordane.* Oslo 1990.

Kynningsrud, Eva : *Balaklava i Fredrikstad. En kulturscene for konferanser.* Reise & Konferansemarkedet 5/1999.

Lexow, Jan Hendrich : *Utstein Kloster.* Stavanger 1995.

Melkild, Arne : *Kunstnarliv.* Skald AS, Leikanger 1993.

Midgaard Berg, Torhild : *Losby Gods. Tradisjon og skaperglede.* Interiør Magasinet 6/1999.

Riise, Arill : *Blå fjordar, blått blod.* Det Norske Samlaget, Oslo 1994.

Simonsen, Tor M. : *Lyd i leire. Historien om Sandnesgauken.* Rocon Forlag, Stavanger 1995.

Stangeland, Gro og Valebrokk, Eva : *Norge på sitt beste.* Wennergren-Cappelen/Den Norske Bokklubben.

Skiaker Mælen, Cathrine : *Hardanger Gjestegard.* Historisk særoppgave. Alsåker.

Storhaug, Hans : *Hotell i særklasse. Victoria Hotel Stavanger 1900-2000.* Victoria Hotel, Stavanger 2000.

Storaas, Reidar: *Trådar attende i tida nr. 7.* T.T.Storaas – Storaas Norheimsund A.S.

Strøm, Kari: *Holmenkollen Turisthotell.* Historisk særoppgave, Oslo 1980.

Sunde, Egil: *Småbruk ble Gjestgiveri.* Hus & Hjem, Bergens Tidende 21. mai 1999.

Sælen, Frithjof : *Kvikne's Hotel Balholm 1877 – 1977,* Bergen 1977.

Sæther, Jon Arne : *Dovrefjell nasjonalpark og Kongsvold Fjellstue.* Trondheim 1990.

Thon, Sverre : *Vertskap i Norge.* Oslo 1994

Underdal, Hans Martin og Eldal, Jens Christian: *Tradisjon og atmosfære – En reise til norske trehoteller.* Kom Forlag, Kristiansund 1996.

Vintervoll, Lene : *Jotunheimen Fjellstue. Fjellstue uten rømmegrøt.* Reise & Konferansemarkedet 5/1999.

Årbok for Gudbrandsdalen 1989.

Kom Forlag
Vågeveien 10
6509 Kristiansund N.
Norway
Telephone: 71 67 83 00
E-mail: komf@online.no
Project leader: Svein Gran

Print: T.I.Trykk, Skien, 2001
Graphic designer: Lilliputt A/S
English translation: V F Stokke – text
                     Melody Favish – recipes

ISBN Norwegian edition 82-90823-75-4
English Edition 82-90823-76-2

Our heartfelt thanks to Hadeland Glass for providing glasses and dishes.

 HADELAND GLASSVERK

A Journey through Norway

Unique places to dine and stay

Hans Martin Underdal
author

Espen Grønli
photographer

Cecilie F. Stang
stylist

Kom Forlag

Preface

"If you must sleep in a good hotel, and sit down at a table d'hôte every day, then avoid Norway!" That was the advice given by the Rev. Frederick Metcalfe in his book The Oxonian in Norway published in London in 1857.

When the first foreign tourists arrived in Norway in the last half of the 19th century, most had to spend the night on a mattress filled with straw and covered with sheepskin. The food available was little better, as Metcalfe attests. "Beyond coffee with sugar and cream, flatbrod and black bread, you can't count on any refreshment for certain."

The first tourists who came to Norway were adventurers and explorers. Full of enthusiasm, they returned home and wrote descriptive travelogues about the untamed and powerful Norwegian landscape, with its fjords, mountains, glaciers, and waterfalls. Mountain climbers, salmon fishermen and artists soon followed. They wrote fishing and climbing handbooks and painted wonderful pictures of dramatic Norwegian nature at its wildest. Norway became a popular destination for the European aristocracy and for royalty from around the world. These new tourists demanded both comfort and luxury, which fuelled frantic building. New, large, and impressive wooden hotels were constructed, and old inns and bed and breakfasts were modernized and expanded. Unfortunately, most of these places no longer exist. Many burned down, while others were demolished or simply closed. Local color and personal service had to yield to ever increasing demands for volume and profitability. The big hotel chains entered the Norwegian market about 25 years ago, and with them came hotels that could be anywhere in the world. Even though these chains are responsible for 80% of all hotel turnover in Norway, there is still an extensive selection of interesting and individual hotels with charm, soul, and atmosphere.

A journey through Norway presents 44 unique places to dine and stay the night in southern Norway, along with some of their best recipes. Historical coaching inns and fashionable beach hotels; traditional, European-style city hotels and mountain lodges. Small and intimate guest houses; well-preserved historical farms, elegant manor houses and magnificent estates. Some old and some new. Places owned and run by the same family for generations. Farms, country houses, and cultural treasures restored and converted into hotels. New hotels that seek to preserve the best of local culture and traditions.

This book is not supposed to be an overview of the best hotels in Norway. Photographer Espen Grønli, stylist Cecilie Fasmer Stang, and I have chosen to present these places because we enjoyed staying there, and because we found an ambience that was genuine and sincere. We have also paid close attention to the food. Caroline Boman Hansen, the first lady of Hotel Continental once said; "If the food is bad, it doesn't matter how good everything else is."

We adopted her motto and have spent the last year traveling around the country, eating and sleeping, trying and failing. We've been both disappointed and impressed. We were especially impressed by how many enthusiastic people there are in Norway – owners and hosts full of creativity and spirit, eager to show off their masterworks. Without these people, it would have been impossible to write this book. We owe them our heartfelt thanks.

And we welcome you to A Journey through Norway. We hope you enjoy your trip!

Øvre Årdal, July 2001
Hans Martin Underdal.

A pearl in historical surroundings
Balaklava Gjestgiveri, Old Fredrikstad

Old Fredrikstad is Northern Europe's best-preserved fortress town. Everything is intact - the grassy dikes, the beautiful old trees, the narrow cobbled streets, the moat and fortress gates; the venerable 300-year-old buildings with bakeries, cafés, and restaurants and small, exciting shops; Saturday markets bustling with life. There are glassblowers and glass works; potters, ceramists and craftsmen; antique dealers, galleries, and museums.

Gamlebyen is the oldest part of Fredrikstad, which lies at the mouth of the Glomma river and was founded by King Frederik of Norway and Denmark in 1567, the first city in Norway to be named after a king. Fires plagued Fredrikstad's first hundred years, and no original building survived. The mid-17th century saw tense relations between the Danish-Norwegian King Frederik III and the Swedish King Karl X Gustav, culminating in 1658, when the Swedes conquered Bohuslän and Bohus fortress. This meant that Halden and Fredrikstad became Norway's border towns to the south. Fredrikstad needed a fortress, and in 1663 King Frederik III decided to build one according to plans drawn up by General Quartermaster Willem Coucheron. That was how old Fredrikstad – with its five bastions, moat, drawbridge, and no less than 130 cannons, came to exist. The outer fort, Kongsten fortress, 500 meters to the east, was built at the same time. The complex was Norway's strongest defense at the time and boasted 200 artillery and 400 soldiers. In wartime, there were 2000 soldiers stationed at the fort.

Today, Old Fredrikstad is one of Norway's most popular tourist attractions. This old garrison town has remained virtually unchanged for 300 years. It is still surrounded by a deep moat on three sides, with three gates leading out to the river. On the inside, there is a drawbridge to the mainland, and 61 cannons are positioned all around the ramparts. But Old Fredrikstad is not just a national historic treasure and tourist attraction – it is a fully functioning city. The fortress was rehabilitated and restored in the 1990s. The 17th and 18th century houses are beautifully preserved and are prize real estate. Business is booming, because you can find almost anything in Old Fredrikstad – even a charming inn.

A MENU OF CULTURE AND GASTRONOMIC DELIGHTS

The Balaklava complex is a handful of historic buildings – an inn, a restaurant, and several cultural venues. The inn is housed in a yellow wooden house facing the moat. It was originally the home of Peder Bull, but it has been a hotel for the last 200 years. It is Balaklava's eldest building and dates from 1783. All the rooms are comfortably and tastefully decorated in the French and Danish rococo styles, with period paintings and furniture. The vicarage, dating from 1803, was designed in the empire style. It houses Prestegården Annen Etage, the main restaurant and Balaklava's flagship, which encompasses the Wilse room, the Malthus sitting room, and the vicar's room. Prestegården Annen Etage is both an elegant restaurant and also one of Norway's best! The dishes served here are traditional with a Danish and international touch. If you prefer to dine surrounded by 3000

bottles of wine, you can do so in the cellar at the vicarage, where courses in wine tasting also are held.

Mulvadgård, the former home of a merchant named Mulvad, was built in 1835 and is now a course and conference center. It also houses a summer café. Balaklava's courtyard becomes a restaurant during the summer and bustles with activity.

Teglhuset, Balaklava's cultural locale, dates from the end of the 19th century. This rough brick building was once both a dairy and a machine workshop, but now it is a venue for music festivals, concerts, theater, and cabarets, as well as for literature, fairy tale, and folk song evenings. You can also view exciting art exhibitions at Gallery Balaklava, across the street from the inn. Balaklava is part of the "The Really Good Life" hotel chain.

People seek out the beautiful, and this is the philosophy behind the "The Really Good Life" chain. And Old Fredrikstad, with its picturesque and historic village atmosphere, is just perfect. Balaklava Gjestegiveri is a very special place.

Left: Guest rooms in the former home of Peder Bull are individually and charmingly decorated. The house, an architectural treasure from 1783, is the oldest of Balaklava's buildings.

Below: Teglhuset is Balaklava's cultural center – a popular arena for artists and hotel guests.

Skate with grilled scallops, asparagus, spring onions and bouillabaisse jus

Bouillabaisse jus
1 onion
2 garlic cloves
2 tomatoes
1 medium leek
olive oil
2 fresh thyme branches
8-10 white peppercorns
1 bay leaf
pinch cayenne
pinch saffron
2 dl (3/4 cup) white wine
5 dl (2 cups) fish stock
100 g (3 1/2 oz) unsalted butter
salt, pepper

Peel the onion and garlic. Chop the tomatoes, leek, onion and garlic and sauté in olive oil with the thyme, pepper, bay leaf, cayenne and saffron. Add the wine and stock and simmer about 1 hour. Strain. Just before serving, beat in the butter with an immersion blender until frothy. Season with salt and pepper.

Skate with grilled scallops, asparagus and spring onions
400 g (1 lb) skate wings
4 scallops
4 large asparagus
4 spring onions
olive oil

Clean the fish and the scallops. Clean and trim the asparagus and onions. Sauté the fish in olive oil 3 to 4 minutes per side.

Grill or pan fry the scallops about 30 seconds per side. Turn off the heat and let them finish cooking with residual heat. Do not overcook.

Steam the asparagus for about 2 minutes, the onions for about 1 minute.

Divide the scallops horizontally and place in the middle of each plate along with the vegetables. Top with fish and spoon jus all around. Garnish with fresh thyme.

Free-range chicken with duck foie gras, potato tart, Savoy cabbage, oyster mushrooms and Calvados jus

4 boneless free-range chicken breasts, about 150 g (5 oz) each
olive oil
1 red bell pepper
1 garlic clove
1 small shallot
1 egg
300 g (10 oz) potatoes
100 g (3 oz) clarified butter
salt, pepper
200 g (8 oz) Savoy cabbage
100 g (4 oz) oyster mushrooms
200 g (8 oz) duck foie gras
1 shallot
butter
1/2 dl (3 1/2 tablespoons) cider vinegar
1 dl (1/2 cup) white wine
1 dl (1/2 cup) red wine
5 dl (2 cups) chicken stock
2-3 tablespoons Calvados
2 tablespoons unsalted butter.

Cut a pocket lengthwise in the chicken breasts and brown in a little olive oil.

Preheat the oven to 200°C (400°F). Place the pepper on a greased oven sheet and bake 15 minutes, until the skin has begun to separate from the flesh. Peel and cut into chunks. Peel the garlic and shallot. Place the pepper, garlic, shallot and egg in a food processor and puree until smooth, adding a little olive oil if necessary. Spoon or pipe the mixture into the pocket in the chicken.

Reduce the oven temperature to 175°C (350°F). Wash, peel and slice the potatoes. Mix with clarified butter, salt and pepper and layer in individual dishes. Bake 20-30 minutes. Season the chicken with salt and pepper, place on a baking sheet and roast with the potatoes for about 15 minutes.

Shred the cabbage. Clean and cut the mushrooms into chunks. Sauté in a little duck fat. Cut the duck foie gras into four pieces of equal size. Sprinkle with salt and pepper and fry quickly in a very hot pan. Transfer to a plate and let rest a few minutes.

For the sauce, peel and mince the shallot. Sauté in butter until shiny, then add the vinegar and wine.

Reduce by half. Add the stock and reduce by half, until rich and slightly syrupy. Thicken with 1 teaspoon cornstarch stirred into 1 tablespoon cold water, if necessary. Stir in the Calvados and butter.

Arrange the vegetables in the center of each plate. Place the foie gras and potatoes on the side. Slice the chicken and arrange on the vegetables. Spoon the jus all around.

Ginger-yogurt parfait with marinated strawberries and raspberry sorbet

Nut base
4 egg whites
100 g (1/2 cup) sugar
100 g (4 oz) finely-ground hazelnuts

Parfait
4 egg yolks
80 g (scant 1/3 cup) sugar
3 dl (1 cup) whipping cream
1 dl (1/2 cup) natural yogurt
30 g (1/4 cup) candied ginger, finely diced

Raspberry sorbet
200 g (1 3/4 cups) raspberries
a few drops lemon juice
100 g (1/2 cup) sugar
3/4 dl (1/3 cup) water
2 teaspoons glucose

Marinated strawberries
120 g (1/2 cup) sugar
1 dl (1/3 cup) water
2 teaspoons glucose
1 teaspoon green pepper berries (canned)
200 g (1 3/4 cups) strawberries

Nut base
Preheat the oven to 180°C (350°F). Line an oven sheet with baking parchment. Beat the egg whites until foamy. Gradually add the sugar, beating to a stiff, thick meringue. Fold in the nuts. Spread the batter in a thin layer over the parchment. Bake 6 to 8 minutes. Cut out 6 circles the same diameter as the parfait rings. There will be cake leftover.

Parfait
Beat the egg yolks and sugar in a double boiler over hot water until light and fluffy. Whip the cream and fold into the egg yolk mixture, then fold in the yogurt and ginger. Pour into the parfait rings and freeze.

Raspberry sorbet
Place the berries in a blender with lemon juice and puree until smooth. Strain and discard the seeds. Bring the sugar, water and glucose to a boil and cook until the sugar is completely dissolved. Strain and cool. Combine the berry puree and sugar syrup. Freeze in an ice cream machine.

Marinated strawberries
Bring the sugar, water, glucose and pepper berries to a boil and cook until the sugar is completely dissolved.

Strain. Clean the berries and marinate in the sugar syrup for a few hours.

Place the parfait in the middle of a flat plate with strawberries all around and a scoop of sorbet on top.

A typical day
Bakkergården, Trøgstad

It's just a normal day at Bakkergården…The big bus filled with foreign tourists doesn't have a choice. Everyone has to wait while a hen and her six chicks cross the farmyard. They move at a leisurely pace, heading toward a small enclosure where a giant warthog is clearly enjoying the attention he is getting from the chickens and the tourists as he rolls in the mud. A little farther down is a larger enclosure housing a flock of wild boar that have been awakened from their nap.

Karistua is a hub of activity. The tourists are here for lunch to try some of antique-filled Bakkergården's specialties, variations on whitefish and wild boar. The tables in the great hall are set. But first, hostess Bente Haraldstad tells the guests a little about Bakkergården's history.

This is always a popular part of the afternoon, and the guests listen carefully.

Bakkergården, in Trøgstad, is an hour's drive from Oslo. People have lived on the farm since the 14th century, and it has been owned by the same family for about 500 years. The current owners, Bente Haraldstad and her husband Nils Sannum, took over the farm in 1990. They were both well aware of the farm's important cultural heritage, but they also wanted to make the most of its resources. They did some research and soon found out that the local ravine areas were perfectly suited to wild boar, so they decided to raise wild boar in addition to cultivating grain and hay.

Wild boars need a lot of space to thrive, so around 25 acres of land were fenced in to make a park for between 35 and 50 wild boars. The ravine area is perfect for grazing, and the animals are outdoors year-round. They are slaughtered when they are about 15 months old and weigh between 55 and 75 kilos (120 and 165 pounds). The meat is very flavorful and is prepared like game.

Food has been produced and prepared at Bakkergården for centuries. Both the farm and local traditions rely heavily on wild game. The area is rich in duck, geese, wild birds and moose. The farm borders Øyeren, the lake with the largest number of white fish species in Norway, so there's more than enough fish.

The local culinary traditions inspired Bente and Nils to open a hotel and restaurant on the farm. It was to be run as part of the farm, not as a hobby, thus they could exploit the rich natural resources there. The food could be prepared and eaten where it was produced. The area was well suited to tourists, and the guests could experience a living farm with traditional farm animals. There was Øyeren Lake, with its sandy beaches and clean water, ideal for swimming, waterskiing, fishing, and kayaking. There was a lush forest where guests could go for walks or pick berries and mushrooms in season. The more they thought, the more they were convinced. This was an excellent idea!

Karistua, dating back to the 18th century, was the first building to be restored, and it was ready for guests in 1995. Karistua now houses the reception, kitchen, restaurant and sitting rooms. It's also where Bente welcomes her guests.

After making sure that the food is ready and all is going according to plan, she runs across the yard to Smia (the smithy), which now houses nine comfortable guestrooms. All the rooms are different – each one with that little something special. Tonight all the rooms are booked, and Bente takes one last look to make sure everything is perfect. On the way out, she checks the temperature in the giant outdoor hot tub, where the guests will enjoy an aperitif before they ride on horseback up to the newly built fireplace room to dine on wild boar ham and schnapps.

This is a typical day at Bakkergården.

The animals are an important part of the milieu at Bakkergården in the agricultural community of Trøgstad.

Right: The restaurant is in the Karistua building. The antique interior contributes to the warm and cozy ambience.

*Above: Bente Haraldstad
and her husband Nils Sannum
welcome you to Bakkergården – a
working farm and a charming
inn in the heart of Østfold.*

*Bakkergården produces its own
wine from berries and fruit.*

*Bakkergården's history
began before the year 1300
and has been in the family's
possession since 1540. Beautiful
Karistua was dates from about
150 years ago.*

Smoked whitefish terrine (appetizer or lunch dish)

1 leek, sliced
5-6 boiled potatoes, sliced
warm-smoked whitefish
fish aspic
toasted almonds

Layer the ingredients in a loaf pan lined with plastic wrap. Brush each layer with fish aspic. Press down lightly and refrigerate overnight. Slice. Serve on a bed of arugula drizzled with a little olive oil. Garnish with almonds.

Herb sauce
natural yogurt
fresh basil leaves
salt, pepper

Combine all ingredients in a food processor and puree until smooth. Season with salt and pepper.

Smoked whitefish with onion compote

shallots
red onions
garlic
olive oil
salt, pepper
whipping cream
warm-smoked whitefish

Peel and slice the shallots, onions and garlic and sauté in oil. Sprinkle with salt and pepper. Add the cream and simmer until thickened. Spoon the compote onto individual plates. Top with smoked white-fish and serve with chanterelles. Garnish with chives.

Wild boar ham sandwich with Parmesan cheese

2 slices whole grain bread
pesto
4 slices wild boar ham
2 slices fresh Parmesan cheese
2 sun-dried tomatoes, finely diced

Spread each slice of bread with pesto. Top with ham and cheese. Sprinkle with sun-dried tomato. 2 servings.

Wild boar ham with lefse

Spread homemade lefse (or flour tortillas) with dairy sour cream and top with thin slices of red onion. Arrange thin slices of wild boar ham over the onion. Roll up and cut into 1 cm (1/2") thick slices. Serve with cocktails or as a snack. Warm-smoked moose can be used instead of ham.

With all the above dishes, we serve ice cold house-brewed beer or "forest wine" made of birch sap and spruce shoot syrup, served cold with ice.

A family jewel in the heart of the capital
Hotel Continental, Oslo

Theatercaféen. The place to see, and be seen. "Those who have never been there have a void in their Scandinavianism" wrote the Swedish newspaper "Expressen" about Scandinavia's most famous Viennese-style cafe, with its turn-of-the-century interior. Another newspaper, "Svenska Dagbladet", went even further, "Paris has the Dome and Rotonde, London has The Antelope behind Sloane Square. Copenhagen has a couple of places around the avant-garde Fiolstræde, and Stockholm has Freden…Oslo has Theatercaféen, and it beats them all…everyone in Oslo goes to Theatercaféen." It's known as the "café with the walls" because of all the portraits that line the walls of the café. Actors from the National Theater started the tradition, and Theatercaféen is still the favorite gathering place of actors and artists in Oslo.

Annen Etage "Annen Etage is Hotel Continental's, and maybe all of Norway's culinary flagship – an institution, a concept, a celebration," wrote Mona Levin in "Aftenposten", Norway's national newspaper, about Hotel Continental's gourmet temple. This exclusive restaurant is a member of "Traditions et Qualité" the famous society of 70 of the world's best restaurants. There is a historic buzz in the cradle of Norwegian gastronomy. Daglistuen – with one of Norway's largest private collections of Edvard Munch graphics. Timelessly continental, intimate and cozy. Lipp – bar, café and restaurant. Trendy atmosphere and a classic milieu with a modern accent and a 12-meter-long bar.

You'll find some of the capital's best and most popular restaurants and bars at the venerable Hotel Continental, where the kitchen is still the heart of the hotel, as it has been since Mrs. Boman Hansen's time. Her business concept was to make good quality food. Her motto was - If the food is bad, it doesn't matter how good everything else is!

BOMAN HANSEN ARRIVES AT CONTINENTAL
Caroline Boman was born in Sweden on August 10, 1860, in Väster Åby, daughter of a fisherman. At 17, she got a job at a restaurant in Gävle, where she quickly decided "to rise as far as any woman could in the field." Caroline became a cook. She worked at the best hotels in Uppsala and Västerås before moving to Stockholm. First she ran the kitchen at Hasselbakken, and then at Gyllene Freden. She moved to Norway in 1887 to work in the kitchen at the Grand Hotel in Christiania. There she met the man she would later marry. Hans Christian Martinius Hansen, son of farm worker Johan Hansen, worked as a waiter at Grand Café. By the time they married in 1891, the groom was working at Martins Hotell in Møllergaten. Caroline continued working at Grand's "delicatessen", a combined restaurant and shop with prepared food, where she had earned a good reputation. When the delicatessen was closed down in 1897, the couple decided open up their own shop.

Boman Hansen's was located in Øvre Slotts gate, in the center of Christiania. Business was good, so they were able to buy Gladtvedt Hotel in Hønefoss in 1900. They moved to Ringerike with their sons Arne and Erik, where, according to a newspaper article, they "made the old place famous". They bought

Above: The interior of "Daglistuen", the hotel's intimate and comfortable bar next to the lobby.

Right: Hotel Continental in the heart of Oslo in the evening.

Modum Spa in 1904, and Sandefjord Spa two years later. They ran all three places together, like a small chain, until 1909, when they moved back to Christiania and rented the Hotel Continental – the capital's small modern hotel, with the great Theater-caféen, and Theatercaféen-Annenetage, as Annen Etage was called back then. Rent was NOK 45 000 a year plus they had to deposit a bankbook worth NOK 25 000 as security. In addition, they had to give up two of their three establishments and promise that one of them would be in the hotel at all times. The Boman Hansens accepted these conditions and took over the hotel on April 20, 1909. That was the beginning of the family-run Hotel Continental.

AN ELDORADO FOR THE PALATE

When the Boman Hansens took it over, the little hotel across from the National Theater was already nine years old. The new theater was finished in 1899, and it was taken for granted that the hotel and theater would be neighbors. Hotel Continental opened its doors a year later, on December 22, 1900. The hotel wasn't a converted mansion, as was usual at the time; it was planned and built specifically as a hotel. This is how a newspaper article described it on December 9, 1900:

"The large, beautiful building on the corner of Stortingsgaden and Klingenberggaden will be opened as a hotel, bar, and restaurant at the end of the month. The building already glows, and one can see that the owners have tried to create something different. There is a cafe on the first floor. It's large, around 800 square ells (1 ell = .62 meter), with a white vaulted ceiling with gilded drawings, supported by tall marbleized pillars. The furnishings - sofas against the walls, etc – will be in red mahogany, and the walls will be covered in silk wallpaper. And of course there will be electric lighting and central heating, and the air in the rooms will be changed three times every hour. The cafe will have two entrances, one from the corner, and one from the side facing the Hals Brothers' shop.

The second floor will include a large dining room, around 600 square ells, and a smaller dining room, around 200 square ells, and four small dining rooms at around 50 square ells each.

The two top floors will house 40 pleasant rooms with very tasteful wallpaper.

Our highly respected painter, Mr. Jens Wang, is responsible for the cafe's simple, impressive decor. Mr. Hessel, the building contractor, will be praised widely for his work.

Mr. Holthe, who designed this building, an eldorado for the palate, is currently in Stockholm studying the newest refinements for Nordic cafés.
In this short description of this magnificent new building, we must not forget the spacious verandas, with their beautiful views…"

Although the Boman Hansens took charge of a beautiful building, the first years of the hotel were not a complete success – more an utter fiasco. Bad finances and constantly changing management had been a headache for the owner, Foss Brewery. Now they hoped for better times!

FROM A FIASCO TO A SUCCESS

They didn't have to wait long. Things started changing as soon as the Boman Hansens took over. They made general improvements, hired and fired staff, did quality control and started marketing the hotel. Hotel Continental was soon an unparalleled success, and when the couple negotiated a new contract with Foss, they ended up buying the hotel with all its contents for NOK 740 000. Christian Boman Hansen died two years later. His elder son Arne was already studying hotel management in Lausanne, Switzerland, and soon his younger son Erik also went abroad. He moved to Paris and used his inheritance to open a car dealership. He married Alice, a French girl, and they had a daughter, Monique. Eric Boman Hansen died young, just 31 years old. Arne moved to America where he studied economics, got a good job, and started a family. In 1917, he married an American,

Grayce LeBert, and their daughter Ellen was born in 1921. And Caroline Boman Hansen continued to run Hotel Continental alone.

She didn't seem to have any problem with that, at least not if we believe the Hotel and Restaurant Owners' Magazine, which wrote the following on her 70th birthday:

"Mrs. Boman Hansen is a strict employer, but we must admit that has only been to her benefit. There is no restaurant in Oslo where such supreme order reigns as at Theatercaféen. The waiters who work there don't give up their jobs lightly; there is even an air of aristocracy among them. Her business can serve as a model for many of her male counterparts. She is a restaurant person with all her heart and soul, and her talent is unparalleled. There are plenty of upstarts in the trade who should go to her for training."

A NEW ADDITION AND MORE ROOMS

In 1927, Arne Boman Hansen and his little family returned to Norway. He went into partnership with his mother, and they reorganized the business together. Even though Caroline ran a model business, there was still room for improvement. Continental wasn't the best run hotel. It needed more rooms and higher standards of comfort to face the future. But expanding the old building was impossible. The only solution was to buy the neighboring building from the Hals brothers and build a new hotel there. And that's what they did. On May, 1932, the new addition, designed by Ole Øvergaard was opened. It housed, among other things, a new central lobby with an entrance from Stortingsgaten, a bar, a shopping arcade, 76 modern guest rooms with baths, and a large banquet division.

The new addition could hardly have been built at a worse time. A large general strike delayed the building by six months, and the Wall Street crash of 1929 and the great depression also affected Norway and caused widespread economic hardship. It could have gone terribly wrong. If it hadn't been for Mrs. Boman Hansen's solid reputation, which enabled her to negotiate credit, the business would have gone bankrupt. But they managed to ride out the storm. Overhead costs were reduced to the absolute minimum, all purchases were paid for in cash, and Mrs. Boman Hansen mortgaged her private property and sold her stocks. Not one creditor lost a single penny on her, and the Hotel Continental got its new addition.

Above: Hotel Continental is the largest training facility in its field, with 41 apprentice chefs and 16 waiters and waitresses in training.

Right.: Theatercaféen is on the New York Times' list of the world's 10 most famous cafés. It is also known as "the café with the walls" because of all the portraits of artists and actors decorating the walls.

ELLEN BROCHMANN – THE NEW MISTRESS OF CONTINENTAL

The years passed. The hotel was taken over by the German occupational forces during World War II, but Mrs. Boman Hansen was back in place on liberation day. "Take down the blackout shades and curtains, light all the candles, let people know that peace has returned!" announced this vital lady who turned 85 in 1945. She reassumed her reins as if it were the most natural thing in the world. She was still full of enthusiasm, but gradually she let her son do more and more, knowing that her hotel was in good hands. Four years later, Christine fell and broke her hip on Christmas Eve. She retained her fighting spirit, but that ended her active participation in the business. Arne, on the other hand, was planning an expansion, this time at the corner of Roald Amundsens gate and Klingenberggate. Construction of Norway's first large cafeteria, Paviljongen (The Pavilion) had already begun when Arne Boman Hansen died in the mountains, on April 1, 1953, just 57 years old. His daughter Ellen, his only heir, had to take over the hotel, but she wasn't exactly unprepared for the job. She began her apprenticeship at Hotel Continental in 1945 and had graduated with top marks from restaurant-service school in 1949. The following year, she received her advanced certificate in hotel and restaurant management, and she had practical experience in every division of the hotel. But the task before her was still enormous, as director and single manager in charge of the entire hotel and a staff of 350. But Ellen proved worthy of the task. The Pavilion opened as planned on May 17, 1953, and it was an instant success.

Eva married journalist Caspar Brochmann in 1955. Both had been married before, and each brought a child into the marriage. Ellen brought her son Erik Shetelig, and Caspar his son Kristen. Caspar soon left his newspaper to devote his time to the hotel.

Caroline Boman Hansen died at the age of 95 1/2 on January 5, 1956. She left the hotel to Ellen and her French cousin Monique, who immediately sold her half to Ellen. Business was good, and soon the hotel needed yet another addition. In 1960, the pavilion was torn down to make room for a new addition that housed two brand new restaurants and 88 sorely-needed guest rooms.

The years passed. Ellen Brochmann, or Mrs. Brochmann as she was now known, kept refining the family jewel. She loved beautiful things, and the hotel's stylish interior became her hallmark. She was soon a legend, just like her grandmother had been in her time. In 1989, she was honored with the medal of St. Olav and could call herself Dame of the First Class for her contribution to the hotel industry.

ELISABETH CAROLINE BROCHMANN – YET ANOTHER MISTRESS OF CONTINENTAL

In 1985, the year Caspar Brochmann died, Ellen Brochmann retired in favor of her daughter, Elisabeth Caroline Brochmann. Her eldest son Erik should have taken over the hotel, but he chose to become a doctor instead. Elizabeth was well prepared for the task, with a business degree from St. Gallen, and work experience from the Berkeley Hotel in London, Hotel Vier Jahreszeiten in Hamburg, and Alain Chapel in Lyon. Caroline Brochmann is very proud of her inheritance. Proud of the traditional restaurants, of the beautiful rooms, and of the inviting interiors. She enjoys being an independent hotel. It gives her the freedom to do what she wants. She wants to continue developing Hotel Continental as a niche hotel for discerning guests – a personal and individual hotel. A hotel where the guests feel well looked after. Hotel Continental is the only hotel in Norway that is a member of the "Leading Hotels of the World" booking service. But she doesn't consider that a chain, it's a stamp of quality, and she's proud of it. Just as proud as she was when Hotel Continental, as the largest training organization in the hotel-restaurant field in Norway with 41 chef-apprentices and 16 waiter-apprentices, was awarded a national educational prize. The new mistress of Continental is genuinely concerned with people and the development of her staff. She knows that if her employees are not happy, then neither are her guests. And her guests' happiness is her primary concern!

Mussel soup

500 g (1 1/4 lb) mussels
2 shallots
1 garlic clove
1 tablespoon chopped
fresh thyme
oil
4 dl (1 2/3 cups) dry
white wine
4 dl (1 2/3 cups) whip-
ping cream
100 g (3 1/2 oz)
unsalted butter
salt, pepper
bok choy
200 g (7 oz) whitefish or
other golden caviar

Scrub the mussels. Peel and coarsely chop the shallots and garlic. Sauté with the thyme in oil in a stockpot. Add the mussels and wine. Cover and simmer until they open, 2 to 3 minutes. Strain the stock and reserve. Remove the meat from the shells and reserve.

Combine the stock and cream in a saucepan. Heat to boiling and reduce to about 6 dl (2 1/2 cups). Just before serving, beat in the butter. Season with salt and pepper. Add the mussels.

Clean and shred the bok choy. Sauté lightly in oil. Divide among deep soup bowls. Spoon the caviar over the greens and pour warm soup all around.

Lightly-smoked char

2 char or trout, about
500 g (1 1/4 lb) each
2 tablespoons sea salt
1 teaspoon coarsely
ground pepper
wood shavings

1 small celeriac
4 almond or other waxy
potatoes
unsalted butter
oil
4 small parsley roots
50 g (1/4 cup) sugar
50 g (scant 1/2 cup)
chopped walnuts
200 g (7 oz) spinach

1 dl (1/2 cup) white
wine
3 dl (1 1/4 cups)
whipping cream
1 dl (1/2 cup) fish stock
chopped marjoram
5 tablespoons reduced
veal or beef stock

Read the instructions thoroughly before preparing this dish.

Wash and fillet the fish. Sprinkle with salt and pepper. Let the fish rest at room temperature for an hour. Turn the oven to the maximum temperature. Arrange wood shavings in a small frying pan and place on a burner set at maximum heat until red hot and glowing. Set fire to the shavings with a match. Smother the flames with a damp cloth. Place the pan with the shavings in a cold oven. Arrange the fish fillets on a rack over the shavings and close the oven door. Smoke the fish in the cold oven 5 to 7 minutes.

Wash and peel the celeriac and two potatoes. Cut into chunks and boil until tender. Just before serving, reheat and season with salt, pepper and butter. Wash, peel and cut the remaining potatoes into strips. Fry in oil until crispy and golden.

Peel the parsley roots, halve lengthwise and blanch in boiling water. Glaze in butter and sugar with the walnuts. Sauté the spinach in oil and season to taste.

Reduce the wine by 2/3. Add the cream and stock and reduce by half. Season with marjoram and strain.

To serve, preheat the oven to 170°C (350°F). Arrange the fish in greased ring molds and bake 4 minutes. Fill to the top with spinach, pressing down lightly. Unmold in the center of individual plates. Remove the skin. Arrange parsley roots, nuts, potatoes and celeriac around the fish. Spoon over the sauce. Season the stock with marjoram and drizzle all around.

Frozen chocolate cake

Base
200 g (1 3/4 cups) vanilla wafer
or graham cracker crumbs
3 tablespoons sugar
2 1/2 tablespoons cocoa
2 teaspoons cinnamon
100 g (3 1/2 oz) unsalted butter

Filling
400 g (14 oz)
bittersweet chocolate
225 g (8 oz) unsalted butter
1 dl (scant 1/2 cup) honey
5 eggs, separated

Base

Combine the dry ingredients. Melt the butter and add, kneading the mixture well. Press into a 25 cm (10") springform pan.

Filling

Melt the chocolate, butter and honey over low heat. Beat in the egg yolks, one at a time. Beat the egg whites until stiff and fold into the chocolate mixture. Pour over the base. Freeze overnight. Cut the cake into serving pieces while still frozen. Glaze with dark chocolate.

A landmark in the capital

Grand Hotel, Oslo

"In the south, in the north, in the east, in the west; Grand Hotel is and always will be best."
Roald Amundsen, September 23, 1912

The venerable Grand Hotel lies on the corner of Karl Johans gate, Oslo's main avenue, and Rosenkrantz gate. When the hotel first opened in 1874, the block consisted of three buildings: the Bordoe, Fuhr, and Heiberg buildings. The latter, a three-story corner edifice facing Rosenkrantz gate was owned by Christiania's leading surgeon, Prof. Dr. Christen Heiberg. The surgeon, who had earned the nickname Chris the knife, had bought the lot on Karl Johans gate 31 in 1842 to build a grand and gracious home for himself and his family on the "new palace road". He sold the property in April, 1873, to grocer Nicolay Dorph Fritzner for 45 000 spesidaler. Fritzner lived in Stockholm, but he wanted to convert the Heiberg building into a hotel for his brother Julius to run. The Fritzner brothers were born and raised at Hafslund Manor in Fredrikshald, where their father, Infantry Captain Nils Dorph Heide Fritzner was the manager. Nicolay became a businessman and settled in Sweden, while his three year younger brother became a pastry chef and ran an extremely popular patisserie in Kongen gate 11.

Julius had neither education nor experience in the hotel field, but Grand Hotel opened its doors on August 15, 1874. It was a grand opening, and the pastry chef proudly presented a modern hotel "with 100 comfortable salons and rooms. Table d'hôte hall, a dining room, smaller dining rooms, reading rooms and a cafe – all tastefully and elegantly equipped." Julius bought out his brother two years later, buying both the building and the business for NOK 252 000. He added an extra floor for staff living quarters, redecorated the cafe and lowered its floor at the end of the 1870s.

Julius Fritzner married Elise Marie Caroline Strøm, and the couple had three children, two girls and a boy. In 1882, Julius died, only 54 years old, and his son Christian took over the hotel. He was a talented manager just like his father, and the hotel continued to develop and flourish under his leadership. He opened "Speilsalen", (the hall of mirrors) on December 15, 1886. The room had a beautifully decorated ceiling, salmon-colored marble pillars, and mirrored panels on the walls. In these elegant surroundings, the citizens of the capital could dine to live music for the first time. Christian, or Kristian as he was now known, bought the neighboring Fuhr property in 1888. After extensive remodeling, it was incorporated into the hotel. The back courtyard was converted into a garden, complete with running water, and the Palm Garden, where guests could enjoy a drink on a shady veranda. The next project was an addition on the Rozenkrantz gate side. This encompassed the "Rococo Room", Norway's finest reception room, which was opened with a grand party in 1894. It was two stories high and richly decorated by the famous artist Wilhelm Krogh. The "Rococo Room" would be the center of Oslo party life for many years. It hosted artistic carnivals, grand balls, and Petra Sand's charity soirees to fund her orphanages. And last, but not least, "The Ball Society", with King Haakon and Queen Maud as their patrons.

Kristian Fritzner died in 1897, and Grand Hotel was supposed to be sold to foreign investors. Meanwhile, his widow Anna decided to sell the hotel to a Norwegian interest group instead. The new owners took over Grand in December, 1897 and the

Palmen was enclosed and covered with a curved glass roof in 1913. It was originally an open palm garden with a shady veranda and a fountain. It was Henrik Ibsen's favorite haunt during the summer.

Grand Hotel became a corporation a few months later.

A CENTER FOR INTELLECTUAL LIFE

When the Grand Hotel opened in 1874, its cafe was two meters above street level. Its doors were on Rosenkrantz gate and guests had to climb exterior stairs to enter. Julius Fritzner had the floor lowered and he also redecorated the cafe. From that moment on, it was the gathering spot for "all of Christiania".

"When we look back, we see that Grand Café left an indelible impression," wrote Leif Huseby in "Excerpts from the hotel's history and development over 100 years, 1874 to 1974," and continues with a quote from "St. Halvard" magazine:

"For decades, Grand Cafe was the most important center for intellectual life in Oslo. The people who left their mark on the city met during the 1880s and 90s; artists and poets trod the stairs that later became a wide avenue. There in the "Daglistue" (the "sitting room"), as the cafe was called, sat Hans and Henrik Jæger, Gerhard Munthe, Hans Heyerdahl, Hjalmar Johnsen, Nils Hansteen, Erik Werenskiold, Edvard Diriks, Ludvig Skramstad, Axel Ender, Gunnar Heiberg, Edvard Munch, Christian Skredsvig, Knut Hamsun, Kalle Løchen, and many, many others. Painters, authors, musicians and actors. Holmboe tells us that Heyerdahl lectured on the four philosophical systems in all seriousness to anyone who would listen. Kalle Løchen dashed in with his arsenal of bizarre jargon, and Skredsvig – the odd combination of farm boy and Parisian – a breath of fresh Nordic air from Eggedal.

GREAT PLANS WERE HATCHED AT GRAND CAFÉ

Author Olav Krohn tells us "It was here that the bullets that would later explode in the form of art exhibits, political oppositions, bohemian movements, etc. were cast. And the owner of the hotel, Julius Fritzner, bowed by the door, and a row of excellent waiters ushered people back and forth. Whisky and soda was the favored drink, and Didriks had a satirical glint in his eye as he looked out over the poplar trees in

Above: Suite number 201 – the Nobel Suite. This is where the Nobel Piece Prize winners stay, and they receive the cheers of the public while standing on its balcony.

The guest rooms at Grand Hotel are tastefully decorated down to the smallest detail.

Student park. 'I think these poplars are so high they should be cut down.' Yes, Grand Café was, according to Macody Lund, "like a new sentence, in a new chapter of Christiania's history, you could even say Norway's, the history of the unusual 80s, when literature and art broke through and sprouted roots. That history cannot be written without the Grand Hotel."

Two famous regulars

Grand has had many famous regular customers over the years, but the first were undoubtedly the writer Henrik Ibsen and the artist Edvard Munch.

Ibsen made the 1890s the most famous decade in Grand's history. After living in Germany and Italy for many years, he moved back to Norway in 1891 and immediately started visiting cafes just as he had done abroad. He took Norway's best-known walk twice daily every day for nine years – down Arbiens gate, past the university clock, where he always stopped to check his watch, then on to Grand Café:

"He was the area's most colorful character, with his long coat, voluminous trousers, his top hat, and umbrella, as he wandered into the café and sat in his special arm chair 'Reserved for Dr. Ibsen'. He was a prime attraction and could be found in the café or reading room between 12:30 and 2 pm and from 6 to 8 pm. Local inhabitants could set their watches by him. During the summer he liked to sit on the shady, cool glass veranda – later "Palmen". For lunch he ate two rolls, bock beer, and a schnapps. And often a whisky and soda, too. Grand was his home away from home…." writes Øyunn Bjaanæs Hrasky in 'Welcome to Grand Hotel'.

Early in 1900, Ibsen fell ill and stayed away from the Grand for several weeks. But the newspaper "Ørebladet" reported that he had returned on April 23 but soon disappeared again. His health deteriorated and he never returned to the Grand….

Edvard Munch was also a regular at Grand Café. The world famous painter told the magazine "Kruset" (The Mug), published by Grand's waiters, about life at the hotel in the good old days: "That's where I got my first patron, waiter Ulleberg. I traded one painting for the rights to chateaubriand with beer and schnapps for 30 kroner – and it was the most delicious chateaubriand for 40 øre with a lump of butter on top. The schnapps cost 10 øre and a half bayer (a beer), 20 øre. I had another patron back then, shoemaker With. One day I was walking down Karl Johan and I heard a voice behind me say:

-Listen here Munch. I'm a shoemaker and I see that your boots are in bad shape. Would you like to make a deal? I'll trade you a pair of new boots for a painting.

-It's a deal, I replied.

I exchanged "Music on Karl Johan" a large painting which is now owned by Professor Curt Glaser in Berlin, for a new pair of boots."

Waiter Olsen wasn't nearly as lucky as the shoemaker. He was offered the famous painting "Sick child" in exchange for 100 steaks, at 50 øre each, but he refused. "Madonna" was sold to another waiter, but he sold it on before Munch became famous and the value increased.

Everything happened at Grand, of that there is no doubt! Or as Munch so fittingly described it: "Grand was the sitting room of the capital back then – there you could feel the pulse of the city."

CONTINUOUS EXPANSIONS AND MODERNIZATIONS

Grand's famous café has been redecorated and modernized many times. In 1932, André Peters wanted to create an entirely new, functional art deco café, so the old French, German, and English inspired café had to go. The caryatids, the painted glass ceilings, the tiled floors, and the marble tables were replaced with simple materials and tables, chairs, and sofas in matte oak, covered in red velour. The walls were plastered, roughly painted in shades of brown and gold from floor to ceiling, while the floor was covered with linoleum. The focal point was Per Krogh's series of large, festive paintings from Christiania's bohemian days. Thankfully, these have been preserved.

The cafe has been refurbished several times since, the last being in 1994, when the redecoration was inspired by Viennese cafes and restaurants throughout Europe

The hotel has also been redecorated and modernized several times, with some fundamental changes along the way. The "Marble Hall" and the "Red Room" were added in 1909-1912, and the entire hotel was refurbished between 1911-1913, when it was given its present facade. The old Fuhr building was torn down in 1911 to make way for a new building and addition designed by architect O. Sverre. The beautiful new building, with its distinctive clock tower and shiny new facade in white granite from Tyin in Sogn, was finished in late summer, 1913. The Palm Garden was incorporated into the new building. It was built in with a glass roof and palm trees and was christened "Palmen". The current vestibule was built in 1946.

Catastrophe hit on May 22, 1957, when a fire destroyed the upper half of the Rozenkrantz wing. It

contained many guest bedrooms, the "Mirror Room", the "Red Room", and the beautiful "Rococo Room". Architect F.S. Platou was hired to design a new wing. It was finished in 1961 and contained more than 100 new guest bedrooms. It also incorporated the rebuilt Rococo and Mirror Rooms. There was even room for a new restaurant, "Grillen". "Grillen" has now changed its name to Restaurant Julius Fritzner and is Grand's gourmet restaurant.

1974 saw more expansions. A new wing with 80 new guest bedrooms, a conference center, and a health club with an indoor swimming pool was built on Arbeidergata.

In 1994, Grand Hotel was bought by Eiendomsspar and is now run by the Rica Hotel and Restaurant chain. The years up to 1999 and the 125th anniversary of the hotel were spent thoroughly refurbishing and modernizing the hotel. Today Grand Hotel stands tall as one of Oslo's best hotels. And the gloomy predictions Julius Fritzner was met with when he decided to build a hotel "a little on the outskirts of town" have been put to shame. Its fantastic location, between the Royal Palace and the Parliament, putting it right in the heart of the city. The founder of Grand Hotel was a very farsighted man!

The beautiful high-ceilinged lobby was rebuilt in 1946.

Pan-fried scallops with asparagus, arugula and tomato salad and dill oil

12 asparagus
8 scallops
2 plum tomatoes
butter
1/2 bunch dill
1 1/4 dl (1/2 cup) olive oil
150 g (5 oz) arugula
olive oil
balsamic vinegar
salt, pepper

Peel the bottom part of the asparagus. Open and clean the scallops. Set aside the muscle and roe. Scald and peel the tomatoes. Halve, remove the seeds and cut into strips. Cook the asparagus in lightly salted water about 2 minutes and glaze in a little butter. Puree the dill and olive oil in a food processor until nearly smooth. Strain.

Sauté the scallops and roe in butter. Sauté the scallops on one side only for about a minute, the roe for about 30 seconds.

Arrange the scallops and roe on individual plates along with the asparagus. Combine the tomato strips and the arugula with a little oil, vinegar, salt and pepper and place on the asparagus. Drizzle dill oil all around.

Squab stuffed with foie gras with spring vegetables and Port wine sauce

10 shallots
butter
4 dl (1 2/3 cups) red wine
8 dl (3 1/3 cups) veal stock
25 g (2 tablespoons) cold unsalted butter
3 tablespoons Port wine

100 g (4 oz) duck foie gras
5-6 spinach leaves
4 whole boneless squab
1/2 head early cabbage

Peel, mince and sauté the shallots in butter in a saucepan until golden. Add the red wine and reduce to about 1 tablespoon. Add the stock and reduce to about 2 dl (3/4 cup). Just before serving, stir in the butter and Port wine.

Divide the foie gras into four pieces of equal size and brown lightly on both sides in a very hot dry frying pan. Blanch the spinach in boiling water for a few seconds. Wrap the liver in the spinach and stuff into each squab. Truss with cotton string. Brown on all sides, lower heat and cook for about 10 minutes.

Shred the cabbage and cook in boiling water until tender, about one minute. Glaze with a little butter and place in a ring on each plate. Halve the squabs and place on the cabbage. Serve with buttered spring onions, tiny carrots, sautéed chanterelles and deep-fried black salsify shreds. Spoon Port wine sauce all around.

Passion fruit trilogy —mousse, sorbet and soufflé

Passion fruit mousse
2 1/2 gelatin sheets
2 dl (3/4 cup) passion fruit juice
100 g (1/2 cup) sugar
2 1/2 dl (1 cup) whipping cream

Passion fruit sorbet
100 g (1/2 cup) sugar
1 dl (1/2 cup) water
1 gelatin sheet
2 dl (1 cup) passion fruit pulp
1/2 dl (3 tablespoons) orange juice

Soufflé
1 egg yolk
1 teaspoon sugar
2 egg whites
2 teaspoons sugar
2 tablespoons passion fruit juice
confectioner's sugar

Passion fruit mousse
Soak the gelatin in cold water 5 minutes to soften. Heat the juice and sugar in a saucepan until the sugar is completely dissolved. Squeeze to remove excess water and melt the gelatin in the hot juice. Cool. When the mixture begins to set, whip the cream and fold into the juice mixture. Pour into individual molds and freeze.

Passion fruit sorbet
Heat the sugar and water in a saucepan until the sugar is completely dissolved. Soak the gelatin in cold water 5 minutes to soften. Try to keep the temperature at 30°C (85°F). Puree the passion fruit pulp. Sieve and discard the seeds. Combine the sugar syrup, fruit puree and juice. Squeeze to remove excess water and melt the gelatin with a little of the fruit mixture. Combine all ingredients and freeze in an ice cream machine.

Soufflé
Preheat the oven to 180°C (350°F). Grease four individual soufflé dishes with butter, then sprinkle with sugar. Whisk the egg yolk with 1 teaspoon sugar. Beat the egg whites until frothy, add the 2 teaspoons sugar, and beat until soft peaks form. Fold the passion fruit juice into the egg whites, then fold in the yolk. Pour into the prepared soufflé dishes. Bake 10 minutes. Sprinkle with confectioner's sugar and serve immediately.

To serve, place the soufflés in the center of individual plates. Serve mousse and sorbet alongside. Garnish with fresh berries, crispy cookies, mint leaves and fruit sauce.

Where the chestnut trees blossom

Rica Hotel Bygdøy Allé, Oslo

Rica Hotel Bygdøy Allé, the former Hotel Norum, lies in Oslo's west-end, just a short walk from city center. Bygdøy allé is the main thoroughfare in Frogner, one of Oslo's most fashionable residential areas with venerable old apartment buildings and large villas. Bygdøy allé itself is lined with large beautiful chestnut trees and with exclusive and enticing shops, as well as some of Oslo's best restaurants.

When it was built at the turn of the century, Bygdøy allé was supposed to be Oslo's main street, complete with a four-meter-wide riding track in the middle. The track was to be lined with trees on both sides to protect it from the six-meter-wide car lanes and the three meter wide sidewalks. But not everything goes as planned. A narrow riding track was placed on one side of the street, but it was removed at the beginning of the 1930s.

Queen Maud often took her daily ride here.

Gjertrud Norum came to Bygdøy allé at the turn of the century to earn her living running a guest house. She had managed to borrow NOK 200, a sizeable sum at that time. There were so many possibilities. There were "to rent" signs everywhere. She quickly chose a ten-room apartment on the third floor of an elegant building at Bygdøy allé 53. The building had been constructed by master bricklayer Simon Borgfeldt at the turn of the century, and was then, as now, an architectural masterpiece of German castle architecture. This beautiful yellow building is German in a romantic Gothic – Wagnerian way. The front gable facade adds a touch of Dutch inspiration, while the towers are reminiscent of the chateaux in the Loire valley.

It was in this beautiful building that Gjertrud Norum prepared to welcome her first guests. The first thing she did was to furnish six rooms as bedrooms. But before she set about running a guest house, she figured she needed some practical knowledge. She rented a room at a guest house on Cort Adelers gate. She stayed one month, paid NOK 50 rent, and felt that she had learned enough. She then took a quick trip back to Råde to fetch provisions. She filled several trunks with home-made food: head cheese, hams, sausages, jam, and other goodies. She also brought her niece back to the capital. She was going to need all the help she could get! And in the fall of 1912, the Norum Guest House finally opened its doors.

A NEW GUEST HOUSE AND A NEW MARRIAGE Gjertrud Norum remarried that same year. Fritz Brotkorb, the building's owner, lived in the smallest apartment. He fell quickly in love with his new tenant, proposed, and she accepted. Fritz Brotkorb worked at the Ministry of Agriculture, so Gjertud was left to run the guest house on her own. She gradually expanded as the tenants in the other twelve apartments moved

Above: There are still many beautiful details dating from the late nineteenth and early twentieth century, when the hotel was built.

Above left: Kristin Rivelsrud (at right) is the director of Rica Hotel Bygdøy Allé, and Sonja Lee is the chef-manager at Magma, the hotel's popular restaurant.

Left: The venerable building in yellow brick at Bygdøy allé 53 is an architectural gem built in the German castle style, with Gothic, Wagnerian and romantic details, a Dutch-inspired gable facade, and towers reminiscent of castles in the Loire valley.

Right: Continental, comfortable furniture and exciting art in the beautiful sitting rooms at the hotel.

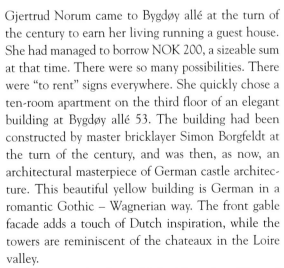

out. "This woman is ruining my apartment building" Fritz used to grumble, but he was really very proud of her.

Gjertud Brodtkorb had been running her guest house for two years when WWI broke out and forced her to close down. She spent the following years as a housewife and mother of two. But Gjertrud did not enjoy staying at home, so she reopened the guest house in 1922.

At that time, hotel standards were rather simple compared to what we expect today. At the Norum, 14 or 15 guests shared one bathroom. The rooms were heated with large coke-burning stoves, and there was no running water, sinks, or toilets. Gjertrud continued to expand her guesthouse while refurbishing the existing rooms. By the end of the 1920s, all the rooms had their own sinks and toilets. Ten years later, she introduced electric heating and installed a freezer in the cellar. She removed the icebox from the balcony and was grateful that she no longer had to crank ice cream every Sunday for dinner. After all the apartment tenants had moved out, she turned the entire building into a guest house with 100 beds.

When WWII broke out in 1940, the German occupational forces requisitioned part of the building as living quarters for their secretaries. The Gestapo moved into the Norum for the final eight months of the war, and regular guests were moved to another hotel.

"A bulldozer and a lady"

Many Norum residents in the 1950s had lived there for years. Over half were old ladies, and the rest were students living two to a room while getting their education in the capital. Old and young enjoyed each other's company, and the rent was certainly affordable – NOK 300 per month with full board. Many permanent guests left in the summer to visit relatives. Then their furniture and personal effects were moved to the attic, and their rooms were rented to tourists. Journalist Arne Hestenes lived at the Norum from 1948 to 1960, and described it and its hostess like this:

"Many cultured single people lived at the Norum, and many brought their own paintings – even their own furniture. It was an entertaining place. A stylish establishment. Mrs. Brodtkorb was a very authoritarian lady who kept a close reign on things. She browbeat me terribly, especially after I did an article on a nudist camp. She almost threw me out! And she didn't like my aftershave, and she let me know it. Mrs. Brodtkorb was both loved and feared as "Grandma", Bygdøy allé's most powerful lady. There was an air of respect around her hotel."

Hestenes described Mrs. Brodtkorb in another article as "a bulldozer and a lady all in one". She was a

perfectionist down to her fingertips. Her philosophy was "if you want to enjoy life, then you have to work for the privilege!" She took an active role in every aspect of the hotel and could appear anywhere in the hotel at any time of day or night. Not even her guests were immune to her behavior, and here we hear from Hestenes again, "Without any consideration of class or status, she would attack any male who by accident was wearing a hat in her presence in an elevator – and perfectly, just on the edge of being an invasion of privacy, she would criticize a tie that didn't harmonize with her piano salon." She loved her house and her guests, and she ran a top-class establishment. She was constantly tearing down walls, removing bricks and putting in elevators. The Norum was an elegant establishment, filled with harmonious interiors and antiques. But the atmosphere was still homey, and the food divine: A sumptuous breakfast, a three-course dinner, and a lovely evening snack. And the hostess was also a perfectionist with the food. She would never serve a Roquefort that wasn't aged at least two years.

In 1962, Gjertrud Brodtkorb received the King's of Merit Medal in gold for her work in promoting the Norwegian hotel industry, and Oslo's mayor, Rolf Stranger, characterized the Norum as "A place for discerning guests, a first class hotel".

A guest house becomes a hotel

Gjertrud's daughter Ellen, and her husband, Per Mathiesen, entered the business in 1946. Both had degrees in hotel management and ran the Norum together with Gjertrud until her death in 1973. In 1952, the name was changed to Hotel Norum, and prices were increased from NOK 1.25 to 4.50, and from NOK 2 to 8. Oslo saw a tourist explosion in the post-war years, and the new visitors expected more creature comforts from their hotels. The Norum installed a switchboard and telephones in all rooms. They also sacrificed a few room on each floor to make room for more bathrooms. The kitchen was also enlarged, and large bedrooms were divided in two to make more single rooms. The rooms facing Bygdøy allé on the first floor were noisy and unpopular, so they were converted into a bar and restaurant. The coming years saw fewer and fewer permanent guests, which meant that the Norum slowly, but surely became a normal hotel.

Most of the furniture at Restaurant Magma, such as these comfortable chairs and sofas in the bar, were designed especially for the restaurant and produced in collaboration with a Spanish furniture factory. Magma means "erupting volcanoes", the glowing, molten rock on its way up. That's how the colors of the restaurant evolved.

These beautiful glass doors lead from the hotel lobby out to Bygdøy allé.

Ellen and Per's son Bjørn gradually entered the business. He became the third generation to run the family business when his parents retired. In 1998, he sold the hotel to I.M. Skaugen ASA, and renovations began almost immediately. In 2000, the hotel was taken over by Rica hotels, Norway's largest hotel chain. A totally refurbished hotel, Rica Hotel Bygdøy Allé opened on April 26, 2000. The renovation may have erased a lot of the hotel's history, but there is still an intimate feeling about the place. And the young hotel director, Kristin Rivelsrud, wanted to create a cozy atmosphere just as her predecessor had done. The

Norum also houses one of Oslo's best restaurants, where chef Sonja Lee reigns supreme. She has worked in some of Europe's finest restaurants and the fruits of her experience can be found at Bygdøy allé 53. Restaurant Magma has been an unparalleled success. It serves real, unpretentious food in a colorful atmosphere that suits its name, Magma, which means molten lava. And the legendary Mrs. Brodtkorb would nod in approval if she could see Kristin welcome the guests and Sonja prepare the daily menu.

Above: The hotel's beautiful staircase is typical of the time the building was constructed.

Right: The charming guestrooms have been refurbished and decorated in the English style, with comfortable furniture and beautiful textiles.

Salad MAGMA

1 black radish
2 carrots
1 fennel
100 g (3 1/2 oz) chevre
2 1/2 tablespoons olive oil
300 g (10 0z) arugula
parsley
chives
crushed black pepper
balsamic vinaigrette (1 tablespoon Dijon
mustard, 1 tablespoon balsamic vinegar,
4 tablespoons (1/4 cup) virgin olive oil)

Wash, clean and cut the radish, carrots and
fennel into fine strips with a cheese plane.
Place in a bowl of ice water.
Mash the chevre with a fork and add the olive oil.
Wash the arugula and parsley. Cut the chives
in half.
Divide the chevre among individual plates and
sprinkle with pepper. Drain the vegetables, then
combine with the vinaigrette. Serve with the
chevre.

Chicken with black truffles, vegetables and jus

3 garlic cloves
6 tomatoes
salt, freshly ground pepper
sugar, thyme
olive oil

2 carrots
4 spring onions
12 tiny onions
150 g (5 oz) fresh peas
chicken stock

1 3/4 kilo (3 1/2 lb) free-range chicken
300 g (10 oz) almond or other waxy potatoes
25 g (1 oz) black truffle
chopped fresh parsley
1-2 dl (1/2 cup) reduced chicken stock

Preheat the oven to 80°C (175°F). Peel and crush
the garlic. Scald and peel the tomatoes. Halve and
remove the seeds. Place the tomatoes, cut side down,
on an oven tray. Sprinkle with salt, pepper, sugar,
thyme and garlic. Drizzle with oil and bake 5 hours.

Peel, wash and cut the carrots into chunks. Clean
the spring onions. Peel the tiny onions. Shell and
rinse the peas. Sauté the carrots in oil for 2 to 3
minutes, turning them constantly so they do not
brown. Add chicken stock to cover and simmer until
the stock has evaporated and the carrots are tender.
Repeat with the other vegetables.

Preheat the oven to 200°C (400°F). Clean and truss
the chicken. Roast 45 to 50 minutes. After the
chicken has cooked for about 20 minutes, place the
potatoes in an ovenproof dish, sprinkle with salt and
pepper and drizzle with olive oil. Roast with the
chicken for 20 to 30 minutes.

Reheat the vegetables in a saucepan with a little
chicken stock. Mash the truffles with a fork and add.
Cut the chicken into quarters and serve with the
vegetables, potatoes and tomatoes. Sprinkle with
parsley and serve with the reduced chicken stock.

Fruit salad

Cut the finest examples of seasonal fruits into large
chunks. Arrange them casually on a platter and serve.

Country romance in the middle of town
Bjørnsgard, Oslo

Bjørnsgård is just a 20-minute drive from Oslo, in Nordmarka, on the edge of Bogstad Lake. It encompasses 19 historical buildings from different valleys in southern Norway all placed around a charming courtyard. Anton Raabe started collecting these beautiful buildings in the 1930s. Raabe was from Oslo, born in 1899, and trained as a surgeon. He was also a sports and nature enthusiast. Even though he lived at Slemdal, close to Oslo's best walking areas, he still wanted a cabin in Nordmarka. He was fortunate enough to buy a lot from the Bogstad estate, then he started searching for the right cabin. Anton Raabe was interested in history and a hopeless romantic. The result of all this was a Norwegian peasant romantic building, in the guise of an old cottage from Sørum. Skihytta (the skiing cabin) was the first building, but others followed close behind. People came from far and wide to be operated on by this skilled surgeon, and he traveled to see his patients and to hunt, his other passion. He was always hearing about old houses that might be for sale. Raabe went to see them, and if he liked them, he bought them and had them moved to Nordmarka.

Storloftet, dating from the 13th century, is the oldest building and one the largest and best-preserved medieval buildings in Norway. It was originally from Su-Saar in Heddal in Telemark and is a combination of storage, living, and sleeping quarters. Today it houses a fantastic collection of regional costumes on display for guests to enjoy. Østerdalsstuen contains a unique and interesting restaurant. The building was constructed in Røros in 1608 and was moved to Dalsbygda in Os in Østerdal valley as part of a dowry. Anton Raabe found Årestuen, or Guristuen as it is often called, at Kruke farm in Heidal. When he arrived at Kruke for the first time, he saw that this 16th century open hearth dwelling had been moved away from the farmyard. He wondered why. He was told that it was haunted by a farm girl who had been killed there.

Raabe was allowed to spend the night in the windowless dwelling. No ghost appeared. But maybe he told ghost stories the next morning just for fun. Shortly thereafter, the house was moved to Bjørnsgard. Today, afternoon coffee is served in this building, which is a perfect example of how Norwegians lived in the Middle Ages both before and after the plague. It is said that Prillar-Guri, the girl who warned farmers with her horn at the battle of Kringen in 1612 and helped them defeat the Scottish mercenaries on their way to Sweden, was born in this building. Teigestuen, the youngest building, dating from 1780, is right on the edge of Bogstad Lake. It comes from Kvam in the Gudbrandsdal valley. It houses charming guest rooms complete with canopy beds and beautiful priceless antiques. Brokkeloftet from the 16th century and Rygnestadloftet from the 17th century came to Bjørnstad from Valle in Setesdal. The 16th century Trollburet came from Vinje in Setesdal, while Harildstadburet came from Skåbu in Gudbrandsdal. Finally there were 19 buildings, large and small. Anton Raabe understood the value of these houses and he understood their importance as cultural treasures. In addition to Bjørnstad, he also had collections at Hulderheim in Bykle in Setesdal and Streitlien in Folldal. Both of these are now state museums.

BACK IN THE FAMILY

Raabe was a widower for many years, but after the war, he married the actress Tore Segelcke. Bjørnsgard was their private home, but in 1947, they decided to make it available to the public. They set up a foundation, which allowed them both to live at Bjørnsgard for the rest of their lives, and both are buried there. Oslo City Council took over the estate after their death, but the property was virtually unused until

unique cultural and historic collection containing many Norwegian treasures. It is part of "The really good life" hotel chain. You really can experience the good life at Bjørnsgard – as we live today and as we lived many hundreds of years ago.

1989. At that time, three of Raabe's grandchildren, Nils, Morten, and Olaf Raabe, together with Knut Kloster Junior, bought the estate. The sales contract stipulated that the new owners were required to rehabilitate the buildings and preserve them with their historical importance in mind. They have certainly kept their half of the bargain. Bjørnsgard is now a

Above: Østerdalsstuen, originally built in Røros in 1608, houses Bjørnsgard's restaurant.

Teigestuen dates from 1780 and came from Kvam in the Gudbrandsdal valley. There are charming guest bedrooms with canopy beds and beautiful rustic antiques in this building, which is right on Bogstad Lake.

Warm-smoked trout salad with apple-celeriac cream

Warm-smoked trout
400 g boneless trout fillet
2 1/2 teaspoons sugar
1 1/2 teaspoons salt

Apple-celeriac cream
1 1/2 dl (2/3 cup) dairy
sour cream (do not use
low-fat sour cream)
1/2 teaspoon sugar
1/2 teaspoon grated
horseradish
100 g (4 oz) celeriac
1 green apple
salt
freshly ground
black pepper

Warm-smoked trout
Divide the trout into four pieces of equal size. Combine the sugar and salt and rub all over the fish. Refrigerate 12 hours. Rinse well in cold water and dry with paper towels. Smoke in a mini-home smoker for 8 minutes.

Apple-celeriac cream
Whip the sour cream with sugar and horseradish. Peel and grate the celeriac. Blanch the celeriac shreds in lightly salted boiling water for about 20 seconds. Plunge into cold water, drain and dry with paper towels. Peel and grate the apple. Fold the celeriac and apple into the sour cream and season with salt and pepper. Serve with a mixed greens, such as lollo rosso, curly endive and arugula, tossed in balsamic vinaigrette. Arrange on individual plates and top with fish and celeriac-apple cream.

Rhubarb terrine with strawberries and vanilla sauce

Chocolate base
3 eggs
100 g (1/2 cup) sugar
60 g (1/3 cup)
potato starch
(or cornstarch)
1 teaspoon baking
powder
2 tablespoons cocoa

500 g (1 lb) fresh
rhubarb
300 g (1 cup) sugar
5 gelatin sheets
3 dl (1 cup)
whipping cream

Vanilla sauce
1 vanilla bean
2 1/2 dl (1 cup) full
fat milk
2 1/2 dl (1 cup)
whipping cream
90 g (scant 1/2 cup) sugar
5 egg yolks

5 dl (2 cups) sliced
fresh strawberries

Chocolate base
Preheat the oven to 250°C (475°F). Line an oven sheet with baking parchment. Grease well. With an electric mixer, beat the eggs and sugar until light and lemon-colored. Sift over the potato starch, baking powder and cocoa, folding lightly until just combined. Spread the batter in a 1 cm (1/2") layer over the parchment. Bake 5 minutes. Sprinkle a sheet of baking parchment the same size as the cake with sugar. Turn out the cake onto the sugared parchment.

Cut the rhubarb into 3 cm (1 1/4") pieces. Cook with sugar until tender. Puree in a food processor. There should be about 5 dl (2 cups) puree. Soak the gelatin in cold water for about 2 minutes. Squeeze to remove excess water and melt in the rhubarb puree, stirring until smooth. Cool slightly. Whip the cream, then fold it into the rhubarb mixture.

Line a loaf pan with plastic wrap. Cut two pieces of cake the same size as the pan. Place one in the bottom. Pour over the rhubarb mixture. Top with the second piece of cake. Press down lightly. Refrigerate until serving time.

Vanilla sauce
Split the vanilla bean lengthwise and scrape out the seeds. Place in a saucepan with the milk, cream and sugar and heat to boiling.

Lightly whisk the egg yolks. Whisk in the hot milk mixture, then return to the pan. Heat until thickened, whisking constantly. Do not allow to boil. Strain, then refrigerate.

Remove the terrine from the pan and cut into even slices. Arrange on individual plates with the fresh berries and vanilla sauce. 8 servings.

Rack of lamb with summer vegetables, new potatoes and thyme jus

Lamb stock
2 kilo (4 1/2 lb) lamb bones
and trimmings
1 carrot, in coarse chunks
2 onions, coarsely chopped
100 g (4 oz) celeriac, peeled and
coarsely chopped
1 medium leek, coarsely chopped
4 garlic cloves
1 branch fresh thyme
1 bay leaf
10 black peppercorns

Rack of lamb
4 racks of lamb, about
250 g (8 oz) each
olive oil
salt
freshly ground black pepper
4 slices day-old white bread,
crusts removed
1 tablespoon fresh thyme
1 tablespoon fresh basil
1 garlic clove

Summer vegetables
assorted small vegetables,
such as cauliflower, broccoli,
baby carrots, and spring onions
salt
1 tablespoon butter
1 teaspoon finely chopped chives
1 teaspoon minced fresh parsley

Roasted new potatoes
600 g (1 1/3 lb)
new potatoes
olive oil
pepper

Thyme jus
5 dl (2 cups) lamb stock
2 tablespoons unsalted butter
1 tablespoon minced fresh thyme

*Trond Skogvoll is both manager
and chef at Bjørnsgard.*

Lamb stock
Preheat the oven to 200°C (400°F). Place the lamb bones and trimmings in an oven pan and brown for 30 minutes. Add the vegetables and brown 15 minutes more. Transfer to a stockpot and add water to cover. Bring to a boil. Skim well. Add thyme, bay leaf and peppercorns and let simmer 4 hours. Strain.

Rack of lamb
Preheat the oven to 200°C (400°F). Brown the racks of lamb in oil and sprinkle with salt and pepper. Tear the bread into chunks, place in a food processor with the herbs and garlic, and process into green crumbs. Place the lamb on an oven sheet and press the crumbs over the fat. Bake 8 minutes. Let the meat rest until just before serving.

Summer vegetables
Wash, clean and cut the vegetables into small chunks. Cook separately in lightly salted water until almost tender. Drain, then combine the vegetables. Just before serving, glaze with butter and sprinkle with chives and parsley.

Roasted new potatoes
Preheat the oven to 200°C (400°F). Scrub the potatoes, cut into wedges if large, and toss with olive oil. Bake about 20 minutes, until tender. Sprinkle with salt, pepper and parsley.

Thyme jus
Return the meat to the oven for 3 minutes. Remove and let rest. Measure 5 dl (2 cups) lamb stock and reduce by half. Arrange vegetables and potatoes on a platter. Cut the meat into chops and arrange on the platter. Remove the stock from the heat and beat in the butter and thyme. Season with salt and pepper. Serve alongside.

Oslo's most spectacular view

Holmenkollen Park Hotel Rica, Oslo

"Forest-covered mountain ridges, and meadows with rivers, ponds and peaceful farms…spreading out for miles toward the north, east, and west. Open to the Oslofjord to the south, with a fantastic view of Norway's beautiful capital, with its islands, skerries, inlets, and blue sea.

That's what you can see from Holmenkollen, the famous hill over Oslo. And that's the setting for Holmenkollen Tourist Hotel & Sanitarium, on the southern slope, against the forest in the background with the impressive panorama in front, as it invites you for a comfortable and invigorating stay.

The impressive hotel sits like a fairy tale castle nestled against the mountain, 350 meters above sea level. A birch tree lined avenue leads up to the hotel. Peaceful, cool walking paths surround the hotel – and extend into the secluded forests – Holmenkollen ski jump, where Europe's most famous skiing competition is held every March – to Frognerseteren, that famous excursion point where sporty youth gather every Sunday and in the evening – to Tryvann Stadium, with Europe's highest altitude skating rink, where you watch Olympic champions practice their skating skills, or even Sonia Henie twirling across the ice on her toes – to Kongsseteren, where the two small princesses tumble in the snow, as their parents, the Crown Prince and Princess, and their grandparents, King Haakon and Queen Maud, look on.

You see the entire city from your hotel window: Oslo with medieval Akershus castle across from the town hall. Oslo, the home of King Haakon and Queen Maud. The home town of Henrik Ibsen, Fridtjof Nansen, Roald Amundsen, and Edvard Munch…"

That's how Holmenkollen Tourist Hotel presented itself in a 1935 brochure. A great deal has changed since then. The capital has grown and Holmenkollen is now a residential district. The two small princesses, Astrid and Ranghild, became adults long ago, and their parents and grandparents are long dead. But the beautiful old hotel is still standing high above the city and still has one of the best views in town. It has been one of Oslo's major tourist attractions for over 100 years – a proud monument to Norway's national romantic dragon style. Now it is the exclusive Holmenkollen Park Hotel Rica, and guests flock from around the world to stay there.

A DOCTOR'S DREAM

It wasn't always like that. In the beginning, it was Holmenkollen Sanitarium, and patients, not hotel guests, followed the path up the hill to the wooden castle.

Homenkollen Sanitarium and Hotel was built by a doctor from Skien, Christian Lund Holm, who wanted to offer healthy living to as many people as possible. To him, healthy living meant light, fresh air, clean water, and outdoor living. He finished his studies in 1872, and opened a practice in Larvik. He soon discovered a source of sulfur by the Farris river, later called King Haakon's Spring, and founded Larvik Spa in 1880. In 1878, Dr. Holm moved to Christiania and founded an inhalation therapy center and practiced as a specialist in respiratory diseases, in addition to running the spa. In 1883, he established Christiania Baths on the site of Torggata Baths today. He was administrative director and chief of medicine there until 1895, and he even installed a sauna. He also worked as a consultant in the construction of spas around the country.

Dr Holm's next large project was opening the Holmenkollen and Voksenkollen area to the population of the capital. He had dreamt of building a sanitarium there since the 1870s, and he finally managed to buy 50 acres from the Holmenkol-Voxenkol-Company for NOK 10 000. His dream would finally become a reality. He founded the Holmekollen Tourist Hotel and Sanitarium corporation together with brewery owner Ellef Ringnes and merchant Alfred Larsen.

HOTEL, SANITARIUM, AND A BIG FIRE

Dr. Holm placed architect Holm Munthe, who had also designed Larvik Spa, in charge of designing the hotel, sanitarium, and the restaurants. The hotel was finished in 1890 and soon became the capital's most popular local excursion destination, and "Aftenposten" newspaper wrote this about it on October 25, 1889:

"The number of visitors this autumn has been so great, that I don't think it would be an exaggeration to compare the road to Holmenkollen on a beautiful Sunday morning with one in Corso. And this isn't just because the novelty of the place has awakened our curiosity. One gets the feeling that this immigration, which it resembles, is because the local population has traded in their parlor life for fresher air and more healthy living. We can only imagine that this traffic will increase in the years that come."

The enormous popularity of the hotel meant that most of the space was used for cafés and restaurants. So much so that there was room for only 15 guests to spend the night. This was not Dr Holm's intention, so he started building a sanitarium next to the hotel. It opened the summer of 1891 and catered to all kinds of ailments, except for tuberculosis and other contagious diseases. Here people could come to enjoy light, fresh air, water, and outdoor activities. And they came in droves!

On January 31, 1892, all of Oslo showed up to watch the first ski jump on newly built Holmenkollen hill. The annual competition was now moved from Huseby hill to Holmenkollen. The new sanitarium quickly outgrew its premises, so Dr. Holm built a new larger one which opened in 1894.

But on March 31 of the following year, catastrophe struck. The popular tourist hotel burned to the ground just five years after it was opened. The cause of the fire was never determined, but one theory was that a candle had fallen onto a carpet and set it alight.

CATASTROPHE STRIKES AGAIN

It didn't take long before rebuilding started, this time with Holm Munthe's assistant, Ole Sverre, as architect. The result was an impressive building twice the size of the previous one. It resembled a Norwegian fairy tale castle decorated with innumerable verandas and elaborate woodcarving, complete with dragon heads adorning the gables. Its perfect setting quickly made it one of Oslo's most popular destinations after it opened in 1896. And when a local railway opened in 1898, carriage drivers stood at the final stop (now Besserud station) waiting to take passengers the short distance up to the hotel by horse and carriage. But this building, like so many other unique national romantic buildings, would also be consumed by fire. On the evening of July 10, 1914 a powerful thunderstorm hit the city, sending a bolt of lightning through the hotel's electrical cables. In just two hours, this beautiful hotel was reduced to ashes.

Dr. Holm had withdrawn from the managing of the hotel in 1905 to concentrate on a new project, Dr. Holm's Hotel at Geilo. Many plans were made for rebuilding the hotel, but nothing ever came of them. Instead, the sanitarium from 1894, which had always been run together with the hotel, took over the hotel side of the business.

WAR AND NEW OWNERS

The years passed. The hotel was a popular destination, both for relaxing holidays, weekend breaks and vacations, but it was also a popular day trip for the citizens of the capital. When World War II broke out in 1940, the Germans occupational forces requisitioned the hotel for living quarters, and they wrecked the beautiful building. The wooden walls and rich carvings were painted over. After the war, the Norwegian military forces took over the hotel for temporary housing for Norwegian officers and their families returning from England and North America.

It wasn't until mid-1947 that the hotel was released and then sold to a corporation formed by superior court lawyer Harald Ramm, restaurateur Hans Telle, and Jakob Berg. They immediately started a thorough restoration and modernization, and the hotel was re-opened in 1948. It was considered one of Oslo's most exclusive hotels, and was a popular destination for royalty from around the world. It was the natural gathering point during the annual Holmenkollen competition, and the Royal Lunch at Holmenkollen Tourist Hotel soon became a yearly tradition.

Many new expansions were planned over the years, but nothing ever came of them. After Harald Ramm's death in 1970, the hotel was sold to NEMI, Northern European Management Institute, which used the hotel as a course center until the organization was disbanded, seven years later. Shipowner Leif Høegh, one of the owners, bought out the others and took over the hotel on January 1, 1978.

He quickly began fixing up the hotel. The newly expanded Holmenkollen Park Hotel opened its doors just before the World Championships in skiing took place in Oslo in 1982. A new addition offered 150 new guestrooms, which Oslo sorely needed. The Høegh family still owns the hotel, but in 1986, they turned its management over to the Rica Chain, Norway's largest privately owned hotel chain. The name was changed to Holmenkollen Park Hotel Rica.

The old sanitarium at Holmenkollen is now a modern hotel. The beautiful old building has been lovingly restored and houses the hotel restaurants, banquet and conference rooms. The gourmet restaurant "De Fem Stuer" is like a miniature national romantic museum – with old Norwegian interiors, beautiful paintings and decorations. The staff at the Holmenkollen Park Fitness & Spa look after the guests' health and well-being, which, after all, was why the hotel was built in the first place. The center opened in 1999 and has a fully equipped fitness center with a variety of machines, a climbing wall, a golf simulator, a swimming pool, a whirlpool bath, a spa and mineral bath, a solarium, saunas, and a hair salon. In addition, there are individual cubicles for facials, manicures, massages, or hydrotherapy. And right outside is Oslomarka, as it has been there all along, with fresh air, breathtaking nature, and well-marked walking paths and skiing trails.

The hotel's gourmet restaurant "De Fem Stuer" is located in the old wooden building which originally housed the hotel's dining and sitting rooms.

Reindeer with mushroom tart and chevre sauce

Game stock

2 kilo (4 1/2 lb) game bones, cut
into chunks
1 carrot
1 onion
1/2 leek
1/2 celeriac
butter

Sauce

1/2 onion
40 g (1 1/2 oz) celeriac
40 g (1 1/2 oz) leek
40 g (1 1/2 oz) carrot
oil
2 dl (3/4 cup) red wine
5 dl (2 cups) game stock
2 dl (1 cup) whipping cream
100 g (3 1/2 oz) chevre
salt, pepper

Mushroom tart

200 g (7 oz) mushrooms
butter
2 sheets (170 g, 6 oz)
puff pastry
4 tablespoons (1/4 cup)
chopped parsley
salt, pepper
3-4 tablespoons grated
Parmesan cheese

Preheat the oven to 200°C (400°F). Place the bones in an oven tray and brown for 15 minutes. Turn the bones and brown 15 minutes more. Transfer to a stockpot and add water to cover. Bring to a boil and skim. Wash, clean and cut the vegetables into chunks. Brown in a little butter in a frying pan. Add to the stock and let simmer about 5 hours, adding water as necessary. Strain, return to the boil and reduce to 5 dl (2 cups).

Sauce

Wash, peel and finely dice the vegetables. Sauté in a little oil in a saucepan. Add the wine and reduce by half. Add the stock and cream and whisk in the chevre. Reduce by half. Strain. Season with salt and pepper.

Preheat the oven to 175°C (350°F). Wash and clean the mushrooms. Sauté in butter until golden. Line four individual tartlet pans with puff pastry. Stir the parsley into the mushrooms and season with salt and pepper. Spoon into the pastry shells. Sprinkle with Parmesan. Bake 5 to 10 minutes.

Reindeer

720 g (1 3/4 lb) filet of reindeer
butter
salt, pepper

Preheat the oven to 175°C (350°F). Brown the meat in butter in an ovenproof frying pan. Sprinkle with salt and pepper. Roast about 5 minutes. The meat should be pink inside.

To serve, slice the meat and arrange in a fan on each plate. Serve with the tarts and sautéed shredded snow peas. Serve the sauce alongside.

Marinated whale carpaccio with lime, carrot puree and caper cream

Marinated whale carpaccio

400 g (14 oz) whale meat
1 tablespoon salt
1 tablespoon sugar
20 g (2 tablespoons) white peppercorns, crushed
mustard seed
juice of 1 lime

Carrot puree

250 g (9 oz) carrots
salt, pepper

Caper cream

150 g (5 oz) capers
3 gelatin sheets
1 1/2 dl (2/3 cup)
whipping cream
salt, pepper
lemon juice

Place the meat in a glass dish and rub with the remaining ingredients. Refrigerate 72 hours, turning the meat after 36 hours. Remove the meat, pack in plastic wrap and freeze. About 30 minutes before serving, remove from the freezer. Cut into thin slices and arrange in a single layer on large plates.

Carrot puree

Wash, peel and boil the carrots in a small amount of water until tender. Strain and mash well. Season with salt and pepper. Form the puree into small eggs with a tablespoon. Reheat just before serving.

Caper cream

Soak the gelatin in cold water to soften, about 5 minutes. Puree the capers in a food processor. Whip the cream until soft peaks form. Fold into the caper puree. Season with salt, pepper and lemon juice. Squeeze to remove excess water and melt the gelatin in a water bath. Stir into the caper cream. Refrigerate until set. Form into small eggs with a tablespoon. Garnish the carpaccio with carrot and caper eggs.

Chocolate sheets layered with blackberries and vanilla cream

200 g (7 oz) bittersweet chocolate

200 g (7 oz) blackberries
1 dl (scant 1/2 cup) sweet liqueur
(Drambuie, Grand Marnier,
Cointreau)

1 vanilla bean
5 dl (2 cups) whipping cream
5 egg yolks
100 g (1/2 cup) sugar
50 g (scant 1/2 cup) cornstarch

Melt the chocolate in a water bath and spread it in a thin layer over parchment paper. When nearly set, cut into squares. Let set completely.

Marinate the berries in the liqueur for a few hours before serving.

Split the vanilla bean lengthwise and scrape out the seeds. Scald the cream with the seeds. Beat the egg yolks with the sugar and cornstarch. Gradually whisk the cream into the egg yolks. Return the mixture to the saucepan and heat, until thickened whisking constantly. Cool.

To serve, make two layers of chocolate, vanilla cream and berries on each plate. Top with a chocolate sheet and garnish with mint leaves.

The elegance of bygone days

Losby Manor, Finstadjordet

Below: From the large, lovely terrace, you can enjoy the view of the golf course and the beautiful landscape.

Lorenz Meyer Boeck and his wife Katherine, nee Brinch, moved to Losby Manor in Lørenskog, not far from Oslo, in 1893. He was heir to Losby, the Munkedammen estate in Christiania (Oslo) as well as Refsnes Manor near Moss. Katherine was the daughter of shipowner and builder Christian Brinch. Losby had been owned by the same family, with only a few small lapses, since the 1830s. It was an important source of income as well as a popular gathering spot for family and friends, especially during the hunting season. Losby was a wedding present from Lorenz's parents and they were the first owners of the estate to actually live on the property. That also marked the beginning of the period that was to be Losby's heyday – and it would last well into the 1920s. The young owners were very hospitable, and the location was perfect, just close enough to the capital to support a glittering social life. Members of society, as well as many diplomats, visited. Even King Haakon VII was a frequent guest. Losby's hunting grounds were ideal, filled with rabbit, hare, woodcock, and other large game birds. But New Year's was also a busy season, with the house filled with guests attending grand parties. Most guests arrived at Lørenskog station by train, where they were met by special carriages driven by uniformed footmen. Transportation was the least of their problems. The estate had 24 horses, in addition to six "fine" horses. The guests were wrapped in giant furs, with hot water bottles to keep them extra warm, before they were transported by horse and sleigh through the dark wintry landscape to Losby. The squire and his wife greeted the guests while the footmen delivered the luggage to the individual rooms. The chambermaids then unpacked all the baggage so

the guests would have enough time to dress for dinner. In the kitchen, the cook and staff were busy preparing an impressive dinner. The dining room table could seat 35, and it was set with Norwegian, Danish, and Swedish silver, huge porcelain dishes, and beautiful Nøstetangen and Biri glasses. These were busy times, not least of all for the servants. After dinner, they wandered from room to room serving hot coffee before setting the table for the late evening snack. The had to be up early the next day to tend to all 35 fireplaces. The guests also needed hot and cold water, which had to be carried to the second story bedrooms in buckets. Outdoor activities were all the rage at the time, so most of the guests went skiing or walking after breakfast. This gave the servants time to clean the rooms and make the beds.

A BUSINESS CRISIS

But there's more to running an estate than hunting and parties. Squire Lorenz Boeck ran a large estate with over 250 acres of sown land. There was also 11 000 acres of forest for timber and a sawmill. He was the richest man in the area, paid the most taxes

Above: Losby Manor stands proud and magnificent in the inviting open landscape which is now dominated by the beautiful 18-hole golf course. And behind it the forests are calling...

Left: "Bound" – Nicolaus Widerberg's beautiful blue torso stands beside the glass doors leading to the golf course.

Right: The large, light breakfast room is the largest of the pavilions around the kitchen.

and was the pinnacle of society. He had many employees, mainly tenants. Tenants were part of an old feudal system that provided the estate with cheap, stable laborers with no land of their own. They were the lowest on the social ladder. They received a cottage and a small plot of land to till and maintain a few animals in return for their labor. The Norwegian tenant system was slowly, but surely, disbanded from the 1860s on, but not at Losby. A 1910 census registered 14 tenants and their families on the estate. Lorenz Boeck was described as a "sympathetic and friendly man", but he was not a talented businessman or administrator. He much preferred partying with his social equals from the capital to running an estate. All the estate's revenues went to supporting his expensive lifestyle, which meant that there was no money for the technical and organizational modernization needed to cope with the new century. When his mother died in 1917, Lorenz and Katherine left Losby. They spent winters at Munkedammen and summers at Refsnes. Losby lay dormant except for hunting and New Year's parties. The 1920s were lean years. The family businesses weren't doing well and Losby was a financial drain on the once wealthy landowner. These financial difficulties also affected the other family properties. Katherine Boeck sold Munkedammen and Refsnes after her husband died in 1936 and moved back to Losby, where she lived until her death on New Year's Eve, 1959.

The couple had no heirs. Their only offspring, a daughter, had died just hours after birth. So Losby went from owner to owner. Losby Manor, once a center of life, was left empty and uninhabited. Soon it started to decay.

A NEW ERA FOR AN OLD ESTATE

Frode, Per, and Tove Fjellheim took over the estate in the mid-1980s. It was in bad shape after so many years of negligence. They wanted to recreate Losby's grandeur. But this time, anyone could experience it, not just landowners and aristocracy. The siblings dreamt of starting a hotel, conference center, and golf course at Losby. They wanted the interesting history of the house, and the house itself, to play a vital role in the plans.

It would take 15 years to turn the dream into reality. They finally reopened the doors in 1999 and welcomed the first guests to a unique modern hotel, an exciting and very successful combination of old and new. The old building had been restored to its former glory, and beside it, they had built a harmonizing addition.

The setting is ideal. Losby is only half an hour's drive from the center of Oslo, but the last kilometers are on a country road that snakes through fields, plains, and forest. Then you see Losby ahead, a fairy tale house set in the middle of a mystical forest. Outdoor life is still in style at Losby, and the local area offers many temptations, including walking paths, tennis, and riding. But Losby is first and foremost a golfer's paradise. The large 18-hole Østmork golf course lies next to the river that runs through Losby valley and offers a challenge to golfers of all levels. There is also a 9-hole course at Vestmork, which is perfect for a quick evening round, or for novice players. Innesvingen golf is Norway's most modern indoor training center and offers training on seven simulators where you can "play" on 33 courses from around the world. Last, but not least, there's Losby Golf Academy, which offers private tutoring. There's also a golf shop at Losby. And if the golfing virus has not bitten you yet, you can try out some of the more traditional activities like hunting, fishing, skiing, and sleigh riding, just as the royals, nobles, and aristocrats did during Losby's heyday.

Left: The beautifully restored ballroom features rococo chairs with gold trim, crystal chandeliers and a sand-scrubbed wooden floor.

Right: The beautiful ladies' salon also functions as an anteroom to the dining room.

Halibut with arugula and soy jus

150 g (5 oz) arugula
1 dl (scant 1/2 cup) virgin olive oil
salt, pepper
4 halibut fillets, about
100 g (3 1/2 oz) each
clarified butter
4 shallots
4 garlic cloves
2 teaspoons minced fresh ginger
1 dl (scant 1/2 cup) sweet soy
sauce (kecap manis) (regular soy
sauce does not work in this dish)

Clean the arugula, removing tough stalks. Refresh in ice water. Just before serving, toss with olive oil, salt and pepper.

Sauté the fish in clarified butter and olive oil. The fish should be golden brown with a small raw core. Keep warm, Mince the shallots and garlic and sauté with the ginger in clarified butter. Add the soy sauce and heat.

Make a bed of arugula on each plate. Top with the fish. Drizzle with sauce.

Wild duck breast with black currant sauce, shallots in red wine, Paulo potatoes and deep-fried black salsify

4 duck breasts

4 baking potatoes
salt, pepper
1 dl (scant 1/2 cup)
clarified butter

2 dl (3/4 cup)
whipping cream
4 dl (1 2/3 cups)
duck stock
100 g (scant 1 cup) black
currants (frozen or fresh)
sugar

4 shallots
2 garlic cloves
1 dl (1/2 cup) beef stock
1 dl (1/3 cup) red wine
fresh thyme and oregano

3 black salsify
soybean oil

Preheat the oven to 120°C (250°F). Brown the duck breasts, skin side down, in a dry hot ovenproof pan. Turn and brown lightly on the other side. Roast in the oven until the meat reaches an internal temperature of 54°C (130°F), about 5 minutes. Let the meat rest for 7 to 10 minutes before serving.

Preheat the oven to 165°C (325°F). Cut the potatoes into cylinders with a small ring. Peel and cut into thin even slices with a mandoline. Layer in cocotte molds, sprinkling salt and pepper between each layer. Fill with clarified butter. Bake about 20 minutes, until the potatoes are tender.

Combine the cream and duck stock in a saucepan. Add the currants. Puree with an immersion blender. The sauce should be bright red. Season with salt, pepper and sugar.

Peel the shallots and garlic and simmer in the stock, wine and herbs until tender.

Peel the salsify. Cut into thin strips with a potato peeler. Deep-fry in almost boiling soybean oil. Drain well on paper towels. Sprinkle with salt.

To serve, cut the breasts into even diagonal slices and serve with the potatoes, sauce and shallots. Serve with sautéed spinach and mushrooms and garnish with deep-fried salsify.

Gratinéed raspberries with cinnamon ice cream

1 vanilla bean
75 g (1/3 cup) sugar
1 dl (scant 1/2 cup)
water
pinch ground cinnamon
4 egg yolks
2 1/2 dl (1 cup)
whipping cream

1 dl (scant 1/2 cup)
white wine
75 g (1/3 cup) sugar
lemon juice
3 egg yolks
300 g (2 1/2 cups)
raspberries

Split the vanilla bean lengthwise and scrape out the seeds. Place the bean and seeds in a saucepan with the sugar, water and cinnamon. Heat to boiling and cook until the mixture forms threads. Beat the egg yolks until light, thick and lemon-colored. Beat in the sugar syrup. Beat until the mixture is room temperature. Whip the cream and fold into the egg yolk mixture. Freeze in an ice cream machine.

Combine the wine, sugar, lemon juice and egg yolks in a small saucepan. Whisk over low heat until light and creamy.

Preheat the oven grill. Divide the berries among four individual ovenproof dishes. Pour over the sauce. Place under the grill until the sauce is golden brown. Serve immediately with the ice cream. Garnish with mint leaves.

With a restaurant in the sitting room, and a guestroom in the storage house!

Trugstad Gård, Holter in Nannestad

"For two centuries, the Vikings tried to subdue this part of England with the sword and the flaming torch. If only they had sent Tove Haga, her stove and her recipes for reindeer, and delicious home-baked made apple cake, one hundred and ninety years of bloodshed could have been avoided, and the only fighting would have been in the queue to get to her dining table."

Sir Thomas Ingilby

There can't be better testimony to the cooking skills of Tove Haga of Trugstad Gård (Farm) than that. Sir Thomas Ingilby is master of Ripley Castle in Yorkshire, where he runs the distinguished Boar's Head Hotel. He is also one of many who have discovered Tove's exciting menus and often unusual flavor combinations. Game is a regular feature at the restaurant she runs with her husband Martin Haga at Trugstad Gård, and she has been chosen Norwegian "game chef of the year" six times.

Trugstad farm, with its fields and meadows, is located at Holter in Nannestad township, only a half-hour drive from Oslo and ten minutes from Oslo Airport at Gardermoen. The farm has probably been inhabited since the 800s and was originally called Strugirstad. The farm was owned by Oslo Cathedral until 1536. It is unknown whether the farm was given to the church as a gift, or if it was claimed by the church against unpaid taxes. At any rate, the property has been an independent farm since 1536.

Martin's great-great-grandfather Christian Halvorsen Trugstad bought the farm in 1850. He was the youngest son of a local farmer and therefore not blessed by the law of primogeniture, so he had to buy a farm. Early on, he decided that none of his four sons should suffer the same fate. He worked hard and managed to buy four farms, one for each son. But the son who was to inherit Trugstad died young, leaving the farm empty. A local vicar saw possibilities in the uninhabited farm, and from 1904 to 1939, it served as Nannestad's first old folks' home

FROM A FARM TO A RESTAURANT

Tove and Martin took over the old family farm in 1978. Martin kept his day job as a businessman in Oslo and worked at night as a farmer for the first 10 years. Tove had worked as a freelance chef since the mid-70s, mainly in restaurants abroad. In 1988, she decided to stop traveling so much and started holding

There's an intimate and cozy dining room as well as a fine collection of vintage bottles in the wine cellar.

cooking courses on the farm. She called them "creative cooking", and they soon became wildly popular, drawing people from a wide area. She toyed with the idea of opening a farm restaurant, and in 1992, her plans were implemented. Martin quit his Oslo job, and they leased out the fields and grazing land. They were going to be full time restaurateurs! Tore appointed herself chef de cuisine, while Martin was a self-educated maitre'd.

Business blossomed. Word of the magnificent food and hospitality at Trugstad Gård spread like wildfire at home and abroad. It is not unusual for the restaurant to serve guests from 20 different nations in one evening. The old 18th-century farm house functions perfectly as a restaurant and as a family home. Both the elegant dining room, which seats 38, and the intimate sitting room, with its cozy fireplace, are filled with beautiful antiques. Some are from the old farm, while others have been brought back from holiday destinations. The tables are decked with damask tablecloths, crystal, and silver – fit for a king!

Tove holds her cooking courses in the old farm kitchen, which can seat ten. You can also spend the night at Trugstad Gård! The old red storehouse has been converted into a unique, luxurious bedroom, which is often used by bridal couples after a wedding reception at the farm.

On most Saturdays, there is an informal café serving lunch, coffee, and cakes at Trugstad. Throughout the year, there are also theme evenings to celebrate the crayfish season and Martin's goose, or to taste a selection of exquisite armagnac. Tove and Martin's philosophy has been to keep things small and intimate, to attend to each guest as an individual. And they have succeeded. And with that we end as we started, with a quote from Sir Thomas Ingilby:

"Visits to Trugstad Gård are for me a privilege, a not-to-be-missed opportunity to expand my waistline and enrich the soul. For me, it is like a second home. Tove's cooking should have been listed as the eighth deadly sin, but some higher authority undoubtedly realized that there was no point in listing commandments that were beyond human temptation."

Salmon in cherry sauce

450 g (1 lb) skinless,
boneless salmon fillet
2 teaspoons pink peppercorns
tablespoon finely chopped dill
1 tablespoon grated lime zest

Cherry sauce
500 g (1 lb) cherries
2 dl (3/4 cup) water
2 dl (3/4 cup) red wine
1 1/2 teaspoons cornstarch
stirred into 1 tablespoon
cold water

Cut the salmon into four pieces of equal size. Place in a low, wide pan and fill with water to cover. Sprinkle with pepper, dill and lime and steam, covered, 3 to 4 minutes.

Cherry sauce
Pit the cherries. Heat the water and wine to boiling. Stir in the cornstarch mixture and cook until thickened. Stir in the cherries.

Arrange the fish on individual plates. Garnish with onion shoots, carrots cut into heart shapes and a puff pastry cage. Serve the sauce alongside.

Grilled filet of deer with black salsify sauce

Wild rice in a basket

4 tablespoons (1/4 cup) wild rice
5 dl (2 cups) water
1 tablespoon chopped sun-dried tomatoes
2 shallots, minced
1 tablespoon chopped leek
1 small bunch parsley, minced

Simmer the wild rice and water for about 30 minutes. Add the remaining ingredients and heat to boiling.

Potato basket

4 large potatoes

Wash and peel the potatoes. Press out excess water in a linen towel. Grate into long, thin shreds. Squeeze the shreds in a linen towel to remove the remaining liquid. Arrange in a potato-nest form and deep-fry at 180°C (350°F) for 30 to 40 seconds.

Black salsify sauce

8 black salsify
2 dl (3/4 cup) full-fat milk
2 dl (3/4 cup) whipping cream
11/2 tablespoons pepper jelly

Wash, peel and cut the salsify into chunks. Simmer in milk and cream until tender. Puree with an immersion blender. Return to the saucepan, add the jelly, and reduce by half. Thin with cream, if necessary.

Grilled deer

800 g (1 3/4 lb) strip loin of deer
oil

Brush the meat with oil. Heat a grill pan until almost smoking. Grill the meat for about 2 minutes per side. Pack in aluminum foil and let rest at least 5 minutes. Slice just before serving.

To serve, spoon the rice into the potato baskets and serve with tiny vegetables. Serve the salsify sauce alongside.

Red wine cake

300 g (10 oz) unsalted butter
300 g (1 1/2 cups) sugar
3 tablespoons baking powder
2 tablespoons vanilla sugar
2 tablespoons chocolate drink powder
2 tablespoons cinnamon
375 g (2 2/3 cups) all-purpose flour
5 eggs
2 1/2 dl (1 cup) red wine
100 g (3 1/2 oz) milk chocolate, chips
100 g (1 scant cup) blanched almonds,
coarsely chopped

Preheat the oven to 150°C (300°F). Grease and flour a 26 cm (10") springform pan. Combine all the ingredients except the chocolate and almonds in an electric mixer. Beat 3 minutes at medium speed. Stir in the chocolate and almonds. Pour into the prepared pan. Bake approximately one hour. Cool on a rack. When completely cold, wrap in foil and store overnight before serving.

Combine all the ingredients in the cream and spoon into a piping bag. Cut the cake into wedges and garnish with the cream. Pipe cream onto each plate and garnish with fresh berries.

Cream

125 g (4 1/2 oz) unsalted butter
1 tablespoon cinnamon
1 tablespoon chocolate drink powder
3 tablespoons sugar
1 egg yolk
6 tablespoons all-purpose flour
approximately 1 dl (scant 1/2 cup) red wine

An Olympic farm with a long and exciting history

Bjerke Gård, Lillehammer

The guest bedrooms are individually decorated with beautiful antiques and textiles.

Below: Ole Henrik Akeleye Braastad and his wife Annikken Stranger Berger run the traditional family farm today.

The XVII Winter Olympic games were held in Lillehammer in 1994. Who doesn't remember the pictures that flashed across our television screens? Joyful medal winners, the thrill of victory, and sportsmanship. A large and enthusiastic audience cheered for all the competitors, regardless of nationality. Spirits, trolls, and a fairytale landscape covered in icy lakes and snow-capped trees. The Lillehammer Olympic Games were the perfect publicity campaign for Norway. Foreigners probably best remember the fantastic pictures from CBS TV's breakfast programming. The hosts sat outside in 20 degrees below zero, freezing, with the steam from all the frost rising like a cloud up to the heavens, broadcasting live from the Olympic city to millions in America. The background view was breathtaking. The Gudbrandsdal river valley, the town of Lillehammer dressed in its finest winter scenery, and the spectacular Lysegård complex with the Olympic ski jumps. It was almost as if they were waiting for someone to land right in front of the camera.

It was no coincidence that the American television company chose Bjerke Gård as its Olympic studio, with its perfect location by the entrance to Gudbrandsdal valley, where the Mjøsa river crosses over to Lågen.

CROWN PROPERTY, CHURCH PROPERTY, AND A PRIVILEGED TRADE CENTER

Bjerke farm was established as a property as early as 500 AD. The first written documents are parchment letters dating from the 13th and 14th centuries, and we know that the farm was church and crown goods until 1660. The farm served as a lodge and coaching inn for pilgrims on their way to Nidaros (Trondheim) during the Middle Ages. The Danish nobleman Peter

Sigvardt Akeleye and his wife Johanne Alette Vibe moved to Bjerke farm in 1762. Akeleye originally came from Verne Kloster and Kambo farm. He was a captain in the Opland Dragoon regiment and had first come to Bjerke as an officer. His son Samuel bought the farm in 1792, and it has remained in the family ever since. Samuel had a commercial education from England, and among other things, had served as Bernt Anker's law clerk for Gudbrandsdal valley. The farm was the administrative center for Bernt Anker's real estate and timber business in the valley. During the 18th and 19th centuries, Bjerke Gård was the center for the forestry industry and timber floating from the Gudbrandsdal valley forests to the coastal sawmills.

Johanne Akeleye and her husband Haagen Ouren took over the farm after Samuel's death in 1809. Haagen came from Toten, and had managed a trade concession in Jørstadmoen. Bjerke farm became a royal trading center with letter of privilege from the Danish king himself. The farm was one of five such trading centers in Gudbrandsdal valley. This was 17 years before Lillehammer received its town status, so Berke was a bustling center of activity during these years. Farm produce was preserved and packaged here, grain was milled, and flour sold. Fruit was harvested from 130 trees and distributed, either in its natural form or as juice or jam. Butter, cheese, and honey cakes were produced year- round and sold on

Above: From the beautiful gazebo in the garden, you can look out over the Gudbrandsdal valley, the town of Lillehammer and the Olympic arena.

Right: The sitting rooms in the old Akeleye building from 1650 are a tribute to the creativity of the hosts.

You can relax in the gazebo and enjoy the fantastic view of Lillehammer and the surrounding landscape.

The hostess at Bjerke Gård, Annikken Stranger Bergerud, has decorated the blue room down to the smallest detail.

One of the four sitting rooms in the Akeleye building is a study in blue.

to Oslo. There was also trade in all sorts of imported items from hardware to furs. Fish was an important part of business. Bjerke farm has always been an important player in the historical inland herring trade. The trade privileges granted by the Danish king via Bulow were later renewed by Count Mørner on behalf of the Swedish king and lasted until 1872. But such privileges also brought with them obligations. Each fall, the farm was required to purchase and store seed grain to secure the harvest for the following year. This seed grain was stored in a silo, which can truly be described as a bank vault, and the activity of the grain silo can be considered as the forerunner of the savings bank in Lillehammer.

From 1790 to 1860 were glory days on the farm. Bjerke had rich resources and there was lots of activity. By the middle of the 19th century, the farm consisted of four agricultural properties in southern Gudbrandsdal valley. Their son Samuel Akeleye Ouren took over the farm in 1840. The trade privileges were renewed and maintained until Samuel's death in 1872.

DIFFICULT YEARS

After Samuel's death, his daughter Johanne Ouren inherited the historical family farm. This well-driven model farm now numbered 25 buildings and housed 25 people. Johanne married Bendik Båberg, from the large farm Båberg in neighboring Biri. Bendik loved to play the fiddle, but his love of partying was a greater vice, and he was soon an alcoholic. One day in 1905, as he was driving his horse and carriage home from the market, he stopped by the river, fell out of the carriage and drowned. He and Johanne had four children together. None of them ever married, and all were bitter toward their father. They even refused to mark their father's grave with a stone. Johanne ran the farm alone for a short time, then she transferred it to her son Samuel Akeleye Båberg and his younger brother Martin. The next 30 years were difficult – the brothers fought continuously, and there was jealousy, intrigues, and irreconcilable arguments. And they didn't just keep their feuding inside. The family feuding turned into fantastic stories at the hands of gossips, and kept the local population entertained. So much so that the intrigues at Bjerke farm became a part of Gudbrandsdal folklore during the first half of the 20th century.

Martin died in 1957, childless, like the rest of his siblings. The property was bought by Agnes and Sverre Braastad on behalf of Agnes's mother, Kari, who was Samuel Akeleye Ouren's granddaughter. She

had grown up on the farm, and by purchasing it, she ensured that it stayed in the family.

Bjerke Gård today

Today, Agnes and Sverre's son, Ole Henrik Akelye Braastad, and his wife, Anniken Stranger Bergerud, run the farm – with help from their children, Henriette, Johanne, and Samuel Akeleye. Ole has both an agricultural and an economics degree, but his background is in national and international research politics. He took over Bjerke Gård in 1974 and now dedicates his time to farming and forestry, while also working as a research strategy advisor. Anniken has worked in commerce and tourism in Lillehammer. She ran the Lillehammer Olympic Information Center and helped set up the Norwegian Olympic Museum, which she managed for its first few years. Now she spends most of her time managing the guest facilities at this lovely old farm. The busy days during the Olympics, when the farm was used both as a TV studio and as the Olympic base for Norsk Hydro's management, left them hungry for more. They enjoyed having a bustling farm, even if it could be tiring at times. They decided to continue receiving guests who wished to spend time in a genuine cultural and historic setting. Since the Olympics, they have had many important visitors, including Hilary Rodham Clinton. There are individually decorated guest rooms in the old Akeleye Building from 1650, in the 19th-century grain silo, and in the Hydro-CBS wing. Each room is special, combining history and the hosts' colorful imagination. Bjerke Gård is no ordinary hotel – it is a journey in time, through history, culture, and beauty.

Bjerke Gård is far from an ordinary hotel. The four beautiful sitting rooms in the old Akeleye building are decorated in different color nuances and have been furnished with creativity, flair and unexpected combinations.

Warm scallops with cockles, mussels and shrimp

4 scallops
8 cockles
1 kilo (2 1/4 lb) mussels
8 jumbo shrimp
1/2 garlic clove
3 dl (1 1/4 cups) dry white wine

4 shallots
6 dl (2 1/2 cups) shellfish stock
3 dl (1 1/4 cups) dry vermouth
1 dl (1/2 cup) whipping cream
75 g (2 1/2 oz) butter
4 egg yolks
juice of 1/2 lemon
salt
thyme branches plus
1 teaspoon minced fresh thyme

Scrub and rinse the shellfish. Remove the beard from the mussels. Place the shellfish in a saucepan with the shrimp. Add the garlic and wine, cover and steam until they open, about 4 minutes. Strain the cooking liquid (stock) and reserve.

Peel and slice the shallots. Place in a saucepan with the stock, vermouth and cream. Reduce to 4 dl (1 2/3 cups). Strain the stock. Beat in the butter in pats. Whisk the egg yolks in a bowl for 2 to 3 minutes (so they will be ready to absorb the stock). Gradually beat in the reduced stock over low heat to make a thick yet light sauce. Season with lemon juice and salt.

Clean the scallops. Use only the white muscle and the coral. Use thyme branches to stabilize the scallop shells, if desired. Return the muscle to the shell and nap with the sauce. Garnish with mussels, cockles, jumbo shrimp and thyme.

Artichokes with beurre blanc

300 g (10 1/2 oz) butter
6-8 egg yolks
1 1/2 dl (2/3 cup) dry white wine
1 teaspoon lemon juice
salt
fresh basil

2 artichokes
fresh basil
rosé pepper

Melt the butter and let it solidify again. Whisk the egg yolks. Gradually add 1/2 dl (3 1/2 tablespoons) of the wine. Whisk over low heat until the mixture thickens. Remove from the heat and whisk in the butter in pats, whisking constantly. Beat in the remaining wine. Season with lemon juice and salt. If the sauce separates, add drops of cold water. Just before serving, add the basil.

Choose artichokes that seem heavy for their size. The leaves should be tightly closed.
Cut off the tips of the leaves and clean the stalks. Boil, stalk up, in lightly salted water for 20 to 45 minutes, depending upon the size of the artichokes. Test for doneness by removing a leaf. If it comes out easily, the artichoke is cooked. Halve the artichokes and remove the choke before serving.

Make a mirror of sauce on each plate. Top with an artichoke half. Garnish with basil and rosé pepper. Remember to use heated plates.

A basket of berries

2 1/2 dl (1 cup)
whipping cream
2 tablespoons sugar
1 1/2 dl (2/3 cup)
all-purpose flour
1/2 teaspoon vanilla sugar

Filling

1 dl (1/3 cup) Drambuie
1 liter (quart) fresh berries
5 dl (2 cups) whipping cream
100 g (1/2 cup) sugar

Whip the cream, then add the remaining ingredients. Bake in a krumkake or pizzelle iron. When done, immediately drape the cookie over the bottom of a glass or cup. Let cool.

Filling

Pour the liqueur over the berries and let steep for 30 minutes. Whip the cream and add the sugar and liqueur.

Fill the baskets with berries and cream.

Kulturstua in Ro, Vestre Gausdal

Kulturstua i Ro is part of the cliff-hanging mountain farm called Ruud, at the top of Bødal in Vestre Gausdal valley. This untraditional and charming inn is run by Tor Jacobsen and Lina Dybdal. Lina moved to Ro in the summer of 2000, and she does all the baking on the premises and tends the herb garden.

The paths of fate can be inscrutable. Tor Jacobsen knows this for a fact. This son of a shoemaker grew up in a bustling agricultural community in Bærum, just outside Oslo, and he never thought he would end up as farmer and host at Ruud Gård, Ro in the local dialect. Tor Jacobsen is actually a licensed surveyor, but he has supplemented his education with different courses. He has studied urban development at Rauland Academy, cultural and nature guiding at the Norwegian State College of Physical Education and Sport, open-air guiding at the Norwegian Mountain School at Hemsedal, as well as log construction and building restoration at the Norwegian Technical Institute. He has worked as a surveyor on Spitzbergen for the Norwegian Polar Institute, a relief man in Vågå, and he has taught about outdoor life in both Scandinavia and the US as well as at a summer camp in Numedal. He has also restored numerous old houses and is an excellent blacksmith.

He would find many uses for his varied skills after he and ex-wife Elisabeth Enge decided to buy Ruud farm, located against a sheer cliff at the top of Bødal in Western Gausdal valley, in 1986. This farm, which dates back to the 12th century, had been well run and maintained, but it still proved to be quite a challenge. He managed to buy and lease extra land, which was an immediate help, but he couldn't escape the fact that Ruud is a difficult-to-run farm with limited resources and significant transport costs. Tor wanted to run a traditional farm complete with milk production, but gradually he realized that he needed to cater to tourists to supplement his income.

A LIVING MOUNTAIN FARM

He knew that this beautiful mountain farm, just 35 kilometers (20 miles) from Lillehammer, was an ideal starting point. The setting was also perfect, with many 18th century houses grouped around a sunny courtyard with a view over the valley and Vestfjell mountain, on the way to Jotunheim mountain. The tourists would love it, but he needed more space. He found two old buildings from the Madslien and Nordgard Aulstad farms in neighboring Olstad and moved them to Ruud, where all the planks, poles, moldings and window frames were carefully

reassembled on an old-fashioned stone foundation. It was a difficult job, and after four years of hard work, the Kulturstua in Ro finally opened in October, 1996. The log building, with its turf roof and tiny window-panes, houses a sitting room with an open fireplace and a dining room on the first floor, and the kitchen, a bathroom, and a large bedroom with wide box beds upstairs. It's come a long way since 1996, and more and more people are discovering this charming and unusual tourist attraction. So much so that more bedrooms are planned.

Guests at the Kulturstua in Ro can choose from many different kinds of activities, including nature walks, dogsledding, sledding, fishing and clay pigeon shooting. They can also eat a meal of game in authentic surroundings and enjoy theatre and literature evenings, and much, much more. But the food keeps them coming back. Kulturstua's reputation extends far beyond Norway's borders. Tor Jacobsen is a skilled cook, and he likes to make old-fashioned Norwegian food prepared in the traditional manner. His food is so good that people from more than 60 different countries have climbed the steep slopes to Kulturstua. He creates excellent dishes from local ingredients such as deer, reindeer, and moose, and freshwater fish like trout, salmon, char, and pike – serving them pickled, salted, or smoked. The dishes are prepared in his own smoke oven and are served freshly smoked straight from the oven. The herbs and spices come from his own garden, or grow wild in the forest. Everything is served with homemade flatbread and almond potatoes.

But a meal at Kulturstua in Ro consists of more than just good food. The host calls it a culinary cultural experience, because each meal is accompanied by his tales about local history, the farm and life

Left: A horse-drawn sleigh is a popular means of transport at the Kulturstua i Ro. Driver Olaf Bjerke is taking Tor Jacobsen and his daughter Kaya for a ride in the beautiful winter landscape.

Right: The Kulturstua i Ro is comprised of two old cookhouses from the area of Olstad, and the cozy fireside room is filled with antiques and beautiful old furniture.

A buffet of smoked foods is Kulturstua's specialty. Moose, deer, reindeer, trout, char, salmon and whitefish – warm-smoked, right from their own smoking oven. These are served with salads, homemade crispbread, bread and lefse.

long ago, and about an old piece of parchment from Gausdal parish dating from 1463 that mentions the farm. He'll gladly tell you about mountain dairy farming on Vestfjell mountain, or about when the farm produced enough to support two tenants, and about when the farm was a cotter's farm. There's a lot to discuss. You can discuss fishing or iron mining 2000 years ago, forestry, old house restoration, or the progress of a moose from forest to plate. All the old stories, combined with the historical buildings, idyllic farmyard, horses and cows, old stone wall and the weather beaten fence with its diagonal beams, the clear and pure mountain water and last, but not least,

the traditional food, tell you that you are at a living mountain farm in western Gausdal. And that is just what Tor Jacobsen, your farmer-host wants to convey at the charming and original Kulturstua.

Spinach-nettle tart

The base for this tart should be made a day in advance.

Dough basis
100 g (3/4 cup) all-purpose flour
75 g (5 tablespoons) butter, melted
1 1/2 teaspoons salt
1/3 teaspoon vinegar
about 1 1/2 tablespoons ice water.

Butter sheet for rolling
100 g (3/4 cup)
all-purpose flour
250 g (9 oz) soft butter

Filling
2 dl (1 cup) blanched spinach or nettle leaves
1 dl (1/2 cup) whipping cream
2 eggs
1 teaspoon salt
1/4 teaspoon pepper

Dough basis
Combine all ingredients and knead until smooth. Wrap the dough in plastic and refrigerate at least one hour.

Combine the flour and butter. Roll out between parchment paper or plastic wrap. Refrigerate at least one hour.

Roll out the dough to twice the size of the butter sheet. Place the butter sheet at one end. Fold over the dough, roll it out and fold into three layers. Wrap the dough in plastic and refrigerate 2 hours. Repeat 2 or 3 times. Refrigerate overnight. Roll out the dough into one large or four small round sheets. Place in pie pans.

Filling
Preheat the oven to 200°C (400°F). Combine all the ingredients and pour into the pans. Bake 20 to 40 minutes, depending upon the size of the pans.

Herb bread

Dough basis
1 liter (quart) water/milk
50 g (2 cakes or envelopes US) fresh yeast
2 teaspoons salt
oil/melted butter
1 egg (optional)
approximately 1 1/2 kg (3 1/3 lb., 10-11 cups) bread flour
fresh herbs in the summer, dried in the winter: oregano, marjoram, basil, parsley, chives, thyme, coarsely ground salt and pepper, garlic, chopped olives

Heat the liquid to 37°C (98°F). Crumble the yeast in the liquid. Add the remaining ingredients and knead (preferably with an electric mixer equipped with a dough hook) until smooth and elastic. Cover and let rise until doubled. Roll out the dough. Brush with olive oil or butter and sprinkle with herbs. Roll up. Cut into slices and place on a baking sheet lined with parchment paper. Cover and let rise 30 minutes. Preheat the oven to 225°C (425°F). Bake about 10 minutes.

The fairytale hotel east of the sun and west of the moon

GudbrandsGard Hotell, Kvitfjell

The XVII Olympic Games at Lillehammer in 1994 put Kvitfjell on the map. The downhill skiing events were arranged on the steep mountainsides above Fåvang in Ringebu township, 50 kilometers north of Lillehammer. The course at Kvitfjell was one of the most challenging and exciting in Olympic history, and later, the Ministry of Cultural Affairs and the Norwegian Ski Association decided that Kvitfjell Alpine Center should be a national center for alpine skiing, in particular downhill and super-G.

But Kvitfjell also has other exciting things for those who aren't world class skiers. That includes 20 kilometers of downhill slopes in every degree of difficulty for both adults and children, as well as seven lifts. There's a slope for free-style skiing and another for off-piste loose snow enthusiasts, as well as half-pipe, three big jumps, three quarter pipes, and a boarder cross for snowboarders. There is a special children's area with instructors and ski lift, so everyone gets safety tips as well as instruction regardless of proficiency and age. Kvitfjell also has 120 kilometers of cross-country skiing trails.

There are many activities and challenges: speed-skiing, downhill, ice-climbing, snowshoe hiking, snow volleyball, parallel slalom, and dog sledding. How about a romantic sleighride? Kvitfjell also offers summer activities, including hiking, alone or with a guide, fishing in mountain streams and rivers, horseback riding with instruction, rafting, paragliding, hang-gliding, tandem jumping, mountain biking, canoeing, mountain climbing, and moose safaris. An 18-hole golf course was inaugurated in the summer of 2001.

And if you get tired of all the sports, you can visit Ringebu stave church dating back to the 13th century, or Ringebu vicarage with its permanent art exhibition displaying more than 40 Jacob Weidemann paintings representing the milestones of his production from 1940 to the present day.

Or you can spend the day in the hotel swimming pool and gym, or just relax in the sun while admiring the fantastic view from the large terrace at GudbrandsGard.

A FAIRY TALE HOTEL

GudbrandsGard Hotell lies just outside Kvitfjell, 745 meters above sea level. The view over the river and the Gudbrandsdal valley is breathtaking. The hotel, owned by financier and investor Einar C. Nagell-Erichsen, opened in 1998 and was the first mountain lodge built in Norway in many years. Its design combines traditional Norwegian elements, giving it a nostalgic ambience. The owner wanted the hotel built in the local style, so that it would blend in with the older buildings. The builder visited Maihaugen, an open-air museum featuring fine examples of traditional architecture and studied stave-joining, a Norwegian building technique dating from the Middle Ages. He was especially interested in Garmo church, and studied how the roof rests on vertical poles, or staves as they are also called, and how these were

connected to horizontal poles at both top and bottom.

Then he returned to Kvitfjell and started building. The pine logs were felled in the high-altitude regions of Skjåk, Lesja and Nord-Østerdalen, so they would contain more tar, then transported to Kvitfjell. A craftsman carved each log individually, and slowly, the building took form. Slate for the floors was shipped in from Fåvang lower down the valley, while the roof was covered in earth and turf and sown with grass. The result was a handsome building indeed.

"Then they came to a castle that was so fine that her father's castle was but a humble dwelling in comparison. There she would be happy and live well, and all she had to do was make sure the fire never died out."

thought the princess when she arrived at the castle of the great white bear, King Valemon, in Asbjørnsen and Moe's fairy tale of the same name. At the entrance to GudbrandsGard Hotell stands a sculpture by Per Ung and Elena Englesen depicting the princess and King Valemon.

And maybe she still feels the same way, as she sits on his back and admires the fairytale hotel east of the sun and west of the moon.

Here she would be happy and live well....

Left: From the lobby. The interiors feature timeless, comfortable furniture and fine art on the walls.

Below: The Norwegian kitchen is king at GudbrandsGard Hotell, with exciting dishes prepared with fresh local ingredients. This table is set for dinner in the fireside room.

Right: The guest bedrooms are decorated with comfortable furniture and beautiful textiles.

Crispy dried ham on a bed of greens with soy-balsamic dressing

5 tablespoons (1/3 cup)
soy sauce
5 tablespoons (1/3 cup)
balsamic vinegar
1 1/2 tablespoons honey

2 liters (quarts) mixed salad
greens, such as radiccio rosso,
lollo and curly endive
12 stalks arugula
8 thin slices dried ham
2 tablespoons virgin olive oil

Heat the soy sauce, vinegar and honey to boiling. Lower the heat and simmer until slightly thickened, about 4 minutes. Cool completely.

Rinse and dry the greens. Tear into bitesize pieces.

Heat a frying pan until almost smoking. Fry the ham in the dry pan for 1 to 2 minutes per side.

Divide the greens among individual plates. Drizzle with oil. Top with ham. Drizzle soy-balsamic dressing over and around.

Baked halibut with smoked eggplant compote and red wine jus

2 shallots
virgin olive oil
3 3/4 dl (1 1/2 cups) red wine
3 dl (1 1/4 cups) veal stock
1 large or 2 small eggplants
salt, pepper

8 medium tomatoes
800 g (1 3/4 lb) halibut
fillets
8 asparagus stalks
2 tablespoons cold butter

Peel and mince the shallots and sauté in oil until shiny. Add the wine and reduce by half. Add the stock and reduce by half. Let cool.

Heat a frying pan until almost smoking. Place the whole eggplant(s) in the dry pan and fry on all sides. The peel will burn and start to crumble. When completely cooked, peel off the skin and mash the flesh with a fork or immersion blender. Season with oil, salt and pepper.

Scald, peel and cut the tomatoes into eight wedges. Remove the seeds.

Preheat the oven to 220°C (425°F). Cut the halibut into four pieces of equal size. Sprinkle with salt and pepper and place on an oven sheet. Bake 10 to 12 minutes. Remove from the oven, wrap in aluminum foil and let rest for about 5 minutes.

Combine eggplant and tomato in a saucepan and heat carefully.

Trim the asparagus and simmer in lightly salted water for 5 minutes. Halve.

Reheat the red wine jus and beat in the cold butter.

Place a mound of eggplant compote in the middle of the plate. Arrange 4 asparagus halves in a square on top. Place the fish on the asparagus and spoon a little jus around the fish.

Sorbets in a chocolate ring with raspberry coulis

200 g (7 oz) white chocolate
200 g (7 oz) semi-sweet chocolate
transparent acrylic sheets (used in
overhead projectors)
7 1/2 dl (3 cups) water
600 g (3 cups) sugar
1 egg white
1 kilo (2 1/4) frozen raspberries
400 g (14 oz) frozen blackberries
3 passion fruits
confectioner's sugar
mint leaves

Melt each chocolate in a separate bowl. Cut the acrylic sheets into 8 strips, about 21x5 cm each. First, brush the white chocolate on the strips, then the dark. Form each strip into a ring and fasten the ends with a paperclip. Refrigerate.

Heat the water and sugar to boiling. Simmer until the sugar is completely dissolved. Let cool, then add the egg white. Divide the sugar syrup into three equal parts. Add 400 g (14 oz) raspberries in one part, blackberries in another, and the contents of the passion fruit in the third. Mash the berries in the sugar syrup and strain into a container. Place the

container in the freezer and stir the sorbets every other hour or freeze in an ice cream maker.

Press the remaining raspberries through a sieve and sweeten with confectioner's sugar to taste.

Remove paper clips and acrylic from chocolate rings and place each in the center of a plate. Place a scoop of each kind of sorbet in each ring. Drizzle a little raspberry coulis all around. Garnish with mint and sift over a little confectioner's sugar. 8 servings.

Once upon a time there was a mountain lodge.....

Kongsvold Fjeldstue, Dovrefjell

Marinated raw trout flavored with wasabi, soy sauce and ginger. A game platter with marinated musk ox, moose and deer. Smoked reindeer tongue. A combination of ptarmigan, musk ox filet, and filet of deer with creamed reindeer lichen, pear poached with lingonberries and a sauce made from mountain herbs. Musk ox pâté. Smoked and marinated trout. Angelica sorbet….

Few mountain lodges offer anything like Kongsvold Fjellstue's menu! But then Kongsvold is not a typical Norwegian mountain lodge either. "A traditional hotel with modern comforts and with an exciting menu based on the ingredients found in the local mountains". That's how the hosts describe the hotel, which consists of 20 well-maintained old buildings. Ellen and Knut J. Nyhus took over the hotel in 1998, but they credit Knut's parents with making Kongsvold what it is today. Kristi and Olav Nyhus ran the hotel from 1979 to 1989 and made extensive renovations. Wash basins and outhouses were replaced with modern plumbing, while the dining room was restored by local craftsmen under the watchful eye of the Central Office of Historic Monuments. They managed to preserve and recreate the atmosphere of the original old coaching inn. Kongsvold Fjeldstue, with its harmonious red and white houses is one of the best-preserved examples of this authentic Norwegian style of architecture.

FROM A CABIN TO A MOUNTAIN LODGE

The road over the Dovre mountain plateau has joined eastern Norway and Trøndelag since time immemorial. Kongsvold Fjeldstue is right on European Route 6, halfway between Dombås and Oppdal, making it a natural destination today, just as it has been for hundreds of years. In the early days, most travelers were on their way to royal capital at Nidaros (now Trondheim). Their numbers increased after Olav Haraldsson was canonized and Nidaros Cathedral became a popular pilgrimage destination.

Back then, all traveling was done on foot or on horseback. Traveling by horse and carriage is first mentioned in 1704, but that did not become common until the late 18th century.

Traveling across the mountains was both exhausting and dangerous. We know from the sagas that King Eystein (1103-23) built a "sælehus" at Dovrefjell. This was a Viking-style self-catering cabin, which helped to make the journey over the mountains safer. Later, these cabins were staffed, and their status changed to mountain lodge. Lodge attendants were hired to maintain the lodges and to guide travelers across the mountains during the winter. The lodges were state-owned, and a list of duties and rights were the backbone of the system. The original duties consisted of housing and feeding those crossing the mountains and showing them the way. From 1734, the king required them to offer postal and coaching services in return for payment through a tax on grain produced by local farmers. There were tax dispensations as well, and fishing, hunting, and grazing rights were important privileges for these lodge attendants. The Dovre area had four mountain lodges – Drivstua, Hjerkinn, Fokstua, and Kongsvold.

NEW TIMES – NEW FOUNDATIONS

Kongsvold fjellstue is the youngest lodge at Dovre. It is now owned by the Norwegian Department of the Environment and was carefully restored under the watchful eye of the Central Office of Historic

Monuments. It was originally called Hullet (the hole) and was two kilometers farther down the valley. Hullet received its official status as a mountain lodge in 1670, but in 1704, King Frederik IV renamed it Kongsvold. During the Great Nordic War of 1718, the Swedes, under the direction of General Armfeldt, took most of Trøndelag, and the Nordenfjeldske (North of Dovre) Dragoon regiment fled south over the mountains. They quickly torched all four mountain lodges, including Kongsvold, along the way. Rebuilding of the lodge at its present site began in 1720, and the first floor of the main building probably dates from that time. The lower building and one elevated storehouse also date from the 18th century. Since 1670, when Jon Eriksen was hired as lodge attendant, the Kongsvold family has run the lodge. They were able to modernize with the times, so it evolved from a simple mountain lodge to a traditional, yet modern hotel.

From the beginning, the lodge was a rescue station for travelers that also served as a simple inn. But the income derived from paying guests was just as important as that from the grain tax. It was, in fact, that tax that made Kongsvold wealthy in the 19th century. In 1845, it was replaced by a set yearly amount paid by the government and the mountain lodges lost an important source of income. Gradually, roads improved and the railroad was extended, so the lodge was no longer so important for travelers. Now the Kongsvold family had to focus on tourism! They were successful in attracting tourists, and they also had an income from the post office and telephone central. So life went on at the mountain lodge.

DOVREFJELL NATIONAL PARK IS FOUNDED
The mountain lodges had always been state-owned, but when the railroad opened in 1921, the Norwegian government no longer saw the need for the lodges. They were then sold to the families who had run them for generations, and it was the eighth generation Kongsvold – Lina Kongsvold and Sigurd Holaker - who bought Kongsvold Fjeldstue in 1935. Lina left her mark on the hotel. She ran a traditional lodge and was widely known for her hospitality. Per Bjørn Holaker, Lina and Sigurd's son, eventually took over the hotel. Although he was a lawyer, he loved nature, hunting, fishing, and the outdoor life. He worked hard to get Dovrefjell, with Kongsvold Fjellstue, designated as a national park. For that reason, he left the property to the state under the auspices of the Department of the Environment. He never saw his dream become a reality. Per Bjørn Holaker died in 1973, just one year before Dovrefjell National Park was established.

Dovrefjell National Park and Kongsvold, at the top of Drivdal valley, 900 meters above sea level, are popular destinations for hikers and nature lovers. There is so much to see and do. Knutshøen Mountain, Europe's most famous "green mountain" rises up from behind the hotel. For 200 years, Dovrefjell has been known for its rich flora. More than 420 different plant species are registered at Dovrefjell National Park and Nature Protection Area. You can see many of these just walking from Kongsvold Fjellstue up to Knutshøen. Thekla R. Resvoll established Kongsvoll Mountain Garden next to the train station in 1923. In 1992, it was moved to the knoll just south of Kongsvold Fjellstue and is now run by NTNU – the Norwegian Technical and Scientific University and the Trondheim Science Museum. They also run Kongsvoll biological station, which was founded in 1975. The verdant and varied vegetation at Dovrefjell has attracted a rich bird life. During the summer months you can study the fieldfare, the willow grouse, the golden plover, the blue throat, the Lapland longspur, and the meadow pipit.

But Dovrefjell National Park and Kongsvold are also home to the musk ox and the wild reindeer. Musk oxen roam the mountains northwest of the hotel. These rare, peaceful, herbivores were released into the Dovre Mountains in the 1930s but disappeared during World War II. Between 1947 and 1953, 23 new calves from eastern Greenland were released into the area. The flock has grown slowly but steadily ever since and today numbers approximately 120 animals. Kongsvold Fjellstue is the perfect starting point for walking tours into Dovre's musk ox and wild reindeer territory. It is also ideal for hunting and fishing. Birds and mammals are protected year-round, but hunting of wild reindeer, grouse, hare, red fox, and mink is permitted in season. And there's plenty of trout in the river for sports fishermen. Kongsvold Fjellstue, in the middle of the Dovre King's hall, is a unique place and definitely worth a visit!

Musk ox paté

100 g (4 oz) well trimmed filet
of musk ox, reindeer or moose
60 g (2 oz) pork fat
20 g (3/4 oz) pork liver
1/2 small onion
1/2 small garlic clove
2 teaspoons port wine
2 teaspoons cognac
salt, pepper
pinch each: crushed juniper
berries, ground nutmeg,
ginger, allspice and celery salt
1 egg
1 dl (scant 1/2 cup) half and
half

Preheat the oven to 140°C (275°F). Coarsely grind the meat and fat in a meat grinder. Transfer to a blender or food processor. Add the liver, onion, garlic and seasonings and pulse several times. With the motor running, add the egg and half and half and puree until smooth. Line a small terrine with plastic wrap. Add the paté mixture, cover with plastic wrap and bake in a water bath until the internal tempera-

ture is 58°C (137°F), 20 to 30 minutes. Cool completely. Unmold and serve cold with a salad and Cumberland sauce, if desired.

Nettle soup

3 dl (1 1/4 cups) fresh nettle leaves
1 tablespoon butter
1 tablespoon all-purpose flour
6 dl (2 1/2 cups) beef stock
1/2 dl (3 1/2 tablespoons) whipping cream
salt, pepper

Sauté the nettle leaves in butter in a stockpot. Stir in the flour. Add the stock and simmer 10 minutes. Puree with an immersion blender. Add the cream, heat to boiling, then season with salt and pepper. Serve piping hot.

Marinated musk ox

1 teaspoon salt
1 teaspoon sugar
200 g (7 oz) trimmed filet of musk ox, reindeer or moose
1 tablespoon fresh juniper shoots
chopped fresh tarragon
1/2 teaspoon coarsely ground black pepper

Birch vinaigrette
1 dl (1/2 cup) apple cider vinegar
3 dl (1 1/4 cups) olive oil
1/2 dl (3 1/2 tablespoons) birch shoot puree
1 teaspoon salt
1 teaspoon ground white pepper

shredded iceberg and lollo rosso lettuce
1 tablespoon lingonberries

Combine the salt and sugar and rub into the meat. Place on the juniper shoots. Sprinkle with tarragon and pepper. Cover with plastic wrap and refrigerate 24 hours, turning the meat several times.

Combine all the ingredients in the vinaigrette. Pour over the lettuce and toss well. Divide the lettuce among four plates. Cut the meat into thin slices with a sharp knife or a slicer and place on the greens. Garnish with lingonberries. Serve with Cumberland sauce.

Right.: Uppigard Sulheim is
undoubtedly one of Norway's most
beautiful large farms. It was given
historic monument status in 1923.
Today, it comprises 20 old, sunburnt
log buildings.

Below: The host at Uppigard
Sulheim, Christian Sulheim, runs
the traditional family farm with his
own family. His son, Jo Kolbjørn, is
a full time agricultural student and
is looking forward to taking over
the farm, which has been in the
family since the 9th century.

Right: From the inner yard at
Uppigard Sulheim. The farm has a
traditional layout with both an
inner yard for the family and an
outer farmyard for the animals. In
the background, you can see the
stables, which usually divided the
two areas. The house belonged to the
inner yard, because it was considered more human than animal.

In the family for over 1200 years

Uppigard Sulheim, Bøverdalen

Facing south, off to the right, a steep and powerful mountain ridge. Behind that blue peaks. Toward the left, a naked slope; many waterfalls below. The leaves were just starting to appear on the trees in the forest, spreading their sweet aroma in every direction with the wind, reminiscent of life in a leafy bower.

There hadn't been a drop of rain in weeks, but farmers still predicted a good year. The fields were plowed but not sown. The earth was warm from the sun.

A wide road cut the valley in two, and ambling down it was an older man with his hands in his pockets smoking a charred clay pipe. Large and bulky he was, and on his head he wore a red cap with the brim pointing forward. Now and then he stopped and made a thoughtful nod with his head, sometime down toward the fields, sometime up through the valley. He probably thought halfway about climbing up, he could use that in this heat, and it could be done without great difficulty. That was probably the reason why he often turned around and brushed off the ever-present mold dust which blew up from the road.

Knut Hamsun: Bjørger

Whether the famous Norwegian author Knut Hamsum really was born at Garmo in Lom, as is often claimed, is a hotly debated topic. We know that he was confirmed in Lom where he spent a couple years in his youth working for his uncle as a clerk. There is no doubt that the great poet was inspired by the wild

and rugged nature in upper Gudbrandsdal valley. In one of his first novels, Bjørger, published in 1878 when he was just 19 years old, he describes beautiful Bøverdal valley in Lom. The "older man with his hands in his pockets" is the peasant farmer at Uppigard Sulheim.

It is not surprising that Hamsun drew inspiration from the area. Narrow Bøverdal valley, with its wild, untouched nature, is considered Norway's finest valley, and Uppigard Sulheim, with its many ancient buildings, is one of the country's most beautiful estates. Its surroundings, plains and fields, the steep, green mountains, and the wild waterfalls just perfect the vision. There was a farm here as early as the 9th century, and it is mentioned in written sources from 1320. It has been owned by the same family ever since, and generation after generation of Sulheim inhabitants have carried on family traditions and carefully looked after the buildings and their contents. Today, Uppigard Sulheim consists of 20 old, sun-bleached, log buildings. The oldest dates from 1250, while most of the others were built in the 16th and 17th centuries. The main building from 1660 is probably the oldest two-story dwelling of its kind in Gudbrandsdal valley and contains some of the finest examples of Norwegian folk art in existence. The many houses contain furniture, weapons and other items dating all the way back to Viking times. It is no coincidence that Uppigard Sulheim was one of the first farms in Norway to be put on the list of historic buildings in 1923.

AN AGRICULTURAL GRADUATE RETURNS HOME

Christian Sulheim is the current master of Sulheim, but he has little time to walk around "with his hands in his pockets". Uppigard Sulheim is still a working farm, and even if the majority of its 6250 acres are pasture, there are still 80 acres of cultivated fields, as well as a great deal of productive forest. The farm also produces a sizeable quantity of milk and meat from both cows and sheep. Sulheim tries to run the farm in a traditional manner. Horsepower was used until 1969, when Dobbin was traded in for a tractor. Hundreds of thousands of kroner are spent every year to maintain the old buildings, so the farm has to make a profit! When Christian returned to the farm just out of agricultural college, he wanted to tear down all the old buildings and build a new barn, but he was stonewalled by the Central Office of Historic Monuments and by his father. There was no question of tearing anything down! That made him angry. If they didn't want an efficient farm he would go elsewhere. He decided to go to Germany to study the language. While there, he also learned to respect and appreciate everything worth preserving. The more fantastic buildings and monuments he saw, the more he understood that Norway had buildings worth preserving, and they weren't being looked after well enough. He changed his mind and returned to Norway where he took degrees in law, ethnology, and history to gain a better insight into these things. Eventually, it was time for him to take over the family

farm. For the first 10 years, he ran it alone with only his family and locals for support. There was a lot to be done and even though he soon learned how to paint, do basic carpentry, and to construct log buildings, most of the farm's income was spent on maintenance and improvements. All that hard work paid off. Nothing in Sulheim's exterior hints of the modern comforts needed to run a modern farm. The buildings stand, as they have stood for hundreds of years, weather-beaten and distinguished.

NORWEGIAN HEIRLOOMS AND TOURISM

The 10 years that Christian Sulheim ran the farm on his own gave him the ballast he needed to start his big project to preserve Norwegian heritage, or as he calls it, "the Norwegian family silver". The "Norwegian Heritage Foundation" was founded in 1993 with Christian Sulheim as the driving force and daily manager, and it receives support from the Central Office of Historic Monuments, the Norwegian Government, the Environmental, Agricultural and Foreign ministries, businesses, and private individuals. The foundation wants to preserve, but more importantly use, Norway's cultural heritage. That means more than just old buildings, rather our

In "Søre Stugu", there are many beautiful cupboards from the end of the 18th century carved by Sylfest Skrinde, teacher of the legendary Skjåk-Ola. The impressive chest was painted by the Klukstad family in 1792, while the beautiful clock is a masterpiece by Peder Bierche from Toten.

Above: The housewife's symbol of power has always been a heavy bunch of keys. This collection of old keys dates from the Middle Ages.

Above right: You can stay in an apartment at Uppigard Sulheim. Each apartment is decorated in a charming mixture of old and new and contains a kitchen, bath, living room and two bedrooms.

Right: The table is decorated for a feast in the impressive hall. The unique seven-meter table dates from before 1350. In the living room, you can see a beautiful carved wall cabinet from 1692, as well as another old table.

entire cultural heritage. The foundation wants these things to be accessible where people live, not locked away in museums. This helps to increase tourism and create new jobs in rural areas.

Now Christian Sulheim has decided to practice what he preaches. He left his job as the manager of "The Norwegian Heritage Foundation" in the spring of 2001 to encourage tourism at Uppigard Sulheim. He created three small apartments in the "Nordre building" which are ready to receive guests by the night or by the week. Each apartment has two or three bedrooms, a sitting room, a kitchen, and a bathroom. He offers either self-catering, or full board with a chef that comes to the apartment and cooks and serves dinner.

There are many activities for guests at Uppigard Sulheim. You can hunt grouse in local privately owned forests, or deer or roe deer in the farm's own woods. Fishermen can hire private stretches of river and fish for trout. 90% of Lom County is covered in mountains and glaciers, with Galdhøpiggen and Glitretind the most famous landmarks. The area offers excellent hiking possibilities – either on one's own or with an experienced mountain guide, who can lead you to the highest peaks and explore the grottoes, gorges and glaciers. Galdhøpiggen summer skiing center is at nearby Juvasshytta and offers stellar skiing conditions

from May to October. For rafting, Sjoa is just a few minutes away. The museum at Lom, the Norwegian Mountain museum, and Fossheim rock center are all worth a visit, and don't forget beautiful Lom stave church which was built around the year 1200. You can also walk up through Bøverdal valley and across Sognefjell mountain, Norway's highest mountain pass, down to Sogn, and on to Urnes stave church, Jostedal glacier and the Sognefjord.

A gourmet dinner and tour of the main house at Uppigard Sulheim awaits after a long day outdoors. Such an evening is part of every stay, and it's an unforgettable experience, sitting in the beautiful dining room at a table from the 13th century set with old porcelain, polished crystal, and the finest antique Norwegian silver.

Pan-fried trout with warm cucumber salad

1 trout, 700-800 g
(1 1/2-3/4 lb) or 2 small
butter

2 dl (3/4 cup) natural
sour heavy cream
1 tablespoon white wine vinegar
1 tablespoon minced parsley
1 tablespoon minced chives
1/2 teaspoon sugar
salt, black pepper
1/2 snake cucumber
1 fennel bulb
2 tablespoons Pernod
juice of 1/2 lemon

Wash and fillet the fish. Scrape off the scales. Pan-fry in butter, skin side down. Sprinkle with salt and pepper.

Combine the sour cream, vinegar, parsley, chives and sugar. Season with salt and pepper.

Peel the cucumber and remove the seeds with an apple corer. Cut into thick slices and stir into the sour cream mixture.

Cut the fennel into very thin slices with a cheese plane. Drizzle with Pernod, lemon juice and salt. Carefully heat the cucumber salad and layer with the fennel. Serve the fish alongside.

Roe deer medallions with wild mushrooms, shallots and creamy pepper sauce

1 teaspoon black peppercorns
12 shallots
200 g (8 oz) wild mushrooms
butter
2 carrots
1/2 dl (3 tablespoons) olive oil
2 dl (3/4 cup) orange juice
800 g (1 3/4 lb) boneless roe deer loin
salt
2 tablespoons minced parsley
1 dl (1/2 cup) Port wine
4 dl (1 1/2 cups) whipping cream

Heat the peppercorns in a dry pan until they begin to "jump" around. Crush.

Clean the shallots and mushrooms and sauté in butter until golden. Peel the carrots, cut into batons and simmer in oil and juice for 20 minutes.

Preheat the oven to 225°C (425°F). While the carrots are cooking, cut the meat into medallions and brown in butter. Sprinkle with salt, crushed pepper and parsley. Roast in the oven for 6 minutes. Remove the meat from the pan and let it rest a few minutes before slicing. Deglaze the pan with Port and reduce until almost completely evaporated. Add the cream and reduce by almost half. Season with salt. Arrange the vegetables on each plate. Top with meat. Spoon sauce all around.

Raspberry mousse and orange jelly with vanilla sauce and burnt hazelnuts

Orange jelly
1/2 teaspoon black peppercorns
2 dl (3/4 cup) orange juice
50 g (1/4 cup) sugar
2 star anise
2 gelatin sheets

Raspberry mousse
5 egg yolks
100 g (1/2 cup) sugar
1 dl (scant 1/2 cup)
whipping cream
2-3 gelatin sheets
3 dl (1 1/2 cups) strained
raspberry puree
2 1/2 dl (1 cup) whipping cream

Vanilla sauce
1 vanilla bean
1 dl (1/2 cup) full-fat milk
1 dl (1/2 cup) whipping cream
50 g (1/2 cup) sugar
3 egg yolks

"Burnt hazelnuts"
100 g (1/2 cup) sugar
8 hazelnuts
wooden cocktail picks

Orange jelly
Heat the peppercorns in a dry pan until they begin to "jump" around. Combine the pepper, juice, sugar and star anise in a small saucepan and heat to boiling. Lower the heat and let simmer about 15 minutes. Soak the gelatin in cold water about 10 minutes to soften. Squeeze to remove excess water and melt in the hot juice. Stir until the gelatin is completely dissolved. Pour into a cylinder mold and refrigerate until set.

Raspberry mousse
Whisk the egg yolks, sugar and cream together in a small saucepan over medium heat and heat to boiling. Cool. Soak the gelatin in cold water about 10 minutes to soften. Squeeze to remove excess water and melt in the raspberry puree. Stir in the egg yolk mixture. Cool completely. Whip the cream and fold into the berry mixture.

Pour half the mousse into a loaf pan, Remove the jelly from the cylinder (dip in hot water for a few seconds) and place on the mousse. Top with the remaining mousse. Refrigerate for at least 2 hours. leskap i minst 2 timer.

Vanilla sauce
Split the vanilla bean lengthwise and scrape out the seeds. Combine the milk, cream, vanilla bean and seeds and sugar in a saucepan and heat to boiling. Beat in the egg yolks. Strain and refrigerate until serving time.

"Burnt hazelnuts"
Melt the sugar in a saucepan until golden brown. Secure the nuts on cocktail picks and dip each into the hot caramel. Remove from the caramel and hold the nut until the caramel has set. Place the nuts on the plate while the caramel is still warm, to glue them in place. Remove the picks.

Cut the mousse into slices and place on individual plates. Make stripes of vanilla sauce all around.

The jewel of the mountains

Røisheim Hotel, Bøverdalen

Tourists and ladies at Jotunheimen
On July 24th, at Gjendesheim in the Jotunheimen mountains, every tourist attraction and cabin are filled to overflowing with tourists and ladies. There is still a lot of snow on the mountain, and during the past week, it has been especially cold – down to -2 and -3°C.
The new road from Vaage to Bærstrandsæter, which is a two-hour walk from Gjendesheim, is especially good and will probably be well-trafficked by visitors from the Lillehammer area.
On the 25th, all the cabins in the area round Røisheim are filled as well. At Røisheim, there are 32 tourists, ladies and gentlemen, and many have stayed for many days expecting good enough weather to climb Galdøpiggen.
From Lom, it is reported that the potato plants have frozen over the past few nights.
"The Lillehammer Observer", August 2, 1884.

That's how conditions at Jotunheimen were described in 1884. The beautiful mountain, with its impressive peaks, glaciers, and passes had never been so popular. Tourism was booming, even if it was the coldest summer in a long time and the potatoes were damaged by frost. Even ladies found their way to the mountains!
    Jotunheimen had been "discovered" in 1820. Local fisherman and reindeer herders had traversed it since time immemorial, but in that year, two students, Carl Boeck and Baltasar Keilhau, explored the area. Their enthusiastic descriptions spread the fame of the mountain far beyond Norway's borders, and students and city folk made their way to Jotunheimen. Most people approached via the Sognefjell road, a simple carriage track that went from Lom to Jotunheimen through Bøverdal valley and down to the Sognefjord. The road was actually an old royal route, the main road from Bergen over Sognefjell to

eastern Norway. Originally, it was just a rough path meant for sturdy horses, interrupted by the occasional rickety bridge over dangerous waters. There were many dangers, including bad weather, snowstorms, bears, and bandits. The farms were far apart, and many people stopped at Røisheim in Bøverdal valley to rest before continuing onward. There was safety in numbers when traveling the mountain road.
    That is really how tourism started at Røisheim, which was originally one of the valley's largest farms, with 40 employees. It was also one of northern Gudbrandsdal valley's largest milk suppliers. Most of the 12 hotel buildings were built in the 18th century, but the oldest dates from the 16th century. The farm itself is much, much older. According to 17 old letters on parchment found on the farm, the Røisheim family have been there at least as far back as the 13th century. And who knows how long they were there before then. Bøverdal valley was settled early, and the Heim name indicates that Røisheim was cleared sometime between 400 and 1200 AD. The original farm lay on the other side of the river, but it was destroyed by an avalanche and flood in 1789 and was then rebuilt where the hotel stands today. But now back to tourism.

THE CLIMBING CENTER OF EUROPE
The discovery of Jotunheimen meant that more people visited Røisheim. Steinar Sulheim, Ola Halvorsen Røisheim's neighbor, was the first person to climb Galdhøpiggen in 1854. Ten years later, Ola set up a route from Røisheim to northern Europe's highest peak. It was the beginning of a new era. In 1858, Ola took over the coaching inn at Hoft, a neighboring farm. In addition to the usual guests - travelers, civil servants, and salesmen – adventurers and hikers began to visit. There was a veritable invasion of eminent English climbers who later returned home and wrote books about their experiences.

Røisheim Hotel

Years passed and Røisheim became a center for climbing. The host himself gained widespread fame as a guide. The famous English climber William Slingsby was a regular guest at Røisheim. He was the first person to climb Store Skagadølstind on July 21, 1876 and is regarded as the mentor of all Norwegian climbers. Ola became his friend and guide, and Slingsby's description of the farm gives us an interesting picture of conditions at Røisheim during the second half of the 19th century.

"The farm consists of a group of painted buildings arranged around a farmyard at the foot of Galdhø mountain, that separates the Bøverdal and Visdal valleys. It is an excellent example of a large mountain farm, and its owner Ola Røisheim is a bold mountain climber and also an experienced mountain guide. I have spent many a happy, lazy day at Røisheim.

The farmhouse and many of the farm buildings balance on the mountain knolls just above a wild, narrow path the river Bøvra has carved out. There are dozens of potholes. An old wooden bridge adds a picturesque feel, and a water channel fills a large wooden trough for washing.

On the other side of the river are potato fields, which are watered almost continuously. Channels spread the water into canals that spread out in all directions down over the hill, forming ponds with spaces in between. The water spreaders are here. Each is equipped with wooden shovel for shoveling the water over the fields. Where they come from is a mystery. The milkmaids give them salt, and there's always a little fight between them in the farmyard. It is just friendly play."

Grieg, Ibsen, Munthe, and many others
Røisheim was idyllic and the guests loved it. And soon a new breed of guest began to visit, artists. Sensitive as they were, they soon fell in love with the picturesque farm, the impressive surroundings, and the friendly hospitality at Røisheim. Norway's greatest painters, poets and composers came, and they stayed, and they returned year after year. Hans Gude, Edvard Grieg, Henrik Ibsen, Fritz Thaulow, Vinje, Garborg, Lars Jorde, and Eilif Pettersen, just to name a few. But the painter Gerhard Munthe would help to make Røisheim famous. He arrived there in 1904, together with Thaulow, and fell in love with the place. Until his death in 1929, he spent 20 summers at Røisheim. He became close friends with the Røisheim family, and he wrote this about his last meeting with old Ola: "When I came out in the morning, he was already chopping firewood from gnarled pine logs – eager and enthusiastic. And did he have a sense of humor; he gave all the logs names, and talked to them at every blow, while he laughed at

me. He wasn't angry at all, just a tough old mountain pine himself."

Protection and a new road
Generation after generation ran the historical coaching inn. The inn always from Ola to Ola, because all men at Røisheim were called Ola. The last Ola, old Ola's grandson, took over Røisheim in 1919. He continued to run the inn with his sisters just as his ancestors had done before him. "Ola's warm, bright smile and wise eyes, Brita's happy, motherly caring, and Torø's home-cooked food, made with love" brought guests to Røisheim year after year. Many royal guests found the way to Røisheim. Queen Wilhelmina of the Netherlands visited three times, her daughter Juliana twice; then Crown Prince Olav of Norway came, and so did Prince Oscar Bernadotte. Two very important things happened during this period. In 1923, Røisheim coaching inn was listed as a national monument. This was done not just because of the old buildings, but also because the setting itself had historical value. In 1938, the old carriage road over Sognefjell mountain was replaced with a proper road for cars. Its highest point, 1434 meters above sea level, made it northern Europe's highest mountain pass. It still is today. The new road brought more tourists to Røisheim. The three siblings ran the place for 45 years. They shut down the farm in 1955, but the hotel lived on. Ola finally retired in 1964. Signe Moland, granddaughter of Ola's cousin, took over the hotel and kept it in the Røisheim family.

Signe Moland was just as interested in preserving the cozy, hospitable atmosphere as those before her. She continued to run the inn as before, but she realized that it needed to be renovated and modernized. For five years, she renovated the hotel under the guidance of the State Office of Historic Monuments. All the farmhouses were fixed up and 1000 quare meters of roof were covered in turf. The old fashioned atmosphere was preserved, while the hotel got the modern conveniences it needed to remain profitable. Signe was lucky to be able to guide the hotel through the changes necessary to take it from an old fashioned coaching inn to today's gem of a hotel. She was a popular hostess, and the regular guests were sorry when she closed the hotel in 1983 to concentrate on her career as a lawyer. It was the end of Røisheim's 125-year history as a family run inn.

"The really good life"
Røisheim remained closed for two years, then Signe Moland sold it to Wilfried Reinschmidt, a German living in Oslo, and his wife Unni Haugen from Lom. What lay before them was no easy task. They had to carry on four generations of hospitality and a

Left: The beautiful sitting room is dominated by the grand fireplace. The furniture are antiques from the valley and the district.

Below: A detail of the dining room.

guests still flock from far and wide to experience this famous hotel set in the shadow of the mountains and the wild nature of Bøverdal valley. Steep mountains rise on either side of this green valley, while the Bøvra river races down it. This is nature just waiting to be explored. You can walk to the top of 2469-meter-high Galdhøpiggen or 2452 meter-high Glittertind, or go skiing on Galdhøpiggen, with its popular summer ski center. Røisheim hotel is truly the gem of the mountains.

The old barn has been converted into a number of charming guest bedrooms, all with private baths. Canopy beds and old-fashioned wooden bathtubs create a nostalgic atmosphere.

reputation as one of the country's most intimate and unique hotels. But Unni and Wilfried proved themselves worthy of the task. Old traditions were maintained and the old buildings were preserved, while they added their own personal touch. Wilfried was soon famous for his culinary skills, and Røisheim gained fame for its excellent kitchen. Unni and Wilfried saw hotel management as a lifestyle and Røisheim as their home. And they wanted their guests to feel at home and to enjoy peace, quiet, and relaxation. Disturbing elements, such as televisions, radios, and newspapers were not permitted. And the guests loved it. Røisheim was once again one of Norway's most exclusive hotels, and diplomats, politicians, and artists flocked there. But the mountain climbers were still their most important clients. In 1995, Unni and Wilfried decided to call it quits. Ten years at Røisheim had left them tired and worn out, and they too wanted to live a peaceful life. Røisheim was sold to Røisheim A/S, a corporation owned by a group of private investors. The company ensures continuous maintenance of the protected buildings and farmyard. Today, Røisheim is part of Knut Kloster's "The Really Good Life" hotel chain and is run by Ingrid and Haavard Lund. Ingrid is an excellent cook, and makes sure that Røisheim lives up to its reputation as one of the country's best restaurants. The couple run Røisheim as it has been run for the last 150 years. They concentrate on hospitality, and

Røisheim Hotel

Pickled hare with apple-celery dressing

Pickled hare
1 large onion
1 small leek
1 carrot
2 dl (3/4 cup) 7% vinegar
2 1/2 dl (1 cup) water
2 dl (3/4 cup) sugar
1 tablespoon dried basil
1 tablespoon dried thyme
3 hare filets

Wash, peel and cut the vegetables into chunks. Bring vinegar, water and sugar to a boil. Add the vegetables and herbs and simmer until the vegetables are tender. Remove from the heat, add the meat and let steep until the brine is room temperature. Refrigerate until serving time. The hare will keep for 2 to 3 days.

Apple-celery dressing
1 apple
2 celery stalks
2 tablespoons dairy sour cream
1/2 teaspoon black currant mustard (or Dijon mustard)
2 teaspoons sugar

Wash, peel and dice the apple and celery. Combine the remaining ingredients and stir in the apple and celery.

Cut the hare filets on the diagonal into even slices. Arrange on mixed greens. Top with the dressing.

Above: After dinner, guests gather for coffee in the sitting room.

Røisheim Hotel has its own wine, and the glass bear the monogram of the hotel.

Left: Every meal is a festive occasion at Røisheim Hotel. Every evening, an exciting three-course gourmet meal is prepared by the hostess, Ingrid Lunde herself.

Baked monkfish with creamy beet sauce, potato puree and buttered vegetables

Fish stock
2 onions
2 carrots
1 leek
2 liters (quarts) water
1 kilo (2 1/2 lb) fish trimmings and bones, preferably from monkfish
2-3 bay leaves

Sauce I
1/2 onion
butter
1 dl (1/2 cup) white wine
3 dl (1 1/4 cups) fish stock
1 dl (1/2 cup) apple juice
2 dl (3/4 cup) whipping cream
1/2 dl (1/4 cup) sour cream

Sauce II
1 beet
2 dl (3/4 cup) apple juice
1/2 dl (1/4 cup) white wine

Potato puree
1 kilo (2 1/4 lb) potatoes
100 g (3 1/2 oz) butter
1/2 dl (1/4 cup) whipping cream
salt, pepper
2 tablespoons chopped chives

Monkfish
800 g (1 3/4 lb) monkfish fillet or 4 small monkfish tails
1/2 teaspoon pepper
1 teaspoon salt

Buttered vegetables
1 leek
2 carrots
salt
butter

Fish stock
Clean, peel and cut the vegetables into chunks. Place in a stockpot with the water, fish trimmings and bay leaves. Bring to a boil, reduce the heat and simmer for about 30 minutes. Strain.

Sauce I
Chop the onion and sauté in a little butter. Add the wine and reduce by half. Add the stock and apple juice and reduce by half. Add the cream and sour cream and cook until slightly thickened.

Sauce II
Peel and dice the beet and place in a saucepan. Add the juice and wine and simmer until tender. Just before serving, combine the two sauces.

Potato puree
Wash and peel the potatoes. Cook in lightly salted water until tender. Drain, then steam the potatoes to remove excess water, then mash well. Beat in the butter and cream and season with salt and pepper. Stir in the chives.

Monkfish
Preheat the oven to 230°C (425°F). Wash and trim the fish, removing all membrane. Place on a baking sheet and sprinkle with salt and pepper. Bake about 15 minutes.

Buttered vegetables
Clean the vegetables and cut into julienne. Cook in lightly salted water with butter until tender.

Make a mirror of sauce on individual plates. Place a mound of potato puree in the center and top with the fish and julienne vegetables.

Ice cream roulade with licorice sauce

Chocolate stripes

40 g (3 tablespoons) soft butter
40 g (1/3 cup)
confectioner's sugar
40 g (2 1/2 tablespoons)
egg white
30 g (1/4 cup)
all-purpose flour
15 g (3 tablespoons) cocoa

Sponge cake

350 g (about 7 large) eggs
120 g (2/3 cup) sugar
140 g (1 cup) flour

Strawberry parfait

4 egg yolks
100 g (1/2 cup) sugar
5 dl (2 cups) whipping cream
5 tablespoons (1/3 cup)
unsweetened strawberry puree

Chocolate stripes

Line a baking sheet with baking parchment. Grease. Beat all ingredients together until smooth. Spread in an even layer over the parchment. Make a striped pattern with a fork. Freeze.

Sponge cake

Preheat the oven to 240°C (450°F). With an electric mixer, beat the eggs and sugar until light, thick and lemon-colored. Sift over the flour, beating to break down any air bubbles. Remove the tray with the chocolate stripes from the freezer. Spread the sponge mixture in an even layer over the stripes. Bake about 5 minutes. Sprinkle a sheet of baking parchment the same size as the cake with sugar. Turn the cake out onto the sugared parchment. Roll up lightly in the parchment. Cool.

Strawberry parfait

Beat the egg yolks and sugar until light, thick and lemon colored. Whip the cream and fold into the egg yolk mixture. Carefully fold in the strawberry puree. Unroll the cake and remove the parchment. Spread the strawberry mixture over the sponge sheet. Place in the freezer until the mixture is stiff enough to roll up. It should not be too stiff or the cake will break.

Licorice sauce

1 stick raw licorice
(available from a pharmacy)
5 dl (2 cups) water
500 g (1 lb) sugar

Chop the licorice in a food processor. Place in a saucepan with the water and sugar and simmer until slightly thickened. The sauce will be even thicker when cool.

Cut the ice cream roulade into slices and arrange on individual plates with fresh berries and licorice sauce. 8 servings.

An urban mountain lodge

Jotunheimen Fjellstue, Bøverdalen

Above: The mountain lodge lies in the heart of the Jotunheimen mountains and is the perfect departure point for fantastic experiences in the landscape.

Right: Even though the style is modern and minimalist, you can still enjoy sitting in front of the fire after dinner.

Below: Åse Wiker (front), Arne Magnus and Gøril Wiker (center), and Petter Gudmundseth are happy hosts at their own mountain lodge.

Jotunheimen mountain lodge isn't like other mountain lodges. It lies 1000 meters above sea level in beautiful Bøverdal valley alongside Sognefjell road, northern Europe's highest mountain pass, with its highest point of 1434 meters above sea level. But that's where the similarities end. You won't fine any sour cream porridge, rose-painting, and traditional furniture at Jotunheimen Fjellstue. Two Oslo couples have made sure of that. Gøril Wiker is a journalist, TV chef, and author of the popular cookbook <u>Leve Livet</u> (Live Life), and her husband Petter Gudmundseth is in advertising. Åse Wiker also has a background in advertising, while her significant other is chief editor at University Press. The four retreat to the mountains at Easter and during the summer, just like other Norwegians. The difference is that while others go skiing, walk in the mountains, and just relax, these two couples spend busy days as hosts at their own mountain lodge.

Gøril and Åse are sisters. They grew up in Bærum, near Oslo, but they spent all their vacations in their parents' home town of Lom. In 1993, they heard rumors that Jotumheien Mountain lodge, just 30 kilometers from Lom, was for sale. The two sisters were very attached to the area, and Petter and Arne had learned to love the place over the years. They had been discussing purchasing something that would give them a good reason to visit more often. A squash hall? A laundry? A shop? They had ideas, but they couldn't decide on anything specific. But a mountain lodge sounded like a good idea. They went up and looked at the place. They liked what they saw. The lodge consisted of a building from 1946 with an addition from 1972, both in sorry shape, but it definitely had potential. What made it extra special was that the girls' grandfather, an former builder in Lom, had helped to build the older part.

Back in Oslo, they spent many long nights discussing ideas and options. All four had to be in complete agreement. In the end, there was no turning back, and they bought the mountain lodge in 1994. Now they had to roll up their sleeves and start renovating and restoring.

SIMPLE AND STYLISH

Their philosophy was simple. The four of them had traveled far and wide and knew exactly what they expected from a hotel. They wanted to create a unique mountain lodge, unlike all the others, a place where they would like to stay themselves. The first thing they did was empty the building of all its contents. Interior architects Beate Ellingsen and Bjørg Aabø came to visit and were met by an empty building. The new owners wanted to keep it simple and plain, with straight lines, natural colors, and modern design. When the lodge opened in 1995, the result was a modern and minimalist hotel in the Norwegian mountains. You won't find any unnecessary decorative objects here, but you will find bookshelves filled with glossy magazines, old classics, detective novels and cookbooks. There is no TV in the fireplace room, but there is a good selection of games and plenty of decks of cards. There are no loud and colorful pictures on the walls, but rather large windows facing out toward the mountains, with their powerful peaks, and toward the idyllic lake just outside the hotel. You can also sit and look out over the panorama of old-fashioned farm life in all kinds of weather. They have planted trout in the lake, so fishing enthusiasts need go no further than the front door to try their luck.

Exciting food and wilderness experiences

Each of the four has defined work duties. Gøril checks the quality of the food, along with the chef and the rest of the cooking staff, who create exciting dishes. Her philosophy is that garlic, pies, and pasta taste just as good in the country as in the city, and Jotunheimen serves modern Norwegian food with an international touch. Everything is homemade, using only the freshest ingredients. Food is an important part of the whole experience and Gøril sees no reason why food served in the mountains should be simpler, less interesting, or of worse quality than that served in Oslo's best restaurants. Åse is the general manger, and Per is responsible for finances and maintenance. Arne is an experienced climber and has spent more than 20 summers as a mountain and glacier guide on Jotunheimen, so he takes the guests out for walks. There are more than 50 peaks over 2000 meters within walking distance of the lodge. Both Galdhøpiggen

(2469 meters) and Fanaråken (2069 meters) have cabins at the top, and if you like a challenge there's Store Skagadølstind (2405 meters) or Loftet (2169 meters). Loftet is just behind the hotel, and you can easily reach the top in just three hours. Arne can tempt more experienced climbers with glacier hiking and trips to the grottoes in Dumdalen – a fairy tale world carved out by the Dumma river over millions of years.

After a long day of breathing fresh mountain air, experiencing nature, and unforgettable impressions, dinner at Jotunheimen Mountain Lodge is the highlight of the evening. At eight o'clock sharp, the curtain is drawn, and the guests enter the dining room. Now teamwork really counts. While Gøril makes sure everything goes as planned, Arne welcomes the guests, and presents the menu – a three-course culinary surprise. Petter moves from table to table recommending wines for the different dishes, while Åse offers hot rolls to the guests. In the simple but beautiful

Above: A detail from the nook in the fireside room.

Right: The guest bedrooms are simple but very functional and practical, with colorful textiles and good mattresses and duvets for a good night's sleep.

Right page: Dinner is served in the beautiful dining room every night at 8. The menu is always a surprise, but it's guaranteed to be a three-course culinary masterpiece.

dining room, the tables are covered in white damask and decorated with fresh flowers and candles. The atmosphere is intimate and the conversation subdued. Blinds cover the large panoramic windows, blocking the view of mighty Jotunheimen. There's enough sensory stimulation right here. You could as well be in an elegant, trendy restaurant in London, Paris, or New York.

Scallops with spinach-mushroom sauce and green beans

8 large scallops
100 g (4 oz) thin green beans
100 g (4 oz) spinach
250 g (8 oz) mushrooms
200 g (7 oz) butter
1 1/2 dl (2/3 cup) full-fat milk
1 1/2 dl (2/3 cup) whipping cream
juice of 1 lemon
salt, pepper
2 tablespoons oil
1 tablespoon minced fresh thyme

Clean the scallops. Top and tail the beans. Blanch in lightly salted boiling water 20 seconds. Plunge into ice water to cool. Clean and rinse the spinach to remove all sand. Chop the mushrooms and sauté in half the butter. Add the spinach, sauté 5 seconds, then pour into a blender. Add the milk and blend until smooth. Pour into a saucepan. Add the cream, heat to boiling and season with lemon juice, salt and pepper.
Brown the scallops on one side in oil in a hot frying pan. Remove from the heat, turn the scallops and add the remaining butter and thyme. Let the scallops rest about 30 seconds in the pan. Season with salt and pepper

Garlic-roasted lamb with rösti potatoes, tarragon carrots and red wine sauce

Garlic-roasted lamb
750 g (1 2/3 lb) filet of lamb
(boneless rack)
soybean oil
2-3 garlic cloves
salt, pepper
butter

Rösti potatoes
4 baking potatoes
clarified butter
1 tablespoon minced
fresh thyme
salt, pepper

Tarragon carrots
500 g (1 lb) carrots
50 g (3 tablespoons) butter
1 tablespoon sugar
salt, pepper
2 tablespoons minced fresh
tarragon

Red wine sauce
2 shallots
1 tablespoon olive oil
2 tablespoons sugar
2 1/2 dl (1 cup) red wine
5 dl (2 cups) rich beef stock
salt, pepper
50 g (3 tablespoons)
unsalted butter

Preheat the oven to 150°C (300°F). Brown the meat quickly on all sides in a small amount of oil in an ovenproof frying pan. Peel and mince the garlic. Sprinkle over the meat with the salt and pepper. Place a pat of butter on the meat. Roast 15 minutes. Check for doneness. If the juices are red, return the meat to the oven for a few more minutes. Let the meat rest 5 minutes before carving.

Rösti potatoes
Preheat the oven to 150°C (300°F). Wash, peel and grate the potatoes. Press out as much liquid as possible. Season with salt, pepper and thyme. Heat an ovenproof frying pan until very hot, then add a little clarified butter. Arrange the potatoes in the pan in an even layer. Fry until brown on one side. Turn carefully and brown on the other side. Bake 10 minutes. Just before serving, cut into wedges.

Tarragon carrots
Peel the carrots and cut into batons. Cook in lightly salted water for 3 minutes, until "al dente". Drain, then add the butter, sugar, salt and pepper. Sauté the carrots for 2 minutes, then stir in the tarragon. Serve immediately.

Red wine sauce
Peel and mince the shallots. Sauté in olive oil in a large saucepan until shiny, about 15 seconds. Remove and set aside. Add the sugar and caramelize. Return the shallots to the pan, add the wine and reduce by half. Add the stock and reduce until 1/4 of the original amount remains. Strain into a clean saucepan. Just before serving, heat the sauce to boiling and season with salt and pepper. Beat in the butter while the sauce is boiling. Remove from the heat and serve.

Tarte Tatin (upside-down apple pie)

Pastry
3 dl (1 1/4 cups) all-purpose flour
1 tablespoon sugar
125 g (4 oz) soft unsalted butter
2 tablespoons cold water

10 tart apples
300 g (1 1/2 cups) sugar
50 g (3 tablespoons) unsalted butter
1 egg yolk

Place the flour, sugar and butter in a food processor and pulse until just combined. With the motor running, add the water and process until the dough begins to form a ball. Do not overprocess. Form the dough into a ball, flatten and wrap in plastic. Refrigerate for at least 2 hours.

Peel, core and halve the apples. Caramelize the sugar slowly in a heavy ovenproof frying pan. Remove from the heat and cover with apple halves. Dot with butter. Return the pan to the heat and cook until the caramel bubbles over the apples. Remove from the heat and let cool. Preheat the oven to 200°C (400°). Roll the pastry into a round sheet just larger than the frying pan. Drape over the apples, pressing down at the edges. Brush with egg yolk. Bake about 45 minutes, until the pastry is golden brown. Remove the cake from the oven and unmold immediately onto a serving platter.

A peaceful and homey atmosphere

Grotli Høyfjellshotel, Grotli

From yesterday
I long for clarity as strongly as anyone
The higher up, the higher the fog

From today
Today I saw a mountain with a glacier on
the edge of the forest
In cold, gray clarity, and froze at the sight
But against the snow, the liveliest heather
And flowers, winking at the red-backed sandpiper:
Sing
And they took me up to their mountain
fresh beauty!
Courage!

Bjørnstjerne Bjørnson, Grotli 1896

In 1896, poet and writer Bjørnstjerne Bjørnson had been traveling around the Romsdal valley and was on his way back home to Aulestad when he dropped by Grotli and wrote those lines in the guest book. That was nine years before the hotel was built, so he had to stay at the old mountain lodge, Old Grotli, two kilometers below the present hotel.

Hans Hagerup Krag, the Minister of Highways, took the initiative on behalf of the state, to add onto Skåre coaching inn and Grotli mountain lodge. These provided food and lodging for travelers journeying over Strynefjell mountain, from Skjåk to Stryn. The state lodge at Grotli was finished in 1870, and Kristen Sperstad was hired to manage it. Grotli, like the other mountain inns, had jurisdiction over large forested areas. These inns were given extensive rights in exchange for looking after the travelers properly. Kristen Sperstad spent winters in town, but summers at Grotli, where in addition to running the inn, he ran a large alpine dairy farm with 300 goats.

Sevald Skiager from Skjåk took over in 1880. He changed his surname to Grotli, and the family have been there ever since. Sevald and his wife Marit were the first people to live at Grotli year-round. The Strynfjell road, now called Gamle (Old) Strynefjellsvei, finally opened in 1894. Its highest point is 1139 meters above sea level and is definitely worth a visit if you're at Grotli in the summer. Now the road has been expanded, and the 26 kilometer stretch on Route 258 between Grotli and Videseter crossing features the Norwegian mountains at their best, with a wild, rugged, powerful landscape. The road was originally built for carts and was only 2.5 meters wide in some parts, but in its time, it was an engineering masterpiece. It was this road Bjørnstjerne Bjørnson traveled in 1896, and there is a boulder and a curve named after him. Bjørnsonsvingen lies just above Videseter, and it was here that our National poet lifted his wife Karoline up onto the Bjørnson boulder.

A NEW HOTEL AND A ROYAL VISIT

The new road brought increased traffic and better times to Grotli. In 1900, Sevald and Marit's son Andreas and his wife Maria took over the farm. Business was good, and soon there were eight or nine larger houses at the lodge. They had 20 horses and employed up to 10 mountain boys in the summer. The most common means of transport was a cart or open carriage, but they also used a buggy pulled by two horses. Andreas decided to build a new hotel two kilometers west of the inn, where the Skjåk-Stryn-Geiranger roads met. Grotli Mountain Hotel was finished in 1905, and an important guest visited just two years later. King Chulalongkorn of Siam was the first head of state to travel the Strynefjell road. The adventurer king wrote a letter to his daughters about his experience. He was especially impressed by the Strynefjell road and he described the road's guard

stones as being "two underarm-lengths high." He spent the night at Grotli Mountain Hotel, and described the hotel as an unpainted wooden building. But the King liked the new hotel because both the building and furniture reminded him of a playhouse he had as a child. "The food is good, but the dining room is cold. The only room that is really warm is the fireplace room. The bedrooms are cold too, and there are no lamps, probably because Norwegian nights are so light in the summer."

CROSSCOUNTRY DRIVING AND FILMING

Eventually, the Strynfjell road was expanded to accommodate cars, and the first car arrived in Grotli in 1910. After 1914, car travel exploded, and soon the tourist industry in Strynefjell mountain was reaping the benefits. Large cruise ships had started docking in the Hjørundfjord, Geiranger and the Nordfjord during the 1870s and 80s. The passengers wanted to explore the natural beauty of the scenery, but the horses and carriages didn't get them far. Cars changed the situation completely. Now the passengers could be transported in small cars from Øye and Hellsylt via Horndal, Stryn, Hjelle, Videseter, and Grotli to Geiranger, where the boat would meet them again. In the mid-30s, on days with many ships, there could be up to 85 cars driving over Strynefjell mountain, and the dining hall at Grotli was decked out for the hungry cruise ship passengers. Cross-country driving is still an important part of business at Grotli, but the small cars have been replaced by large tourist buses.

There was another royal visit in 1936, when Norway's own King Haakon stopped at the hotel on his way to open the new Trollstigen road. In 1939, Grotli got its own power station. This marked the end of carrying wood and stoking fires. Electric lights replaced all the old paraffin lamps that had to be cleaned and filled every day. That summer, camera crews left their mark on the area. The mountain along the old road served as the backdrop for the filming of a movie and the cast and crew lived at Grotli and Videseter.

SNOW SCOOTERS AND AN
ALL-WEATHER ROAD

The old lodge remained in use even after the new hotel was built in 1905. Andreas and Maria's son, Sevald Grotli and his wife Bertha took over both the hotel and management of the lodge in 1950. In addition, they also ran a cattle farm, tourist services and a youth hostel at old Grotli, and they had a mink and fox farm and a herd of reindeer. There was more than enough to do. Sevald managed to buy old Grotli from the Norwegian government in 1962, so now the family owned both the hotel and the old inn.

It wasn't always easy living in the Stryn mountains year-round. Grotli Mountain Hotel lies 900 meters above sea level, and the winters are definitely white. Back then, the Strynfjell road was open only in the summer, and the road was often closed by October. Skis were the only means of transportation when there was snow on the ground, and the nearest neighbor was at Pollfoss, 20 kilometers away. In good weather, they skied to Pollfoss once a week to pick up the mail, and from there the road was ploughed to Skjåk. But Berta and Sevald's children had to live with relatives in town while they attended school and came home for Christmas and Easter. But the Grotli family is used to snowstorms, bad weather, and closed roads. In 1961, the couple's daughters, Mari Grotli Bergheim and Liv Grotli Skogen took over the hotel. The first snowscooter arrived at Grotli the following year and changed life there forever. Now Pollfoss was just an hour's drive away! More and more tourists found their way to Grotli each summer. The sisters decided to expand the hotel, and in 1967, they opened a new wing with 50 modern guestrooms. In 1977, a year-round road was opened between Skjåk and Stryn. King Olav presided over the official opening at Grotli on October 17, 1978. That meant that Grotli could be open year-round, and the years until 1982 were spent insolating the building for winter use. The old building was also completely renovated and restored to its original style.

ANTIQUES AND EASTER WHO-DUNNITS

Today, Mari's son Are Bergheim and his wife Berit run Grotli, the fifth generation at the hotel. Both are concerned with preserving Grotli's unique character and traditions – especially those regarding food. They serve well-prepared, home-made dishes based on local products and traditions. In 2001, they opened their new "Storstugu", with a bar, dance-floor, and warm, cozy sitting rooms. They've also taken over the old "Kjos cabin", the 18th-century dwelling from Heggebotten farm in Skjåk, which rural doctor Kjos had moved to the Breidalsvatn lake outlet in 1929, when he got a plot of land from Andreas Grotli. Kjos collected old interiors and antiques from the area around Sjåk, and Lom, and his collection is on display here. The house was neglected after the doctor's death, and Berit and Are bought it in 1998. The old log building was moved to an idyllic plot just above the hotel and is used for special occasions. It was renamed "Andreas-Stugu" after Andreas Grotli, who gave the doctor his plot of land.

CULTURE, NATURE, AND SUMMER SKIING

Its location between eastern and western Norway make Grotli Mountain Hotel the perfect starting point for excursions and day trips. The mountain towns of Skjåk and Lom are renowned for their beautiful landscape, unique building style, and rich cultural heritage. A visit to Uppigard Skjåk is a must, and you can't visit Lom without visiting Lom stave church, the Norwegian Mountain Museum, the Stone Center, and the Lom Museum. Beautiful Stryn is just 63 kilometers away, and you can visit the National Park Center in Oppstryn along the way. The main building is in the iron age style and lies next to Stryn lake. It houses both a natural and cultural historic museum, with films and exhibits, and Inger Fure's botanical mountain garden. It's just a short trip to Geiranger in the summer. What is perhaps Norway's most popular destination lies just 36 kilometers from the hotel, but along the way, you should take a detour along Nibbe road. The road features 13 hairpin turns along the way to Dalsnibba, 1495 meters above sea level. The view out over the mountains, Geiranger, and the Geirangerfjord is breathtaking.

Grotli Mountain Hotel is surrounded by powerful mountains, excellent hiking paths, and nature at its best – in summer and winter. Jotunheimen, with famous destinations such as Galdhøpiggen and Besseggen, isn't far away. You can rent a bicycle and explore on your own, or you can follow one of the marked walking paths that depart from the hotel

door. The trout frolic in the lakes and rivers, and if you want to go river rafting, then Sjoa, Norway's best rafting river, isn't far away.

Grotli is paradise for skiers, offering lots of snow, varied terrain with endless flat plains and steep mountains, and there's a 1.3 kilometer long ski tow just outside the hotel. Stryn Summer ski center is at Tystigen, along the old Strynfjell road. Here you can enjoy all kinds of skiing activity – cross country, alpine, Telemark, and snow boarding, even in the middle of summer.

Dr. Kjos, the previous owner of "Andreas-Stugu", was an enthusiastic collector. Some of his treasures include wonderful antiques from Skjåk. This beautiful sideboard is one of many carved by Sylfest Skrinde, one of Skjåk's best-known woodcarvers.

To serve with coffee and Port wine

Deep-fried Rosettes
6-8 eggs
1 liter (quart) full-fat milk
about 500 g (4 cups) all-purpose flour
150 – 200 g (about 1 1/2 cups) potato starch or cornstarch
2/3 dl (1/4 cup) sugar
1 1/3 kilo (3 lbs) lard or vegetable shortening

Beat the eggs, then gradually add the milk. Stir in
the flour, starch and sugar, mixing well. Heat the lard
in a deep-fryer to 180°C (350°F). The temperature is
very important. If it's not hot enough, the batter won't
stick to the iron, and if it's too hot, the rosettes will
be soft. Dip the rosette iron into the batter and fill
to the level of the batter. Fry in the hot fat about
1 minute. 75 rosettes.

Sour cream crackers
Although these are called sour cream crackers, they
do not contain sour cream.

500 g (2 1/4 cups) lard or vegetable shortening
250 g (9 oz) stick margarine
(do not use low-fat margarine)
4 dl (1 2/3 cups) sugar
1 teaspoon hornsalt/ammonium carbonate
or 1 tablespoon baking powder
1 teaspoon cardamom
1 dl (scant 1/2 cup) barley flour
900 g (about 7 cups) bread flour
2 1/2 dl (1 cup) full-fat milk

Beat the lard, margarine and sugar until light and
fluffy. Sift all the dry ingredients together. Add
alternately with the milk, reserving a little flour for
rolling out. Roll the dough into thin sheets with a
patterned rolling pin. Place on a griddle over
medium heat, rolled side down. Bake 3 to 4 minutes.
Turn and bake 3 more minutes. These need to bake
for 6 to 7 minutes or else they get soft. 100 crackers.

Cone or cylinder cookies
These cookies are best if the batter is made a day
ahead of time.
2 eggs
100 g (1/2 cup) sugar
65 g (4 1/2 tablespoons) margarine
65 g (1/2 cup) all-purpose flour
65 g (1/2 cup) potato starch or cornstarch
2 teaspoons vanilla sugar (or 1 teaspoon vanilla extract)
3/4 dl (1/3 cup) water

Beat the eggs and sugar until light, thick and lemon-
colored. Melt the margarine and add along with the
flour, starch and vanilla. Stir in the water. Bake in a
"krumkake" or pizzelle iron. Roll around a cone or
roll up while still warm. Serve with whipped cream,
cloudberry preserves and sour cream. 20 cookies.

Potato-barley flatbread

2 kilos (4 1/2 lb) boiled potatoes, mashed or ground
200 g (1 2/3 cups) rye flour
200 g (1 2/3 cups) coarsely ground whole wheat flour
800-900 g (6 – 6 2/3 cups) barley flour
a little all-purpose flour
2 1/2 dl (1 cup) cultured buttermilk

Place the potatoes in a large bowl. Gradually mix in the flour. Add the milk. Roll into very thin sheets in a blend of barley flour and coarsely ground whole wheat flour. Bake on a griddle over medium heat, rolled side down. When done, fold into quarters while still on the griddle. Remove and place under a weight. Serve with dried ham and sausages. 20 to 25 sheets.

Sour cream porridge with Sjåk wafers

Sour cream porridge
1 liter (quart) cold whipping cream
2 dl (3/4 cup) cold buttermilk
200 g (1 2/3 cups) all-purpose flour
3 1/2 dl (1 1/2 cups) full-fat milk
1 1/2 teaspoons salt
1 1/2 tablespoons sugar
1 1/2 ss sukker

Combine the cream and buttermilk in a large saucepan, bring to a boil and simmer 10 minutes. Sift over the flour, whisking constantly until the porridge is smooth and thick. Cook the porridge over low heat until butter begins to seep out. Add the milk and cook, stirring constantly, until more butter is released. Season with salt and sugar. 5 servings.

If the porridge is too rich, remove some of the butter and serve alongside, or add more milk. Serve with sugar and cinnamon.

Sometimes the butter doesn't seem to be released so easily. Using cream which has been frozen can help.

Sjåk wafers
The kind of flour used here is a matter of taste. In the olden days, barley flour was used, but today most people prefer wheat flour.

3 dl (1 1/4 cups) whipping cream
3 dl (1 1/4 cups) natural sour heavy cream
(do not use low-fat sour cream)
6 dl (2 1/2 cups) water
1 teaspoon salt
12 dl (5 cups) all-purpose flour

Combine the whipping cream and the sour cream. Add the remaining ingredients. The batter should be slightly thicker than waffle batter. Bake in a wafer iron. Do not let the iron get too hot, as the wafers are supposed to dry out while they are baking. 80 wafers.

Cured meat

A fine family-run hotel

Visnes Hotel, Stryn

It's very early, not yet 6 am, and the hostess at Hotel Stryn, Kristin Visnes, is busy preparing breakfast. The bread dough was prepared hours ago, and the heavenly aroma of freshly baked bread wafts from the oven. Fragile old glass bowls are filled with fresh raspberry jam and homemade orange marmalade, while the paté is gently released from its pan onto an antique platter. The food at Visnes Hotel is always homemade: fresh salmon and ocean catfish, roast deer, and grandmother's prune surprise for dessert – homemade, healthy and hearty food made from fresh Norwegian ingredients. That's Kristin's philosophy. Even the potatoes are peeled by hand. It takes time, but Kristin feels that it's time well spent! It's easy to see that she enjoys her job. It's hard to believe that she hasn't been doing it her whole life!

When she inherited the old family hotel in 1986, she didn't know what to do. She had a life in Oslo. Should she take the chance and leave a well-paid secretarial job to move back to the country and take over the family business? She knew that managing a hotel was no easy task, but she was born and raised at Visnes Hotel, and her roots were in Stryn. Her great-great-grandfather, Anton Arnesen Visnes, had built the hotel in 1850, and it had been passed down the generations ever since. The old white wooden building had been changed and extended several times since 1850, but it still retained its charm. It certainly had a great location – in the middle of Stryn in the shadow of powerful mountains, with a fantastic view of the fjord. But no guests had entered its doors for 29 years. Kristin's father decided to close the hotel in 1957, when the local authorities expropriated most of the hotel grounds for a road and houses. During the hotel's heyday, the grounds had extended all the way down to the sea, with a private beach and a large, lush garden with many fruit trees. Kristin considered

this both an advantage and a disadvantage. Since the hotel had been closed from 1957 to 1986, that meant that it hadn't been destroyed by merciless modernization, and no one had added on a concrete extension. But that also meant that the old building had not been properly maintained and was in desperate need of an overhaul. What should she do?

A SECRETARIAL JOB, OR HOTELLIER – A DIFFICULT CHOICE

She saw the potential! Stryn, with its mountains, fjords and glaciers, is one of western Norway's top tourist destinations. It attracts lovers of wildlife and nature. Some come to fish in Stryn river, famous for its salmon. Others come to hike in the mountains and trek across the glaciers. And many come to ski, even in the summer. Tystig glacier has the best summer skiing conditions in all of Europe, and there is a 975-meter long chair-lift to carry you from Stryn straight up to the glacier. Once there, you can ski along a 775-meter long glacier path. For those who prefer alpine skiing, there are several different courses with varying degrees of difficulty, the longest of which is 2100 meters long with a drop of 518 meters. On the glacier plateau are several kilometers of well prepared and maintained cross country skiing trails. Briksdals glacier, with its fantastic setting between soaring mountains and powerful waterfalls, attracts tourists from around the world. It can be explored on foot or in a horse-drawn carriage. Either way it's an unforgettable experience.

There were certainly many good reasons to reopen the hotel, and Kristin decided to give it a try. But she needed an extra income to make ends meet, so for the first three years, she ran the hotel in the summer and worked as a secretary in Oslo during the winter. Eventually, tourists returned to the hotel, and in 1989, she was able to move to Stryn and run the hotel

Visnes Hotel

full time. Since that time, she has invested all her time and money in the hotel, and little by little, she has restored it to its former glory.

After careful consideration, Kristin's daughter, Vibeke Visnes, took over the hotel in 1999. She continued rehabilitating the hotel, and for the summer season in 2000, she opened the third floor, with eight new guest rooms and baths.

At the same time, the Visnes family took over King Oscar's Hall, a former hotel built in 1896 in the national romantic dragon style. It was renamed Villa Visnes and is now used for banquets and special occasions.

Kristin admits that there has been plenty to do over the years, but she had a lot of help. Her daughter Vibeke, mother Emma, and ex-husband Roar Berger all moved to Stryn to lend her a hand.

Today, Hotel Visnes is managed by Kristin and Vibeke, and Roar is both host and handyman. This old traditional hotel can once again call itself a true family-run hotel.

Left. The cozy, nostalgic atmosphere which is the hallmark of Visnes Hotel in Stryn greets you at the door.

Below: All the guest bedrooms are individually decorated. Kristin Visnes loves to browse in antique shops in search of special items for the hotel.

Visnes Hotel

Left: Hearty Norwegian fare made with fresh local ingredients is prepared in the large old-fashioned kitchen.

Baking is Kristin's specialty. The aroma of freshly baked bread, rolls and cakes, is just one aspect of the wonderful experience of staying at Visnes Hotel.

Liver paté

250 g (9 oz) pork liver
75 g (3 oz) boneless fresh pork
100 g (4 oz) fresh pork belly
1 onion
1 1/2 teaspoons salt
2 tablespoons melted butter
1 dl (1/2 cup) all-purpose flour
2 1/2 dl (1 cup) milk
1 egg

Preheat the oven to 140°C (280°F). Cube the liver, meat, belly and onion and place in a food processor with the remaining ingredients. Process until not quite smooth. Pour into a 1-liter (quart) mold and bake in a water bath for about 2 hours.

Orange marmalade

3 oranges
1 grapefruit
1 lemon
2 dl (3/4 cup) water
750 g (3 3/4 cups) sugar

Cut the fruit into strips. Simmer in the water until soft, about 1 1/2 hours. Add the sugar, bring to a boil and let simmer until thick. If the marmalade becomes too thin, add 1 tablespoon pectin mixed with a little sugar. Pour into sterilized jars and seal.

Raspberry preserves

1 kilo (2 1/4 lb) raspberries
750 g (3 3/4 cups) sugar
1 tablespoon pectin

Clean and rinse the berries and place in a saucepan. Heat to the boiling point. Combine the sugar and pectin and stir into the berries. Let cool. Pour into freezer containers and freeze for up to one year.

Multi-grain bread

1 3/4 liters (7 cups) water mixed with a little whole milk
1 dl (1/2 cup) oil
50 g (1 3/4 oz, 2 US cakes) fresh yeast
2 kilos (4 1/2 lb) all-purpose flour
1 kilo (2 1/4 lb) coarse whole wheat flour
3 dl (1 1/4 cups) rolled oats
1 1/2 dl (2/3 cup) fine whole wheat flour
3/4 dl (1/3 cup) barley flour
4 teaspoons salt

Heat the water and oil to lukewarm and crumble in the yeast, stirring to dissolve. Combine the remaining ingredients in a large bowl and stir in the yeast mixture. Cover the dough and let rise for about 2 hours. Knead the dough, preferably with a heavy-duty mixer with a dough hook. Divide into 5 equal parts and form into individual loaves. Place in a well-greased oven pan. Let rise 1 hour. Preheat the oven to 200°C (400°F). Bake the breads in the center of the oven for about 1 hour.

Apple cake

100 g (3 1/2 oz) butter
1 1/2 dl (2/3) cup full-fat milk
4 eggs
3 dl (1 1/4 cups) sugar
4 dl (1 2/3 cups) all-purpose flour
2 teaspoons baking powder
2 apples

Preheat the oven to 180°C (350°F). Grease a 22 cm (9") round cake pan. Melt the butter in a saucepan, add the milk and heat to the boiling point. Let cool. Beat the eggs and sugar until light and lemon-colored. Sift in the flour and baking powder alternately with the milk mixture. Spread the dough in the pan. Peel and slice the apples and press the slices into the dough. Bake the cake on the lowest oven rack for about 1 hour.

Rolls and a wreath

100 g (3 1/2 oz) butter
1 liter (quart) water mixed with a little whole milk
50 g (1 3/4 oz, 2 US cakes) fresh yeast
about 2 kilo (4 1/2 lb) all-purpose flour
2 eggs
2 teaspoons salt

Melt the butter. Heat the water to lukewarm. Crumble the yeast in 1 cup (2 1/2 dl) of the water, stirring to dissolve. Combine the butter with the remaining liquid and add the flour and eggs. The dough should be rather loose, so use only a little flour at a time. Stir in the dissolved yeast and salt. Cover the dough and let rise until doubled. Divide the dough into two equal parts. Use one half for rolls, the other half for a wreath.

Rolls
Divide the dough into 25 pieces of equal size. Roll into balls and place on a baking sheet. Cover and let rise until doubled. Preheat the oven to 225°C (425°F). Bake about 15 minutes.

Wreath
1 batch dough
100 g (3 1/2 oz) soft butter
sugar
1 tablespoon cinnamon
confectioner's sugar

Roll the dough into a large rectangle, spread thinly with butter and sprinkle with 1 tablespoon sugar. Fold in two. Repeat twice, but sprinkle generously with sugar and the cinnamon the last time. Fold over and place, seam down, on an oven sheet. Shape into a ring. Cut with a scissors every other centimeter (1/2") and fold each piece out in opposite direction. Cover the dough and let rise 30 minutes. Preheat the oven to 200°C (400°F) and bake about 25 minutes. Do not let the wreath get too brown. Garnish with confectioner's sugar, either in a glaze or sprinkled.

Ghosts and garlic

Hotel Union Øye, Norangsfjorden

The German Kaiser Wilhelm II loved Norway and visited here every summer from 1888 until the outbreak of World War I in 1914. The only exception was in 1905, when he was frightened that trouble would break out after Norway dissolved her union with Sweden. He usually stayed in Norway for a month, from the beginning of July to the first week in August. He always traveled aboard the "Hohenzollern", a 117-meter (about 460 foot) long ship manned by eight officers and a crew of 295, and he loved to cruise the beautiful Norwegian fjords. One of his favorite places was the lovely Norangsfjord and Hotel Union Øye. One of the Kaiser's officers onboard was the German Count Filip. One summer while staying at Hotel Union Øye, the count fell in love with one of the chambermaids. Linda was as pale and beautiful as a Norwegian summer evening, much to the Count's delight, his love was returned. Count Filip always stayed in room number seven, now called "The Blue Room". After the affair had been going on for a few years, Linda moved into the room whenever the Count was in residence. Everyone could see how much in love they were, and even though everyone knew that the Count had a wife back home in Germany, the local population accepted this affair between a German count and a Norwegian chambermaid. The Count's marriage had never been a happy one. It was an arranged marriage between two wealthy, noble families. One summer the count gave Linda a valuable gift. It was part of a priceless sautoir – a set of jewelry he had inherited from his father to one day give to the woman he loved. The sautoir consisted of a beautiful brooch set with an oriental pearl and a matching ring. The brooch was an engagement present, while the ring would be a wedding present when they eventually married. Count Filip asked Linda to wear the brooch until he came back to Norway the following summer. By then he would be divorced from his wife and could offer the ring to Linda as a free man. He gave her his word. He left, and Linda wore the brooch all winter while she waited for her beloved to return. Spring came, the hotel reopened, and Linda returned to her job as a chambermaid. She lived on a farm just above the hotel, and she had to cross a river to and from work every day. Early one May morning, she took her usual route to the hotel. The river was swollen and wild after a

particularly heavy winter. Linda slipped on a wet stone and fell into the river. Luckily she was a strong girl and managed to pull herself out of the river, only to discover that the brooch had fallen off into the river. She was beside herself. Hour after hour, day after day, week after week, she went up and down the river hoping to catch sight of the brooch. She looked everywhere but never found it. The date of the Kaiser's visit drew near, and Filip would be coming with him. The "Hohenzollern" docked at the hotel on a beautiful, sunny day, and the whole village was there to greet the Kaiser, who was the first to land. He went straight to Linda, kissed her hand, and in a sad tone told her that Filip would not be visiting the hotel that year. Filip was dead. One evening during the voyage, the young Count asked the Kaiser to deliver a letter from him to Linda. When the Kaiser asked why he couldn't deliver the letter to Linda himself, Filip replied that he would never see her again. With those words he left the cabin never to be seen again. The ship was searched, but everyone soon realized that the Count had committed suicide by jumping overboard.

Linda's hands trembled as she opened the letter, and her eyes welled with tears as she read it. Filip wrote that he had asked his family for permission to divorce his wife and marry Linda, and they had been furious. They threatened to disown him, take away his title, power, and money if he went through with his plans. The also reminded him of the marriage vows he had given his wife. Filip was an officer and a gentleman. Promises were meant to be kept, but he had also promised Linda. In the letter, he also asked for her forgiveness, but he couldn't live with that. In the letter was the ring. Linda cried so hard that day that no one present on the dock could ever forgot her sobs.

As soon as she was finished reading the letter, Linda ran away from the dock and no one ever spoke with her again. She kept to herself and spent her days looking for the brooch in the river. One beautiful day after the Kaiser and his men had left the village, her body was found floating in the river near its mouth at

Above: Physiotherapist Per Ola Ratvik from Ålesund rescued this venerable hotel. When he and two others, Idar Nordang and Johan Øye, took over the hotel in 1998, it had been neglected for years and was in complete decay. Now it has been recreated in all its former glory.

Right: When the new owners took over, the hotel had been stripped of its original interiors. Since then Per Ola Ratvik has traveled all over Europe in search of antiques for this beautiful building.

Right page: The guest bedrooms are a dream! Tastefully and individually decorated, most feature period canopy beds.

Hotel Union Øye

Øye. Dressed as a bride with flowers in her hair, she had taken her own life. In her hand was a bridal bouquet, and she wore Filip's last token of love on her finger, the pearl ring. And, wonder of all wonders, the beautiful brooch was fastened to her dress. Linda and her beloved Count were joined in death.

The story should have ended there, but it didn't. From that day on, Linda took up residence in "The Blue Room" at Hotel Union Øye, and she has never left. You can still hear her occasionally, sometimes even see her hovering above the floor, and hear her painful sobs in the dark night...

It is so quiet you could hear a pin drop in the salon at Hotel Union Øye. Dinner is over and the guests have gathered to hear hotel owner Per Ola Ratvik tell the story of the ghost in "The Blue Room". The fire is aglow and the flickering candles cast ghoulish shadows over the lavish furniture, large statues and magnificent flower arrangements. The white gauzy curtains flutter in the early evening breeze coming through the open windows, bringing with it the fragrance of wild strawberries and newly cut grass. The faint rushing from the powerful waterfalls plunging into the Norangsfjord helps to conjure up the image of Linda searching the river for her beautiful brooch. He is a good storyteller. The amount of truth in all these fantastic stories is debatable, but they are well-told and very entertaining. There is always an element of truth in them, even in the story of Linda and her German count. At the end of the 19th and the beginning of the 20th centuries, Hotel Union Øye, which lies at the innermost point of Norangsfjord, an arm of the better known Hjørundfjord, was a very popular gathering place for royalty, the aristocracy, and other wealthy individuals who could afford to travel at the time. There is no doubt that Kaiser Wilhelm II visited the hotel on several occasions, and on June 22, 1896, Oscar II, who was then king of both Norway and Sweden, visited the hotel with a staff of 12. King Haakon, Queen Maud, and Crown Prince Olav all visited the hotel in 1906 on their coronation trip around Norway. Other famous guests included Queen Wilhelmina and Crown Princess Juliana, later queen of the Netherlands, and the authors Karen Blixen and Bjørnstjerne Bjørnson.

Like many other places in Norway, the Norangsfjord and its surrounding areas were "discovered" by the first tourists who came to Norway. These were mostly explorers, adventurers, and mountain climbers, and the powerful mountains, especially Slogen and Smørskredtind made an indelible impression on them. Although these first tourists were in search of rough and rugged nature, they expected more from their lodgings. They wanted good food, comfortable

beds, and vintage port served in crystal glasses, while they enjoyed looking at all this wilderness from their wicker deck chairs. And it was to meet these demands that a modern hotel was built in this remote fjord arm in Sunnmøre.

A MOTLEY HISTORY

A corporation led by Adolf Schjelderup was responsible for the building of Hotel Union Øye. The same group also was behind Hotel Union in Geiranger. This venture proved to be too large and risky. Hotel Union Øye was prefabricated in Trondheim and moved by boat to Øye. The company went bankrupt before the first guest arrived.

Fortunately, the building did not remain vacant for long. That same year it was purchased by the Norwegian consul in Spain, and the hotel opened as planned on June 1, 1891. Consul Tonning had neither the time nor the inclination to run the hotel himself, but he did pay regular visits and often brought along Spanish friends. But the running of what was then considered one of Norway's most modern hotels was left to his sister and her husband, Peter Stub.

In 1913, Consul Tonning decided to sell the hotel. At that same time, Martin Laurits Dahl, a Geiranger native who had spent the previous 18 years in the US, decided to return to Norway. He had been in the hotel business for many years, working both in the US as well as one year in Germany. When his wife Birgitte got pregnant in 1913, he decided it was time to move Ørsta. On his way, he spent the night at Hotel Union Øye and ended up talking with Consul Tonning. He offered the Dahls the hotel, lock, stock, and barrel. Martin and Birgitte agreed immediately. The hotel remainind in the Dahl family for 68 years. Martin Laurits Dahl died in 1954, his son Karl and daughter-in-law Aslaug ran the hotel until Karl became ill in 1972. Then they rented it to Ingvald Rørnes until 1976, when Aslaug and Karl's son Leif took over. In 1981, the Ørsta Free Church purchased the hotel and added a course and conference center, which they ran until 1989.

A PHOENIX HAS RISEN

The present owner, Per Ola Ratvik, a physiotherapist and acupuncturist from Ålesund, had driven past the old hotel many times and simply fallen in love with it. So when the church decided to sell in 1989, he jumped at the chance. People thought he had lost his mind and thought he was doomed. The building had not been repaired in years, and there had been little to no maintenance. The exterior was in decay, and the interior wasn't much better. The wallpaper hung in shreds and the once beautiful salons were filled with shabby furniture, but Per Ola took on the

challenge. This mythical hotel would regain its former pride and rise like the phoenix from the ashes. He was able to recruit two local shareholders, farmers, and two local fur farmers, Idar Nordang and Johan Øye, and a researcher Ivar Lødemel. The interior of the hotel was stripped entirely before they started the painstaking restoration. Today the owners readily admit that they had no idea of what they were getting themselves in for, and that it would cost blood, sweat, and tears. But it was a success. Both the interior and exterior are just like those of the original hotel where kings, emperors, writers, and explorers drank their vintage port. They might even be nicer. Per Ola Ratvik personally trawled through Europe looking for antiques, and he returned home with countless chandeliers, furnishings, and decorative objects from Berlin, London, Paris, and Barcelona. The guest rooms are like something from a fairytale – individually decorated in an ornate style – just like a Real Belle époque hotel. And if you get the keys to "The Blue Room", don't despair. A bowl of garlic comes with the key, because all ghosts are allergic to garlic….

Below: With his creativity and attention to detail, Per Ola Ratvik has made Hotel Union Oye one of Norway's most interesting hotels.

Right:

Grapes in Champagne aspic

12 grapes
4 gelatin sheets
3 3/4 dl (1 1/2 cups) semi-dry white wine
1 dl (1/2 cup) Champagne or other sparkling wine

Rinse and halve the grapes and remove the pits. Place six grape halves in each of four wine goblets. Soak the gelatin in cold water to soften, about 4 minutes. Squeeze to remove excess water and melt in the wine. Stir until the gelatin is completely dissolved, pour over the grapes, but leave enough space for the Champagne. Refrigerate the goblets until the aspic is partially set – it takes a little longer than usual because of the alcohol. Carefully pour the Champagne into the glasses and watch the bubbles enter the aspic.

Cream of crayfish soup

1/4 onion
3 liters (quarts) water
4 teaspoons salt
1 bay leaf
8 white peppercorns
750 g (1 2/3 lb) freshwater
crayfish
1 shallot
butter
2 tablespoons all-purpose flour
1 liter (quart) crayfish stock
2 dl (3/4 cup) dry white wine
2 dl (3/4 cup) whipping cream
salt, pepper
1 small carrot
1/4 small celeriac

Peel and coarsely chop the onion. Place in a stock-pot with the water, salt, bay leaf and pepper and heat to boiling. Add the crayfish, reduce the heat and simmer for 10 minutes. Remove the crayfish, strain the cooking liquid and set aside. Clean the crayfish, removing the tails and the black veins. Cover the tails with plastic wrap and refrigerate.

Crush the rest of the crayfish and shells. Mince the shallot. Sauté in a little butter a stockpot. Add the cooking liquid and simmer for 30 minutes. Strain. Measure the stock and pour 1 liter (quart)

back into the stockpot and heat to boiling. In a large saucepan, melt 1 tablespoon butter, then stir in the flour. Whisk in the hot crayfish stock and wine and let simmer 20 minutes. Add the cream and boil 3 to 4 minutes. Season with salt and pepper. Wash, peel and shred the carrot and celeriac. Blanch in boiling water for about 1 minute. Just before serving, sauté the crayfish tails and vegetables lightly in butter and divide among the individual bowls. Reheat the soup, but do not allow to boil. Pour over the crayfish and serve with freshly baked bread.

Fish braid Hotel Union Øye

700 g (1 1/2 lb) boneless,
skinless trout fillet
700 g (1 1/2 lb)
boneless monkfish fillet
5 dl (2 cups) fish stock
300 g (10 oz) fresh
spinach leaves
1 shallot
2 tablespoons butter
2 tablespoons
all-purpose flour
1 dl (1/2 cup)
whipping cream
salt, pepper

Remove any small bones and membrane or skin from the fish. Cut each fillet into 12 finger-thick strips, about 20 cm (8") long. Weave 3 and 3 fillets. Repeat 3 more times. Place in a low frying pan and poach in fish stock for around 5 minutes, until just done. If the braids are cooked too much, they will fall apart. Remove and keep warm. Strain the stock and reserve.

Rinse the spinach, removing any stalks. Peel and mince the shallot. Sauté spinach and shallot in butter until soft. Stir in the flour. Add the reserved stock and the cream. Boil 5 minutes. Puree with an immersion blender and add salt and pepper to taste.

Make a mirror of sauce on each plate. Top with the fish and serve with boiled almond potatoes.

9 egg yolks
185 g (scant 1 cup) sugar
5 dl (2 cups) full fat milk
1 teaspoon vanilla
10 gelatin sheets
1 1/2 dl (2/3 cups)
whipping cream
1 1/4 dl (1/2 cup) dairy sour
cream (do not use
low fat sour cream)
20-25 long sponge biscuits
(lady fingers or cat tongues)

Chapeau la Belle Époque

Beat the egg yolks, gradually add the sugar and beat until thick and lemon-colored. Scald the milk and vanilla. Gradually beat the milk into the egg yolk mixture. Pour into a clean saucepan and heat until almost boiling, stirring constantly. The mixture must not boil!

Soak the gelatin in cold water to soften, about 5 minutes. Squeeze to remove excess water and melt in the hot egg mixture. Stir until the gelatin is completely dissolved. Cover with plastic wrap and refrigerate.

Whip the cream and the sour cream until thick. Fold into the egg cream. Refrigerate for about 1 hour, stirring several times. The cream should be quite thick.

While the cream is setting, line a 2-liter (quart) Charlotte mold with baking parchment. Line the inside of the mold with biscuits, cutting them to fit, if necessary. Pour the egg cream into the prepared mold and refrigerate overnight. Just before serving, unmold or remove sides of mold. Decorate with berries, fruit and whipped cream. 8 servings.

It all started with the English salmon lords

Gloppen Hotel, Sandane

Above: Traditional Gloppen Hotel is in the center of Sandane at the end of the Nordfjord. The oldest part of the present hotel building was constructed in 1890.

Right: In "Stovene" you can enjoy a good meal or just relax in the nostalgic setting.

They lie, brag, exaggerate, and argue. There is a charged atmosphere in the fireside room of Gloppen hotel. It's the end of a long day on the river and now they're discussing the day's catch – including the ones that got away. The sports fishermen are gathered over a four-course fish dinner, just as enthusiastic sport fishermen the world over have done at this traditional hotel in Nordfjord for over 100 years.

Salmon and trout fishing in the Gloppen river spurred the development of this hotel set in the heart of the Gloppenfjord. Fishermen have come from around the world to Gloppen to try their luck. Gloppen was named one of the best fishing spots in all of Norway in the English guidebook "Salmon fishing in Norway", published in 1904, but the English salmon lords already knew that. They'd been going there for years. In England, salmon fishing was a luxury reserved for estate owners and the aristocracy, while in Norway, anyone could pay the local farmer a few kroner for the privilege of fishing in a good river. As early as 1872, the local farmers in Sandane understood that renting out fishing rights on the Gloppen river could add to their income. Soon sports fishermen flocked to the area, and of course, they needed a place to stay while they were in Sandane.

There had been a hotel in Sandane since 1846, on the same lot where Gloppen Hotel now stands. For the first 20 years, it was just a simple coaching inn, but in 1866, Joakim E. Sivertsen was granted a license to run a country store at:

"Sanden in Gloppen Parish, Sønd- and Nordfjords District, Nordre Bergenshus County with the obligation to:

1. run an inn, without licensing rights to hard liquor or any other kind of mixed drink.
2. if required, to hold court and to serve as the shipping agent for the postal steamer as paid for by the Royal Mail.
3. pay the yearly sum of 8 spesidaler to the government. Other requirements:
a) that he will keep the place adequately supplied with essential goods.
b) that he keeps the inn in good condition and provides travelers with lodging, good food and drink, the latter within the laws and regulations as stated. Or else he would lose the rights."

The new inn quickly became popular, and in 1890, Sivertsen built the first part of what is now known as Gloppen Hotel. At that time, it was called Sivertsen's Hotel, after the owner. It became a natural congregating place for the English salmon lords, but equally important were the streams of immigrants going to America in the late 19th and early 20th century. This was because Sivertsen's Hotel also housed the Cunard Line ticket office. This meant that Sivertsen's Hotel was often the last Norwegian residence of many immigrants before they set out across the Atlantic.

Business increased, and by 1925, the hotel was too small. An addition was built in the same style as the old building. It now houses the sitting rooms and salons. According to the standards of the day, Sivertsen's Hotel was a modern hotel with running water and electricity. The years between 1925 and the outbreak of World War II were the most profitable in the hotel's history.

Below: Dag and Irene Moen purchased Gloppen Hotell in 1994. Here they are with their sons Preben and Dag Håkon.

NEW OWNERS AND A NEW NAME

The Sivertsen family left the business in the 1980s, and the hotel was turned into a corporation. The next eight years saw many owners and as many bankruptcies. In 1988, the hotel was purchased by K. Strømmen's salmon farms in Bremanger, and the name was changed to Gloppen Hotel. Dag Moen was hired as manager and millions of kroner were invested in the hotel to recreate the traditional ambience that had so appealed to the salmon lords.

Six years later, on December 1, 1994, Dag Moen bought out his employers and took over the hotel with his wife Irene. The new owners were fascinated by the hotel's history, and since they took over, they have tried to go back in time. They have restored the interior and have fixed up the beautiful white wooden building to look just as good as it did in its heyday. The last big project, 10 new bedrooms on the third floor of the old building, was completed in May, 2000. All the rooms are different and have been decorated with wallpaper in historical patterns dating from between 1820-1890, antique furniture and lace curtains, as well as unique bathrooms with modern equipment.

In addition to preserving the old building, the new owners have worked hard to maintain Gloppen Hotel's reputation as a fine place to dine. They concentrate on serving good food using local Norwegian ingredients, and the hotel has an excellent wine cellar.

In 1996, the hotel took over the fishing rights in Gloppen River, and even though times have changed, and most of the winter guests come for courses and conferences, salmon fishermen are still in the majority from June to September. They still want good old-fashioned service at this traditional salmon hotel deep in Nordfjord!

Left: Chef Serge Dykmans makes the most wonderful dishes with local products, and Gloppen Hotell has one of the best restaurants in western Norway.

Right: For years, salmon fishermen have been enjoying four-course lunches in this beautiful old room.

Gloppen's fish chowder

Fish stock
small chunk celeriac
1/2 medium leek
1 kilo (2 1/4 lb) fish bones and trimmings
1 dl (1/2 cup) white wine
1 1/2 liter (quarts) water
1 bay leaf

Fish soup
200 g (7 oz) salmon and cod fillet
4 scallops
fish stock
1 small onion
small chunk celeriac
1/2 medium leek
150 g (5 oz) shrimp in their shells
50 g (3 1/2 tablespoons) butter
1/2 teaspoon salt
1/2 teaspoon pepper
3 tablespoons tomato paste
60 g (1/2 cup) all-purpose flour
1 dl (1/2 cup) cognac
4 cooked ocean crayfish
chopped fresh parsley

You will need a good fish stock to start.

Fish stock
Wash, peel and chop the celeriac and leek. Place in a stockpot with the remaining ingredients and heat to boiling. Reduce the heat and let simmer about 1 hour. Strain and reserve the stock.

Fish soup
Cut the fish into fine dice. Clean the scallops. Heat the fish stock to boiling, then add the diced fish and scallops. Reduce the heat and let simmer about 5 minutes. Remove the fish and scallops. Keep the stock warm.

Clean the vegetables and cut into chunks. Chop the shrimp, shells and all. Melt the butter and sauté the vegetables and shrimp about 5 minutes. Sprinkle with salt and pepper and stir in the tomato paste. Sprinkle with the flour, stirring to coat. Add the cognac and the hot stock. Let simmer about 40 minutes, stirring now and then. Puree with an immersion blender, then strain. Serve in deep bowls with the fish, scallops and crayfish. Sprinkle with parsley.

Salmon and cod roulade

600 g (1 1/3 lb) salmon fillet
400 g (14 oz) cod fillet
5 ice cubes
2 egg whites
1/2 teaspoon salt
1/2 teaspoon pepper
2 1/2 dl (1 cup) whipping cream
4 ss (1/4 cup) finely chopped fresh dill
1 1/2 tablespoons finely minced fresh parsley

Dressing
3 tablespoons mayonnaise
1 teaspoon pesto
1 dl (1/2 cup) full fat milk
1 tablespoon lemon juice
salt, pepper

Trim the fish, removing any small bones. Split the salmon fillet horizontally to make two relatively large thin sheets. Place on separate sheets of plastic wrap. Cube the cod and place in a food processor with the ice, egg whites, salt and pepper and puree for 2 minutes. With the motor running, gradually add the cream, then the herbs. Spread a 1 cm (1/2") layer of mousse over the salmon, except for a 1 cm (1/2") border. Tightly roll the fish up like a jelly roll. The roulades should be no more than 5 cm (2") in diameter. If the rolls are too thick, they will not cook evenly. Pack the rolls in plastic wrap and seal at the ends. Simmer in water to cover for around 15 minutes. Do not allow to boil. Refrigerate overnight. To serve, remove the plastic wrap and cut the roulades into 1 1/2 cm (3/4") slices.

For the dressing, whisk all ingredients together until smooth.

Serve the fish roulade with boiled asparagus, endive and cherry tomatoes. Serve dressing alongside.

Left: Breims tront is one of many delicacies served at Gloppen Hotell.

Breims trout with Sandefjord butter and potato puree

Potato puree
1 kilo (2 1/4 lb) potatoes
50 g (3 1/2 tablespoons)
butter
2 egg yolks
1/2 teaspoon salt
1/3 teaspoon ground white
pepper
pinch ground nutmeg
1 egg yolk mixed with a
few drops of water

Sandefjord butter
1/2 dl (3 1/2 tablespoons)
whipping cream
3-4 tablespoons chopped
parsley
250 g (9 oz) soft butter
lemon juice

Breims trout
2 large Breims trout
or char
50 g (1/3 cup)
all-purpose flour
50 g (3 1/2 tablespoons)
butter
1/2 dl (3 1/2 tablespoons)
oil

Vegetables
1/2 yellow squash
1/2 zucchini
10 cherry tomatoes

The potatoes take the most time, so they should be prepared first.

Potato puree
Preheat the oven to 180°C (350°F). Wash, peel and slice the potatoes. Boil in salted water until tender. Drain, then return to the heat and let the remaining water evaporate. Mash the potatoes, then beat in the butter, egg yolks, salt, pepper and nutmeg. Spoon into a pastry bag and pipe mounds onto a baking sheet. Brush with egg yolk and bake about 15 minutes.

Sandefjord butter
Heat the cream and parsley to boiling. Remove from the heat and beat in the butter in pats. Season with lemon juice. Do not allow to boil after the butter has been added.

Breims trout
Wash and fillet the fish. Dip the fish in flour and sauté in butter and oil, skin side down, for 5 minutes. Turn and fry on the other side for 3 minutes.

Vegetables
Wash and cube the squash. Boil in lightly salted water until "al dente". Wash and halve the tomatoes. Mix together.

Serve the trout with potatoes, vegetables and Sandefjord butter.

Caramel pudding

300 g (1 1/2 cups) sugar
3 dl (1 1/4 cups) water
5 eggs
100 g (1/2 cup) sugar
5 dl (2 cups) full fat milk
2 teaspoons vanilla sugar

fresh fruit

Caramelize the sugar in a frying pan. Let simmer about 10 minutes until completely caramelized. Pour into a 1-liter (quart) loaf pan to a depth of 1 cm (1/2"). Combine the rest with the water to make caramel sauce.

Preheat the oven to 125°C (250°F). Whisk the eggs, sugar, milk and vanilla sugar until just blended. Pour into the prepared form. Place in a water bath and bake 1 1/2 hours. Refrigerate overnight. Just before serving, unmold onto a platter. Slice and serve with caramel sauce and fruit.

Sea, health, and a very salty experience

Selje Hotel & Spa Thalasso, Selje

Gerd Kjellaug and Harald Berge came to Selje Hotel in 1976, and since that time, the sea, weather and wind have been their most important resources in marketing the place.

Algae baths in hot seawater. Shower jets with powerful, massaging streams. Seawater, and algae oil effusion showers followed by a manual massage. Cold or warm algae wraps with a remineralizing effect. Algae oil body massages. Sauna. Aromatherapy with ethereal oils.

Selje Spa Thalasso, Norway's first thalassotherapy center, opened in Selje Hotel in October, 2000. Thalasso is Greek for "sea" or "sea-water", and "spa" is Latin for "health through water". Thalassotherapy uses healing preparations derived from algae and other products of the sea, and well as medicinal mud baths.

In 1899, a Frenchman, Dr. Bagot, discovered that heated seawater was beneficial to stiff joints. It promoted flexibility, which was very beneficial to arthritis sufferers. He established the world's first thalassotherapy center in Roscoff. It was to be the first of many. Today, thalassotherapy is an accepted treatment not just for rheumatic and joint pains, but also for asthma, psoriasis, and different psychosomatic ailments. It is also used to treat stress, depression, sleep problems, obesity, cellulite, headaches, menopause, elephantiasis, and poor circulation.

But you can be healthy and still enjoy a stay at a thalassotherapy center. Most of us need a break from reality at some time or another. Thalassotherapy cleanses and invigorates the body. It replenishes vitamins, minerals, and trace elements, while eliminating fat, toxins, and other waste products that suppress energy. In this way, the body is revived and put into balance again.

Treatment always starts with a check-up and a chat to help tailor a specific plan of action. Four different therapies for a total of two hours a day is usual.

The spa also offers foot therapy, advanced skin treatment, light therapy, modeling masks, as well as wax and paraffin treatments. There is also an outdoor swimming pool with pure seawater heated to a pleasant 38°C (99°F) facing the sea. You can even combine thalassotherapy with a round of golf at the nine-hole course near the hotel.

The hotel west of the sea

Not just anyone can open a thalassotherapy center. There are many rules and regulations to be met. One of the most important is location - the center must be by the sea. This wasn't a problem at Selje hotel. Its location is ideal, with 600 meters of beach and the sea as its closest neighbors.

But you may well ask what possessed anyone to build a hotel and thalassotherapy center here, on the edge of the Nordfjord, in what is essentially the middle of nowhere.

It all started in 1975, when local entrepreneur Wald Drageset decided to fulfill a lifelong dream. He wanted to build a "great hall" at Selje, where locals could gather for both private and public functions. The following year, husband and wife Gerd Kjellaug and Harald Berge were hired to run the new hotel. The came to a beautiful building site which would eventually evolve into a hotel. The location was fantastic, but sadly there were no guests. Something had to be done! But how were they going to tempt guests into coming to this stormy backwater? There were many late nights, and many ideas were aired before they came up with a plan of action. The sea, wind, and weather were their most important resources in devising a marketing strategy. They came up with the slogan "Selje Hotel – The hotel west of the sea – in good weather an idyll, in bad weather a powerful experience. They needed a lot of supplies, from fishing gear to wet suits and water-skis. They wanted their guests to experience the coastal landscape and culture in all kinds of weather. Guests could fish in the sea around Stad, then clean and freeze their catches in the hotel's own fishing cabin, and take them home when they left. Selje beach was particularly inviting, and the hotel sea sport center offered activities such as diving, windsurfing, and water-skiing. The restaurant served everything the sea could offer, and then some: lobster, crab, crayfish, mussels, scallops, salmon, and trout.

Gerd Kjellaug and Harald bought the hotel in 1983 and immediately started building a health center with an indoor swimming pool, a whirlpool bath, infra-red therapy, a sauna, skin and body treatments, aromatherapy, massage, a solarium, and a gym. This

Left: There is a fantastic view of the sea around Stad from the outdoor swimming pool which keeps a constant temperature of 38 (99) comfortable degrees.

Below: Thalassotherapy is treatment employing the healing qualities of water, mud, algae, sand and other substances derived from the sea.

center changed the whole concept of the hotel. Selje Active – a vacation with health, culture, and well-being on the menu. The concept was an instant success, and people came from all over Norway to experience a few healthy days at Selje.

But Gerd Kjellaug and Harald had additional plans. Their dream came true when they finally opened the thalassotherapy center in 2000. They see the pipes that pump the salty seawater into the therapy center as another great step for the hotel. They don't fear the powerful ocean at Stad. This stormy section of the sea is probably their most valuable resource and represents the future of the hotel.

AN IRISH PRINCESS, RUINS OF A MONASTERY, ART AND ANTIQUES

Whether you come to Selje Hotel & Spa Thalasso to spend lazy vacation days or for treatment, you should take some time to look around the area.

The legendary island of Selja is just a 15-minute boatride from the hotel. Selja is best known for its association with St. Sunniva, the Irish princess who fled Ireland during the 900s when her father promised her in marriage to a heathen king. Catholic Sunniva could not face such a future and fled to sea with neither sails nor oars. She let God lead her forth, and she landed on Selja. According to legend, she settled on the island, living off the land as God had taught her. But she came into conflict with the heathens. One day she saw the fleet of Håkon Jarl heading toward her island. She ran into a cave and prayed to God to save her from the heathens. Her prayers were answered when a large boulder fell from the mountain and covered the entrance to the cave. This saved her from the Vikings but not from death. She died a martyr in the cave. Olav Trygvasson found Sunniva's remains in 996 and canonized her the same year, making her Norway's first saint. Selja was the Episcopal residence for all of western Norway from 1068 to 1170, and a Benedictine monastery, St. Alban's was built on the island in the early 12th century in honor of St. Sunniva. Today, these are the best-preserved monastic ruins in Norway. You can also visit the cave in which Sunniva died a martyr's death.

North of Selje is Vestkapp, Norway's westernmost lookout point connected to the mainland. The view of the sea, with the Sunnmøre Alps, Hornelen mountain and the Ålfot glacier in the background is breathtaking from the 500-meter high mountain plateau.

But while you're in Selje, you should also visit the Gallery by the Ocean owned by painter Kjell Stig Amdam and textile designer Vigdis Wåge. This artistic pair live and work right on the rocks by the water.

They arrange permanent sale exhibitions, and you can see the powerful nature film "Stad – the pearl of the west – in bad weather and wind-tossed at its best" in the new "summer barn" in the courtyard.

If you like old furniture, lamps, glass, clocks, and old porcelain, you should visit Gammel Sjarm (Old Charm) at Flataker, a 20-minute drive from Selje Hotel. You can find all sorts of interesting things at this antique store owned by Belgian Werner van der Brendan and his wife Bodil Flataker.

There's a lot to do in Selje, making it a complete experience, for both body and soul, in both good weather and bad.

Avove: A trip to Selja island with its monastery ruins is a popular excursion for hotel guests.

Below: Delicacies from the sea! Fish and shellfish, in all shapes and sizes, are richly represented on the menu at Selje Hotel & Spa Thalasso.

Right: The hotel west of the sea – in good weather an idyll – in bad weather a powerful experience! Nature and its forces are an important part of the experience when you visit Selje Hotel & Spa Thalasso.

Selje Hotel & Spa Thalasso

Blanched tomatoes with lumpfish caviar and dried herring

4 tomatoes
3 dl (1 1/4 cups) dairy sour cream
1 teaspoon sugar
salt, pepper
3-4 tablespoons lumpfish caviar (or other kind of caviar, such as salmon caviar)
chopped fresh parsley
2 dried herring, about 200 g (7 oz) each) or dried cod or haddock, filleted and sliced

Do not use low-fat sour cream in this dish. The only sour cream which can be whipped successfully has a butterfat content of more than 30%.

Scald and peel the tomatoes. Remove the seeds with a teaspoon. With an electric mixer, whip the sour cream to stiff peaks. First it will become quite thin, then it will form peaks. Add the sugar, salt and pepper. Carefully stir the caviar into the cream. Spoon the mixture into a pastry bag and pipe into the hollowed-out tomatoes. Place on individual plates with the herring and garnish with parsley. Serve with flatbread.

Cold glazed salmon with Chantilly sauce

3 dl (1 1/4 cups) water
500 g (1 1/4 lb) skinless salmon fillets
1 fish bouillon cube
1 tablespoon butter
2 tablespoons all-purpose flour
40 g (5 tablespoons) light aspic powder
165 g (3/4 cup) mayonnaise
3 dl (1 1/4 cups) whipping cream
salt, white pepper
lemon juice
pinch sugar

1 lemon
1 red bell pepper
parsley

Bring the water to a boil, add the salmon and simmer 8 to 10 minutes. Do not allow the water to boil. Remove the fish from the water and set on a platter to cool.

Dissolve the bouillon cube in the water. Melt the butter in a saucepan, add the flour and mix well. Add the bouillon and heat to boiling, stirring constantly. Add the aspic powder, stirring until dissolved. Pour over the salmon. Refrigerate a few minutes. Spoon any aspic which has dripped down the side back over the fish. Refrigerate until firm. Cut the salmon into four pieces of equal size.

Whisk the mayonnaise and cream together. Season with salt, pepper, lemon juice and sugar.

Place a piece of salmon in the middle of a plate and garnish with lemon, pepper and parsley. Spoon the sauce into a pastry bag and pipe around the fish.

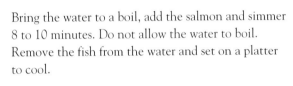

Mussels in white wine

800 g (1 3/4 lb) live mussels
1 red onion
5-6 garlic cloves
200 g (7 oz) butter
2 dl (3/4 cup) white wine
chopped fresh parsley

Scrub the mussels under cold running water. Discard any shells which do not close when touched. Peel and mince the onion and garlic. Sauté in all the butter in a large saucepan until shiny. Add the mussels and wine, cover and steam until they open, 3 to 4 minutes. Serve in deep soup bowls and top with a generous handful of parsley. Serve with bread and butter.

Grilled halibut

1 leek
2-3 carrots
1/2 small rutabaga
small chunk celeriac
1 bunch fresh parsley
3 dl (1 1/4 cups)
whipping cream
250 g (9 oz) softened
unsalted butter
salt, white pepper

850 g (2 lb) halibut
(or turbot) fillet
all-purpose flour
1 lobster tail, cooked and sliced
4 cooked fresh water crayfish
1 lemon, in wedges

Wash, peel and cut the vegetables into julienne strips. Set aside 4 parsley sprigs for garnish, then chop the rest. Pour the cream into a small saucepan and reduce to about 1 dl (1/2 cup) Beat in the butter in pats. Add the parsley and season to taste with salt and pepper. Do not allow the sauce to boil after the butter has been added.

Wash and clean the fish and cut into four pieces of equal size. Coat the fish on both sides with flour. Grill in a grill pan or sauté in butter in a frying pan for 2 to 3 minutes per side. Do not use too high heat!

Cook the vegetables in lightly salted boiling water for about 1 minute. Pile in the middle of the plate with the sauce all around. Place a few lobster slices on the sauce, then place the fish on the vegetables. Garnish with a fresh water crayfish, a lemon wedge and a sprig of parsley.

Sunnfjord's "parlor"

Rica Sunnfjord Hotel, Førde

Below: Odd Erik Gullaksen is the director of the Rica Sunnfjord Hotel.

"When you come down to Førde from Halbrendslia, you soon realize that this is one of those places where God changed his mind. At first he thought it should be a pleasant little settlement with a few scattered farms, a church, a vicarage, and a few nice cottages, in an idyllic setting next to the mouth of the Jølster river. But then he threw in large-scale industry and a commercial center, a regional hospital, and houses climbing up the side of the mountain. But Førde city center is still outback Norway, condemned to the bottom of a cauldron with mountains as its walls, with heavy gray clouds draped over the mountain walls for most of the year, cold and frosty in winter, and too hot on the warmest summer days. It's no wonder they need a good social services office there."

That was how author Gunnar Staalesen described Førde in his book The Dead Have It Good. Whether it was God, local industrialists, or county politicians who changed their minds can be discussed at length, but Sunnfjord and the surrounding countryside have developed at an astounding rate. Førde was granted "city" status in 1996, and it is now the center of culture, communications, services and commerce for Sogn og Fjordane county, thanks to its location right in the center of the county. Førde is the most important commercial center between Bergen and Ålesund, and what was once an agricultural community is now full of cars, asphalt, concrete, shopping centers, and concrete buildings from the 1970s. Førde was once voted the ugliest populated area in Norway. But you can still find small gems between the asphalt and concrete – an old stone bench along an idyllic stretch of the river, small and cozy cafes, exciting art galleries, and the many statues spread throughout the town. The most famous is perhaps Norway's longest single statue, "The Salmon", a 65-meter-long granite sculpture made by Jørn Rønnau in 1989. There are advantages to town status, and now Førde has a cultural center, a county art gallery, a county library, as

well as the Sogn og Fjordane Theater. Førde is the place to be during the first half of June every year, when the town hosts the Førde International Folk Music Festival, with singers, dancers, and musicians from around the world.

WILDERNESS EXPERIENCES AND ACTIVITIES

That Førde is not an architectural masterpiece makes its surroundings all the more beautiful. The best western Norway has to offer of ocean, fjords, mountains, glaciers, and waterfalls are less than an hour from Førde.

A drive toward central Norway brings you to Sunnfjord Museum, a restored farmyard with 25 historical buildings in a time-typical idyllic setting. If you continue on a little farther, you arrive at Jølster, where the painter Nikolai Astrup (1880-1928) found inspiration. His home on the eastern side of the lake is now a museum, where you can see how he lived as well as admire his paintings, graphic works, woodcuts, and sketches. The Eikaas Gallery, which features about 100 works by Ludvig Eikaas, and the Jølstra Museum, a private estate with many local buildings as well as about 3000 objects in its collection, are both located there as well. The museum has a gift shop which sells art by local artists Ludvig Eikaas and Oddvar Torsheim. If you visit Skei, Jølstad's regional center, be sure to stop at Audhild Viken's weaving

Above: Rica Sunnfjord Hotel is right in the middle of Førde. With its characteristic blue and white facade, the hotel is a beloved landmark in this Sunnfjord community, which was granted town status in 1996.

Left: There's a swimming pool, tennis court, miniature golf course and a play area on the grounds of the hotel.

Right: A canopy bed in a rustic romantic setting. From the bedroom in one of the fantastic suites at Rica Sunnfjord Hotel.

studio. She specializes in woven table runners and bedspreads based on traditional local patterns, but she also sells crafts, souvenirs, and Christmas ornaments year-round. It's not far from Skei to the Sognefjord and the village of Fjærland with its prizewinning Norwegian Glacier Museum, where you can learn about ice, snow, and glaciers. It is also the home of the Norwegian book town with second-hand book stores, as well as book cafes. Last, but not least, you can stop at Bøya glacier, an arm of the famous Jostedal glacier, the largest glacier on the European continent.

If you choose to drive west from Førde, along the Førdefjord, you will reach the open sea in no time. Svanøy, the southernmost island in Flora county, as well as its most verdant, is well worth a visit. It is the site of a stone cross raised in honor of St. Olav, and there was a Viking sacrificial site here as well. Here you can also visit Svanøy Manor, a noble seat from 1685, as well as Eiriksgård, where the Viking king Erik Blood Axe is said to have grown up. Svanøy, known as the pearl of Sunnfjord, is also the home of the Norwegian Deer Center which raises both roe deer and regular deer. The waters around the island are so dangerous that three lighthouses were built very early on, and a visit to them is an exiting and exotic experience.

Førde and its surroundings are the perfect place for those interested in an active vacation. Jølstra, Nausta, and Gaula are three of Norway's best salmon rivers, and there are more than 1000 lakes full of trout. The Jølstra, Stardal, and Våtedal rivers offer rafting in all degrees of difficulty. Sunnfjord Golf Club offers a 9-hole course in spectacular surroundings, and there are miles of cross country ski trails at Langeland as well as an alpine center at Blomlia and Jølster, just to name some of the possibilities.

A CITY HOTEL IN THE COUNTRY

"I checked in at Sunnfjord Hotel" Gunnar Staalesen continues in his book The Dead Have It Good. We followed suit, and checked into the Rica Sunnfjord Hotel, as it is called today. The hotel first opened in 1968 and had been extended nine times since. The hotel is still owned by 450 shareholders, most of whom are local. The Rica hotel chain took over the running of the hotel in October, 1999. It is a hotel full of contrasts. The main door leads straight into the center of Førde, to one of the busiest shopping streets in town, while the back door leads to a large comfortable garden, an oasis with a swimming pool, a tennis court, a miniature golf course and a playground. Rica Sunnfjord Hotel is a modern city hotel with comfortable rooms, excellent restaurants, a night club, a pub, a discotheque, an indoor swimming pool, and a gym. But at the same time, it's a country hotel with respect for local traditions. The stylish interior is decorated with pale colors, classic furniture, and the hotel's extensive art collection. The hotel owners have been collecting art for years and are especially interested in local artists, but they have also bought works by national and international artists. Look around the hotel and you will see works by Ludvig Eikaas, Oddvar Torsheim, Klara Søgnen, Malvin Berqvam, Gunnar S. Gundersen, Knut Rumohr, B. Hegranes, Arvid Eikevik, Jacob Weidemann, Hans N. Dahl, Torstein Rittun, and Salvador Dali.

The hotel has always been known for fine food at its many restaurants. "Baronens Spisestue" (The Baron's Dining Room) has an international a la carte menu, while the hotel's main restaurant "Laxen" (The Salmon) was designed especially for buffets. Buffet style dining is a tradition at Norwegian west coast hotels, and Rica Sunnfjord is keeping that tradition alive. The buffet at "Laxen" is a sumptuous experience, both for the eye and the palate! Here you find all your heart desires – including every local specialty you can think of, often with a modern touch. Because food is also art, says the chef at the art hotel Rica Sunnfjord Hotel in Førde.

4 walnuts, finely chopped
6 tablespoons walnut oil
1/2 shallot, minced
1/2 teaspoon grated lemon zest
1/4 teaspoon salt
1/4 teaspoon freshly
ground white pepper
160 g (6 oz) skinless,
boneless trout fillet
150 g (5 oz) arugula
4 tablespoons (1/4 cup) crème
fraîche or dairy sour cream
4 chives

Homemade flatbread
1 kilo (2 1/4 lb) coarsely
ground whole wheat flour
250 g (9 oz) finely ground
whole wheat flour
1 1/2 dl (2/3 cup) all-purpose flour
1 teaspoon sugar
1 teaspoon salt
1 liter (quart) warm water

Trout carpaccio with arugula, walnuts and homemade flatbread

Whisk together the first 6 ingredients.

Cut the fish into paper thin slices and arrange in a single layer on four large plates. Brush with the walnut mixture and let rest about 20 minutes at room temperature before serving.

Place some arugula in the center of the fish. Pipe small dots of creme fraiche on the arugula. Garnish with chives.

Homemade flatbread
Combine all ingredients in the bowl of a mixer with a dough hook. Knead thoroughly. Divide the dough into 14 pieces of equal size. Roll the dough into thin sheets. Use additional finely ground whole wheat flour as necessary. Bake on a griddle over high heat, first for 20 seconds on one side, then for 10 seconds on the other side.

Medallions of deer with wild mushroom cream sauce, baked vegetables and bouillon jus

Deer stock
5 kg (11 lb) deer bones,
chopped into coarse chunks
3 carrots, peeled
and coarsely chopped
3 onions, peeled
and coarsely chopped
1/2 leek, sliced
100 g (4 oz) celeriac,
peeled and coarsely chopped
1 tablespoon black peppercorns
1 tablespoon salt
1 bay leaf

Baked vegetables
150 g (5 oz) carrot, thinly sliced
150 g (5 oz) kohlrabi,
thinly sliced
150 g (5 oz) zucchini,
thinly sliced
1 shallot, minced
1 1/2 dl (2/3 cup) good olive oil
2 teaspoons freshly ground salt
1 teaspoon freshly ground pepper

Medallions of deer
600 g (1 1/3 lb) trimmed strip
loin of deer
butter

Wild mushroom cream sauce
300 g (10 oz) coarsely chopped
wild mushrooms
(chanterelles, cepes)
1 red onion, sliced
50 g (3 tablespoons) butter
6 dl (2 1/2 cups) whipping cream
2 dl (3/4 cup) deer stock
salt, pepper

Bouillon jus
7 dl (3 cups) deer stock
50 g (3 tablespoons) unsalted
butter
salt, pepper

Deer stock
Preheat the oven to 300°C (550°F). Place the bones and vegetables in an oven tray. Brown on all sides, about 30 minutes. Transfer to a stockpot and fill with water to just cover the bones. Add the seasonings. Heat to boiling, skimming well. Lower the heat and let the stock simmer 6 to 8 hours. Strain.

Baked vegetables
Preheat the oven to 150°C (300°F). Layer the vegetables, sprinkling each layer with shallot, oil, salt and pepper. It pays to do this directly on a baking sheet. Cut cylinders about 5 cm (2") high and 5 cm (2") wide. Bake about 40 minutes.

Medallions of deer
Preheat the oven to 150°C (300°F). Cut the meat into four pieces of equal size. Brown in butter in an ovenproof pan. Roast 10-12 minutes. Wrap in foil and let the meat rest several minutes before serving.

Wild mushroom cream sauce
Sauté the mushrooms and onion in butter. Add the cream and stock. Simmer 15 minutes. Season with salt and pepper.

Bouillon jus
Reduce the deer stock to 2 dl (3/4 cup). Beat in the unsalted butter. Season with salt and pepper.

3 gelatin sheets
150 g (1 1/4 cups) frozen black
currants
150 g (3/4 cup) sugar
1 1/2 dl (3/4 cup)
whipping cream
4 egg whites

Spiced pears

150 g (5 oz) unsalted butter
2 pears, peeled, cored and
cut into batons
70 g (1/3 cup) sugar
1/2 teaspoon ground cardamom
1/2 teaspoon ground cinnamon
1/4 teaspoon ground cloves
1 1/2 teaspoons grated lemon zest.

Yogurt sauce

1 vanilla bean
1/2 dl (3 tablespoons) honey
2 dl (3/4 cup) natural yogurt

Black currant mousse with spiced pears and yogurt sauce

Soak the gelatin in cold water to soften, about 5 minutes. Place the currants in a saucepan and sprinkle with the sugar. Heat carefully to 80°C (175°F). Squeeze to remove excess water and melt the gelatin in a little currant juice. Stir into the currants and cool completely, stirring occasionally. Whip the cream to soft peaks and fold into the currants. Beat the egg whites until stiff and fold into the currant mixture. Pour into a 1-liter mold and refrigerate at least 3 hours.

Spiced pears

Melt the butter. Carefully brown the pears, then sprinkle with sugar and spices. Simmer over low heat 10 to 15 minutes, stirring occasionally.

Yogurt sauce

Split the vanilla bean lengthwise and scrape out the seeds. Combine with the honey and heat to melt. Stir in the yogurt. Serve the sauce lukewarm.

To serve, make a nest of pear batons. Make eggs of the mousse with a tablespoon and place in the nest. Pour the sauce all around.

Southern idyll on the west coast

Walaker Hotell Gjestgivargarden, Solvorn

Urnes Stave Church, which dates from around 1150, is Norway's' oldest preserved stave church. Urnes is often called the queen of stave churches, and rightly so, as it towers on its perch 120 meters above sea-level looking out over Luster and the Sognefjord. Urnes' decoration is unique, and the heathen animal carvings which adorn it are now called the Urnes style. This stave church is one of the four Norwegian sites on UNESCO's list of valuable cultural heritage monuments.

JOSTEDAL GLACIER AND THE BREHEIM CENTER IN JOSTEDAL

The Jostedal glacier is the largest glacier on the European continent and covers 487 square meters, making it six times greater than the largest glacier in the Alps. Both Jostedal and the surrounding areas were designated as a national park in 1991. Internationally certified guides offer glacier and climbing courses, guided ski trips, and walking trips across the blue ice. There is also a comprehensive exhibit at the Breheim Center in Jostedal. It is a journey through 20,000 years, from the ice age to the present day, and sound and light show takes you inside the glacier.

MUNTHE MANOR - A NOBLE ESTATE AND ARTIST CENTER

The more than 200-year-old manor house at Ytre Kroken in Luster is newly restored and open to the public. Ytre Kroken, a large estate with history back to the Middle Ages, belonged to the Munthe family from the 1700s until 1884. Officer, historian, and cartographer Gerhard Munthe (1795-1876) was born on the estate and was the driving force behind the rich cultural life that developed there during much of the 19th century. The stylish Munthe House was the gathering place for researchers, geographers, and especially Norway's best mid-19th century national romantic painters. Johannes Flintoe, Joachim Frich

and Johan C. Dahl all stayed there, and Adolph Tidemand and Hans Gude, who worked together on some of Norway's best-known historical paintings, met for the first time at Munthe Manor.

It's not far from Solvorn in Sogn to some of Norway's best-known tourist attractions. Solvorn was a busy place at the end of the 19th century. The wealthy Hafslo farms shipped their wares from here. Trade blossomed, and the town even supported six or seven businessmen at one point. It was also the local court seat, and sessions were held four times a year in the old courtroom at Walaker Hotell Gjestgivargarden. The hotel, which was classified as an inn, was the center of this little community.

But times changed. The area surrounding the Lustrafjord, an arm of Europe's longest and deepest fjord, the 200-kilometer long Sognefjord, eventually got a road network. Boats gave way to cars and trucks, and the need for a steamship office in Solvorn disappeared. Today, Solvorn is a sleepy village, the epitome of idyllic country life. The beautiful old wooden houses lie in terraces up from the water's edge, and the weather-beaten fishing huts cast long shadows on the still water of the fjord.

A DELICATE BEGINNING

Walaker Hotell lies next to Solvorn quay, where the ferry M/S Urnes docks to unload its cargo of tourists. It has been owned by the Nitter family for all of its 300 years. It has been passed down from generation to generation, and is now a tourist attraction in its own right. The Nitter family is thought to have immigrated to Norway from Scotland. An ancestor arrived in Bergen during the 16th century and established himself as a trader on Norway's western coast. Parts of the

Above: Walaker Hotel is known for its excellent kitchen.

The evocative garden is an important part of life at Walaker Hotell. There's nothing quite like spending a beautiful summer evening sitting around one of the old stone tables in the garden.

family moved to Sogn during the 17th century. Christen Nitter, founder of Walaker Hotell, grew up in inner Sogn. He left the village to learn a trade and was an apprentice goldsmith for several years before returning to his home and renting premises at Vollåker in 1690.

He set up a business with is his wife Birgitte, and they earned enough to buy the premises in 1696. Christen bought Vollåker farm at the same time and would later buy several other farms. Christen and Birgitte had seven children together, but it was their youngest son Ludvig, born in 1709, who inherited the trade and innkeeper's license from his father. He received his royal innkeeper and tradesman's license on June 11, 1734. It was renewed in 1758, and it was noted that: "Ludvig Nitter must continue to run an inn and restaurant at Vallaker, and he must offer travelers and customers food and drink at reasonable prices, with the condition that he may brew beer for the premises, but that he not be allowed to distill alcohol." And Ludvig did brew beer. He brewed it from barley in the winter and then stored it in a cold cellar so it would last through the summer. He brewed a stronger beer for special occasions.

GENERATION AFTER GENERATION

Ludvig Nitter married "demoiselle" Øllegård Klingenberg. After his death in 1776, his widow continued to run the in on her deceased husband's license, which was her right. The couple produced six children, but it was their youngest son, Henrik, who received the deed to the property in 1790. He was married to Mette Råum and lived in Sogndal. A local official wrote these lines when Henrik applied for his innkeepers license in 1799:

"I hereby recommend the current owner and resident, Henrik Nitter, as worthy of his father, Ludvig Nitter's privileges. He owns Åroy Farm in Sogndal, and the inn at Solvorn must therefore be externally managed, as long as he lives on the farm, but as soon as his eldest son takes over Årøy, that will relieve him of his other duties. Then he must move to Solvorn. The highest yearly tax is two riksdaler." Henrik moved back to Vollåker in 1808.

Henrik and Mette produced eight children. Erik Vollåker took over the farm from his parents in 1821. He applied for his innkeeper's license that same year, and the town administrator told the department that a coaching inn at Solvorn was a vital necessity. His application was granted, and in 1831, he was also granted a license to open a country store. Erik married Malene Mo of Hafslo in 1824. The couple had one son who died in infancy and four daughters. Their eldest daughter, Mette Malene, inherited the

property. She married Jacob Sjursen Talle in 1845, and they ran Vollåker coaching inn together. During this period, the first tourists came to western Norway. In 1865, the Swedish-Norwegian Crown Prince, later King Carl XV, toured Norway. He traveled over Sognefjell mountain and out the Sognefjord. Photographer Mathias Hansen accompanied him, and this was probably when the first pictures of Solvorn and Walaker Hotel were taken.

Mette Malene Nitter died in childbirth in 1868, just 40 years old. It was her 11th birth during her 23-year-long marriage. Four of her 11 children died early. Their eldest son Erik paid his father NOK 15 000 for the property in 1878 and married Barbra Wilkensdotter Hereid from Årdal that same year. The couple had six children, and their eldest son Wilken was the next generation of Nitter at Walaker.

Wilken married Inga Ranghild Mo from Luster, who eventually became a hotel legend in her own right. She was educated at the State College for Home Economics Teachers at Stabekk and had a lot of professional experience, both from a tuberculosis sanitarium in Luster and from Helgheim County College in Sogndal. Both Wilken and Inga were local politicians, and she was the first woman to sit on the local council at Hafslo. In addition to the guesthouse, they ran the shipping office in Solvorn and the post office. They also rebuilt the old guesthouse into a more functional, modern hotel in the 1930s. In 1964, they built a one-story bungalow-style addition in the garden next to the old courtroom and added large, comfortable guest rooms.

AN ART GALLERY IN THE BARN

Times and generations have passed, but little or nothing has changed at Walaker Hotel. The old courtroom is still there, but now it contains a meeting room and several guest rooms. Just a few meters away is the main building carefully restored by Inga and Wilken in 1934. It is surrounded by a lush garden enclosed by green hedges and white picket fence. Virginia creeper climbs up the walls, and lilacs and fruit trees blossom in the garden, casting spooky shadows over the old stone tables. It's easy to understand why so many guests eat breakfast in the garden. Just below the hotel is a beautiful sandy beach, which is very popular with hotel guests on sunny summer days.

The cozy nostalgic atmosphere at Walaker Hotell greets you at the door. This small, privately run hotel is more like a private home than a hotel. The current hosts are the eight and ninth generations of Nitter at Walaker Hotell. Hermod was born and grew up at Solvorn, while his wife Oddlaug Marie, nee Bringe, is from Numedal. They took over the hotel in 1978, but they had run it, together with Hermod's mother Inga, since 1968. Now they run the hotel with their son Ole Henrik, and all three are involved in keeping the traditions of the old family hotel alive. They use the winter to maintain and restore the buildings, and in May, 1990, they turned the old outbuilding behind the hotel into Galleri Walaker 300 to celebrate the 300th anniversary of the hotel. The building, dating from 1882, had been a cow-shed, stable and hayloft in earlier days and had been constructed with materials from 17th century Solvorn church which was torn down in 1883. Now this building, designated as worthy of preservation, has regained its status as a popular gallery exhibiting national and international artists. The Walaker family invited the first guests to a newly redecorated dining room in May, 2001. When the guests sit on the veranda after dinner, enjoying their coffee while looking out over the powerful mountains and the blue fjord, and the notes from Ole Henrik beautiful piano playing stream out through the open window, there's no doubt! It's summer at Walaker Hotell.

The old sitting room, filled with antiques and older landscape paintings collected over generations, was incorporated into the new hotel building in 1934.

Potato soup

1 liter (quart) vegetable stock
400 g (14 oz) potatoes
100 g (3 1/2 oz) bacon rind
1/2 onion
butter
salt, pepper
pressed garlic
lovage
100 g (3 1/2 oz) reindeer filet
1 dl (1/2 cup) whipping cream

Make a good vegetable stock first with carrots, celeriac, leek, onions and celery. Wash and cut the vegetables into chunks. Sauté in a little butter in a stockpot. Add water, heat to boiling, cover, reduce heat and let simmer for 1 to 2 hours. Strain and season with salt and pepper. Measure out one liter (quart) for the soup.

Peel and slice the potatoes. Dice the bacon rind and onions. Sauté in butter in a stockpot until golden. Add the stock and potatoes and cook until the potatoes are tender. Pour the stock into a bowl, then mash the potatoes by hand to a fine puree. Beat in the stock. Season with salt, pepper, garlic and

lovage. Brown the reindeer in a little butter on all sides, but do not overcook. It should be pink inside. Cut into thin slices. Just before serving, stir the cream into the soup.

Serve the soup in warm deep bowls. Top with reindeer and garnish with lovage.

Veiled country lass

3 dl (1 1/4 cups) applesauce
2 dl (3/4 cup) bread crumbs browned in butter
2 dl (3/4 cup) whipping cream

Layer the applesauce and the bread in a glass bowl. Whip the cream and spread over the top. Sprinkle a little brown breadcrumbs over the top.

Applesauce
At Walaker Hotel, we make applesauce from rather tart apples such as Gravenstein. For a small portion, you need only a few apples. Core and dice the apples. Simmer in a few drops of water. Add sugar to taste – the fruit's own sweetness determines how much you need. The shorter the cooking time, the fresher the taste. Cool. Applesauce keeps for about a week in the refrigerator and it freezes well.

Browned breadcrumbs
Dry bread, zwieback or rusks are best. Grind or crush the bread. Sprinkle with sugar and cinnamon and brown in a little butter in a hot skillet. It may be difficult to avoid hard lumps if the mixture caramelizes too quickly, but practice makes perfect! Cool before using.

An artist's paradise by the Sognefjord

Kvikne's Hotel Balholm, Balestrand

Balestrand. Paintings with images from Balestrand can be found in museums, galleries, palaces, and private art collections around the world. For centuries, both Norwegian and foreign artists have flocked to Balestrand to paint the wild landscape and historic surroundings. Documentary landscape painters first arrived in the 18th century, but Johannes Flintoe's journey to Sogn in 1819 marked the artistic discovery of western Norway. Others soon followed – J.C. Dahl, Thomas Fearnley, Hans Gude, Adolf Tidemann, Anders Askevold, Gerhard Munthe, Adelsteen Normann, Hans Dahl, and many, many more. Leading Scandinavian and European artists soon joined them. They painted lofty mountains and snow-covered peaks, wild waterfalls and shiny glaciers, green meadows and blue fjords, and the local folk on the farms.

After the Swedish poet Esias Tegner published "Frithiof Saga" in 1825, people also came searching for ancient stone monuments, burial mounds, and national symbols. The book was based on a Viking saga, but most of it is fiction. It's the story of a love affair between Frithiof the fearless, son of a large landowner from Vangsnes, and Ingeborg, daughter of King Bele, with his seat at Balestrand, which is probably how the place got its name. The book became a pillar of Norwegian national romantic literature and was widely translated. It was also an inexhaustible source for both Norwegian and foreign artists seeking Nordic themes. And what was more natural than to go to Balestrand where it all took place? There was so much to paint – so much that there was an artists' colony living at Balestrand at the beginning of the 20th century. Adelsteen Normann and Hans Dahl built beautiful villas in the national romantic dragon-style at Balestrand, but most of the other artists stayed at Kvikne's hotel, a fairytale castle on the banks of the Sognefjord. A hotel as colorful as an artist's palette. It is the story of a family and their hotel.

THE BOY WHO BECAME AN INNKEEPER

During the middle of the 19th century, three brothers lived at Kvigne farm in Lærdalen in Sogn. Two left early in search of work, while the third remained on the farm. Knut immigrated to America, while Ole moved to Balestrand, or Balholm as it was called, to work as a clerk in a shop.

The shop was called Holmen and had been founded in 1752 by Nicolai Gerlow of Bergen, but there had been a number of owners in the interim. Johannes Danielsen owned and ran the shop when 18-year-old Ole arrived. Danielsen's trade license from 1863 stated that he had to "offer lodging and food to travelers", so he wasn't just a shop owner, he was also an innkeeper. Ole enjoyed his job right from the start, and he had a good working relationship with Danielsen. He was hard-working and industrious, and it wasn't long before he had earned enough money to buy a shop of his own. He saw that many English tourists visited Balestrand and knew a good opportunity when he saw one. He was ready to start up for himself.

When Danielsen heard of Ole's plans, the older man, who had no family or heirs, offered him Holmen instead. On February 26, 1877, Ole took over the general store and inn with room for four guests from Danielsen.

Above: Below: With its long veranda facade facing the Sognefjord, Kvikne's Hotel Balholm is the largest and most impressive of Norway's old wooden hotels.

Left: Sigurd Kvikne is the fourth generation of Kvikne to run the traditional hotel at Balestrand.

Right: The old wooden building at Kvikne is one of Norway's finest examples of the gingerbread architecture, also called the chalet style.

Kvikne's Hotel Balholm

Above: A detail from one of the beautiful glass doors in the Høivik room.

Right: Ivar Høivik of Balestrand carved all the ornamentation as well as the beautiful dragon-style furniture in the Høivik room between 1910 and 1959.

LETTERS FROM AMERICA

Ole had married Kari Gurvin from Sogndal two years earlier. Now he had both a wife and an inn. He was now ready to receive the flood of tourists he had dreamt of since he saw his first steam ship enter the Sognefjord in the 1850s. The only thing that worried him was that he only had four beds to offer to all those tourists. But a rescuer soon appeared. One day Ole received a letter with US stamps on it. It was from his elder brother Knut, who had immigrated to America and done very well there. He had saved a sizeable sum of money which he wanted to invest in his brother's business. Was Ole interested? Ole accepted, and Knut returned to Norway with a bulging wallet and a new name. Americans couldn't pronounce the "g" in Kvigne, so he had changed it to a "k", and was now called Kvikne. Ole thought of all the foreign guests who would be visiting and he changed his name to Kvikne, too. They may have been brothers, but they were quite different in both appearance and temperament. The Englishman F. Scarlett, a pioneer in the Norwegian tourism industry, described the brothers in his book Norway - tourist destination: "Ole was stocky, clean-shaven, with rosy cheeks, while Knut was swarthy as a Spaniard, with jet black hair and a large moustache." Ole was outgoing, while Knut was quiet. But they worked together very well. Ole and

Kari looked after the day-to-day running of the inn and saw to the needs of the guests, Knut maintained the buildings and organized guest activities. He knew the local area well, and his English was excellent after all those years in America. That made Knut a popular guide with foreign visitors, so popular that he married one of them in the 1880s – an English vicar's daughter, Margaret Green.

NORWAY'S LARGEST FJORD HOTEL

During the first few years that Ole and Knut ran the inn, the ferry landed at Balestrand once a week. But as Balestrand became a more popular destination, more and more tourists arrived, and the ferry docked more often. Four beds just weren't enough. The two brothers expanded and added to the inn many times. In 1912, they began work on the large wooden building which is Kvikne's Hotel today. In 36 years, the number of beds increased from four to 200, making it Norway's largest fjord hotel. Today the old wooden building is considered one of Norway's finest examples of the "chalet-style" or "gingerbread" architecture.

But the stress of building the hotel had sapped Ole's strength and he died in September, 1913 of a heart attack, only 64 years old. Norwegian superstition says that accidents always come in pairs. WWI broke out just a few months later. Knut Kvikne died within the first few months of the war, leaving Ole's son Theodor, who had studied hotel management abroad, to run the hotel. That same year, he installed electricity at the hotel. But another tragedy was just around the corner. Theodor Kvikne died in 1916, just 34 years old, and his mother Kari died the following year. His brother Sigurd, who also had studied hotel management and trained at Kvikne's, took over the hotel. He and his wife Marta ran the hotel just as Knut and Ole had done. These were good years. Tourism blossomed and Balestrand was a popular destination. Englishmen, Germans, and even Americans joined Scandinavian tourists. The Norwegian-America Line was founded in 1912, and direct routes to Norway were established after WWI. Many Norwegian immigrants used this chance to visit their homeland.

A STRONG WOMAN

The autumn of 1935 saw a new tragedy at Kvikne's hotel. Sigurd died suddenly, leaving Marta with four children and a large hotel. But the years of running the hotel with Sigurd stood her in good stead. Although Kvikne's Hotel had an excellent reputation, both at home and abroad, Marta realized that the hotel needed modernization to keep attracting guests. In 1937, hot and cold running water were

fashioned charm. This fairytale hotel draws people from around the world to Balestrand. As you sit on the terrace and look out over the water, you can imagine what life was like at the hotel 100 years ago, when the first "floating hotels", ships larger than any local had ever seen before, first came to Balestrand. Back to the time when prominent Norwegians and foreigners built large villas in the national romantic dragon-style in Balestrand and arrived at them on private yachts. Back to when gentlemen in white suits played croquet on the lawn of the hotel, while the ladies walked along the beach with their long white dresses, hats, and parasols. Back to the elegant garden parties held every evening. Back to when the leading artists of the day came to Balestrand to paint the wild and wonderful western Norwegian landscape, and when kings and emperors, including King Haakon, Kaiser Wilhelm of Germany, Queen Wilhelmina of the Netherlands, and the Prince of Egypt, came to admire this magnificent hotel.

Left: Every room in this old wooden hotel is rich in details. These are the beautiful windows in the hotel dance-bar.

Right: "A room with a view". They're lots of those at Kvikne's Hotel Balholm! The "lacy" construction of the verandas is just as beautiful from the outside as on the inside.

installed in all the guestrooms, with showers and bathrooms in the corridors. She also gave the dining room a much-needed facelift. Marta became a Kvikne's legend, just as Kari had been before her. Marta held fast during the difficult war years and the harsh Norwegian post-war economy. She closed the hotel in the summer of 1940, after the Germans invaded Norway, but she kept it open for the rest of the war. It was a holiday retreat for those Norwegian who were able to leave the cities and the horrors of war. The years after liberation brought food shortages, rationing, and price controls, but she never gave up. Thanks to her, Kvikne's retained its popularity and its unique position in the Norwegian tourist industry.

A MODERN HOTEL WITH AN OLD-FASHIONED ATMOSPHERE

Marta and Sigurd's son Per and his wife Mulla took over the hotel in 1961. The hotel had become too small for its audience in the final years. The salons and recreation rooms were big enough, but the need for guestrooms with private baths was ever increasing. Mulla and Per decided to expand the hotel, and in 1973, a new, modern addition was ready for the public. The new wing behind the grand old wooden building housed 165 sorely needed guestrooms.

After Per died in 1991, their son Sigurd is the fourth generation of the Kvikne family to run the hotel. He renovated all the rooms in the old wooden hotel, adding baths and showers, but he retaining their old-

Ocean crayfish with curly endive salad and chef's dressing

Chef's dressing

1 1/2 teaspoons sweet mustard
salt, pepper
sugar
2 tablespoons red wine vinegar
2 tablespoons soybean oil
1 1/2 dl (2/3 cup)
hot brown gravy
1/2 dl (3 1/2 tablespoons)
Port wine

Ocean crayfish

1 1/4 kg (2 1/2 lb) live crayfish
1 curly endive
80 g (3 oz) fresh chanterelles
2 tablespoons butter
40 g (1 1/2 oz) pork filet

Chef's dressing

Combine the mustard, salt, pepper and sugar in a bowl. Stir in the vinegar. Whisk in the oil in a thin stream. Add the gravy and wine, combining well.

Ocean crayfish

Cook the crayfish in boiling water for 8 minutes. Remove the head, tail fins and shells. Remove the black vein from the tails. Cut off the root of the endive and wash the leaves. Clean the chanterelles. Dice the meat.
Sauté the crayfish tails in 1 tablespoon of the butter. Remove from the pan and set aside. Sauté the meat in the same butter. Sauté the chanterelles in the remaining butter in a clean pan. Place 3 small clusters of endive on each dish and arrange the crayfish between the endive. Place the chanterelles in a ring in the center. Drizzle dressing on the endive and around the edge of the plates. Top the endive with the diced meat.

Flambéed Balholm Surprise

6 dl (1 pint) vanilla ice cream
1 teaspoon cinnamon
1 tablespoon black currant jelly
30 large fresh raspberries
30 cherries with stems
1 tablespoon blueberries
2 dl (3/4 cup) 60% golden rum

Remove the ice cream from the freezer to soften slightly. Stir in the cinnamon. Fill 6 small coffee cups half-full with ice cream. Make an indentation in the ice cream with a spoon. Place 1/2 teaspoon jelly in each. Fill with remaining ice cream. Freeze for 1 hour. Rinse and halve the raspberries. Rinse the cherries and slice off the bottoms, so they can stand on the dish without falling. Halve the blueberries. Remove the ice cream from the freezer. Arrange cherries alternately with two half-raspberries around the edge of each plate. Place half-blueberries in the center. Unmold the ice cream and place in the center of the blueberries. Pour rum over the ice cream, light with a match and let the alcohol burn off as the flames extinguish themselves. 6 servings.

Monkfish with saffron sauce

Puff pastry fish
1 sheet (about 100g/3 oz) puff pastry
1 egg yolk, lightly beaten

Saffron sauce
1/2 onion
1 teaspoon butter
pinch saffron
2 dl (1 cup) dry white wine
1 dl (1/2 cup) creme fraiche (or whipping cream)
1 dl (1/2 cup) whipping cream
salt, pepper
juice of 1/2 lemon
hot pepper sauce

Rice timbale
160 g (3/4 cup) long grain rice
2 dl (3/4 cup) whipping cream
salt, white pepper

Monkfish
800 g (1 3/4 ib) monkfish fillet
2 large carrots
3 tablespoons soybean oil
salt, pepper
1 dl (1/2 cup) all-purpose flour
12 shelled shrimp
4 dill sprigs
4 teaspoons black caviar

Puff pastry fish
Preheat the oven to 200°C (400°F). Cut out four fish shapes and brush with egg yolk. Bake 8-10 minutes.

Saffron sauce
Peel and mince the onion. Melt butter in a saucepan and sauté the onion and saffron for a few seconds. Add the wine and reduce by half. Add the crème fraîche and cream and reduce to a full-bodied sauce. Season with salt, pepper, lemon juice and hot pepper sauce.

Rice timbale
Boil the rice in a generous amount of water for 12 minutes. Strain, then return the rice to the pan. Add the cream and cook, stirring constantly, until thick. Season with salt and pepper.

Monkfish
Cut the fish into 12 medallions. Peel and cut the carrots into 4 x 1/2 cm (1 1/2 x 1/2") strips. Blanch the carrots in boiling water for 1 minute. Sprinkle the fish with salt and pepper, dredge in flour. Fry in hot oil for about 3 minutes per side.

Arrange the carrots in a small stack in the middle of each plate. Spoon saffron sauce all around. Place three monkfish medallions around the carrots. Top one medallion with three shrimp, another with a puff pastry fish, the third with a teaspoon of caviar. Dip a timbale mold or a coffee cup in cold water. Fill with rice and unmold over the carrots. Garnish with dill.

The Cider House, anno 1898

Hardanger Gjestegard, Utne

Above: Hardanger Gjestegard, right at the edge of the Hardangerfjord is surrounded by fruit trees and the powerful scenery of Norway's west coast.

Below: Torild Skiaker Mælen and her husband Per took over the old cider factory in Ålsaker in 1989. After thorough renovation and restoration, it is one of Norway's most interesting hotels.

Hardanger Gjestegård lies in a sea of fruit trees at Alsåker, right off the idyllic road between Utne and Jondal on the edge of the Hardangerfjord. It is nestled in the shadow of the impressive Gråfjell and Såta mountains, 1100 above sea level. It was fruit cultivation at the end of the 19th century that laid the foundation for this unique hotel.

Sjur Ålsaker, the young owner of Ålsaker farm, was a creative and progressive-minded man. He was very interested in the cultivation of fruit and berries and was constantly experimenting with fruit in his attempt to develop new varieties of apples. He was, among other things, the "inventor" of the Red Torstein apple. He was also interested in fruit products and preservation, and in 1898, when he was only 22, he opened a juice factory and winery or cider factory, as it was called back then. Most of his fruit and berry harvest was turned into juice and wine here, and he also produced wine, juice, and preserves from locally picked strawberries, blueberries and gooseberries.

His project proved fruitful. Production steadily increased through to the 1920s and he built three additions onto his factory. But he needed better distribution channels, so he built a large steamship dock. From there, he shipped his wine to local and international dealers until the end of November, 1922, when the Norwegian government created the national Wine and Liquor Monopoly. From that date, all the wine produced at Ålsaker was sold through the monopoly shop in Bergen.

Sjur was planning a fourth extension to the cider house when his bank declared bankruptcy. This marked the beginning of the great depression, and Sjur lost a lot of money. He decided to abandon juice and preserves production and concentrate on wine instead. Many commendations and awards attested to the excellence of his wine. He continued to produce wine until the beginning of World War II. With war came widespread rationing - sugar was strictly rationed. Since sugar is a main ingredient in wine, production became impossible. The factory shut down, and over the next 50 years, the building was a warehouse for fruit and crates, a workshop, and even living quarters for the odd fisherman. The building began to decay, and the family had to decided whether to demolish or restore it. What would they use it for?

FROM FACTORY TO GUEST HOUSE

The decision fell on Torild Skiaker Mælen and Per Mælen, the grandson of Sjur Alsåker's sister, who had run Ytre Alsåker since 1975. The farm had been in the family for 15 generations.

They took over the factory in 1989. Per was a full-time farmer specializing in fruit production, primarily apples, but he also had land to maintain which left him with little spare time. Torild was a farmer's wife, the mother of four, and a teacher working full-time at the local primary school. What were they going to do with the old factory?

Cabinetmaker Sjur Solheim of Noreheimsund made new chairs and a table for the cozy "Tap Room" dining room. All are copies of old furniture found there. The large old slate slabs on the floor come from a barn roof at Hesthamar, while Geir Vetti designed the new fireplace.

Old juice and wine bottles decorate the window sills and remind guests of bygone days when cider was produced in these very rooms.

For years, Torild had dreamt of opening a little hotel at Alsåker, a place where guests could come to enjoy the silence, the impressive Hardanger scenery, go for mountain walks, ski across Folgefonn glacier, fish for salmon in Alsåker river, or fish in the fjord. There were certainly enough activities, but there was nowhere to stay. Could they turn the old factory into a hotel?

They started planning. After many study-trips both at home and abroad, they knew exactly how to create a cozy, distinctive, and intimate hotel. They wanted to offer all the modern comforts and facilities as well as create a living museum based on the old cider production. It was important to preserve the old factory, which was unique in Hardanger, perhaps unique in all of Norway.

Then the ball started rolling. They worked closely with Olav Fagerbrekke from Odda Agricultural College, the chief architect at the Hordaland County Curator's office, Kjell Andresen, and master builder and interior designer Geir Vetli from Folgefonna Design Center in Jondal. They started building in 1991, after just two years of planning.

Work went quickly. The roof and the external paneling were replaced, the old windows were replaced with exact copies, and the walls were refurbished both inside and out. Then the building was divided into separate rooms that were named after their previous functions. There was "the office", "the barrel warehouse, "the workshop", "the tap room" and "the pressing room". The interior was also important. They used some of the old machines and wine casks along with antiques and handmade copies of old furniture to create a cozy, unique interior.

Hardanger Gjestegard today

Per and Torild welcomed the first overnight guests in the spring of 1994. It had been a lot of hard work, but their dream was a reality. Not only had they converted the old factory into bedrooms, apartments, a restaurant and wine cellar, but they had also transformed the old foreman's house into a cozy apartment. They had also refurbished two old mill houses and the old boathouse where guests could rent vintage wooden rowboats. The old dock had been rebuilt to accommodate larger boats, and there was even a helipad.

They have since built a new boathouse with large comfortable apartments. Hardanger Gjestegard is a unique hotel experience set alongside the picturesque Hardangerfjord. It offers mainly self-catering apartments, but Torild is an excellent cook and will gladly prepare and serve local delicacies. She specializes in traditional home-style Norwegian cooking, with a few local twists. She will be happy to serve you different kinds of flat breads and crackers, sour cream porridge, potato dumplings or dried meat. And if you're really lucky, she'll offer you a glass of the excellent wine that the farm used to produce in the old cider house.

Above: Beautiful old porcelain is displayed on open shelves and serve as decoration when not in use.

Hardanger Gjestegård also offers self-catering accommodation. Old and new harmonize together to create an intimate and exciting ambience.

Next page: More than a hundred old wine and cider bottles have been placed on a shelf in the wine cellar.

Sour cream porridge

7 dl (3 cups) dairy sour cream (do not use low-fat or artificial sour cream)
2 dl (3/4 cup) all-purpose flour
1 liter (quart) full-fat milk
1 teaspoon salt

Place the sour cream in a saucepan, heat to boiling, cover and simmer 5 minutes. Sprinkle with half the flour, stirring well. Cook over medium heat until droplets of butter begin to leach out. Pour off about 1/2 dl (3 1/2 tablespoons) of this butter to serve with the porridge. Stir in the remaining flour. Heat the milk and add in 2 or 3 increments, stirring well and allowing the mixture to boil each time. Simmer 8-10 minutes. Add the salt. Serve the porridge with sugar, cinnamon, raisins and the melted butter. Norwegians like dried country sausage with their sour cream porridge.

Salt meat and barley

500 g (1 1/4 lb) salted, smoked lamb or pork, in one piece
2 dl (3/4 cup) pearl barley
1 1/2 liters (6 cups) water
500 g (1 1/4 lb) fresh beef, veal or deer meat (from the shoulder), in one piece
1 leek
2 tablespoons vegetable oil
1 teaspoon pepper

Soak the salt meat overnight. Combine the barley and water in a saucepan and soak overnight. Bring two pots of water to a boil. Add the salt meat to one, the fresh meat to the other. Cover and simmer over low heat until tender, at least 1 1/2 hours. Simmer the barley in the soaking water for an hour. Remove the meat from the water and cool slightly. Remove any bones from the meat. Grind the meat (with the fat) once. Rinse and slice the leek and sauté in oil. Combine the barley and ground meat in a stockpot. Add a little cooking liquid and season with pepper. Stir in the leek. This dish should have the consistency of thick porridge. Serve with fresh potato griddle cakes or flatbread. This dish also can be served for dinner with potatoes, rutabagas and carrots.

Crispbread (also called flatbread)

1 kg (8 cups) coarsely ground whole-wheat flour
100 g (3/4 cup) cracked rye
300 g (2 1/2 cups) finely ground rye flour
1 teaspoon salt
1 liter (quart) lukewarm water
finely ground rye flour

Combine all ingredients. Knead well, preferably with an electric mixer equipped with a dough hook. Divide the dough into pieces of equal size. Roll each into a round, thin sheet on a floured board. Use a rolling pin with a grid pattern, if desired. Bake on both sides on a griddle over medium heat. The baked bread should still be pale. Fold each sheet twice. Stack the sheets under a light weight. Store air-tight to retain crispness.

Potato griddle cakes

2 kilo (4 1/2 lb) potatoes
1 teaspoon salt
2 tablespoons light sugar or corn syrup
15 dl (6 1/2 cups) all-purpose flour
all-purpose flour

Boil the potatoes in their jackets. Peel and grind with salt twice in a meat grinder. Cool. Add the syrup and knead in the flour. If the dough softens, knead in more flour. Divide the dough into pieces of equal size. Roll each into a round, thin sheet on a floured board. Use as little extra flour as possible. Bake on both sides on a hot griddle. The baked griddle cakes should be flecked with light brown. Stack and cover with a cloth to keep soft.

The garden of Hardanger

Hotel Ullensvang, Lofthus

Lofthus lies on the eastern side of the Sørfjord, part of the Hardangerfjord. This beautiful area is often called the orchard of Hardanger. And rightly so! Thousands of fruit trees blossom every May to create a glorious vision. All this in the shadow of the Hardanger plateau with its mighty mountains and Folgefonn glacier. It was here that Cistercian monks, who lived in a monastery in Lofthus until the Reformation in 1537, planted the first fruit trees in Hardanger between 1200 and 1210. We don't know whether the monks intended this to be the start of an industry, but now there are more than 600 000 fruit trees. Approximately 512 000 of these lie around Sørfjorden, and fruit production is the most important local industry.

Lofthus was an early tourist destination because the beautiful surroundings and the rich hunting and fishing opportunities. The local preacher, Niels Hertzberg, was largely responsible for the development of tourism in Lofthus and Hardanger. At the beginning of the 19th century, he was the only person in the area who spoke and understood English and French, so he greeted and took care of all the tourists. And he enjoyed it. He was proud of his parish and gladly showed people around. He usually took them back to the vicarage for food and lodging. Thus the vicarage became the first inn in the area. Hertzberg was a visionary man. As the tourists increased, he understood that they represented the future, both for Lofthus and the rest of Hardanger. He felt that publicity would attract more tourists, so he sat down and wrote a brochure about Lofthus and Hardanger. At first, it was distributed only in Norway, but it soon found its way abroad through Norwegian embassies and consulates. Hertzberg is often called the "First Norwegian Tourist Commissioner" because of his pioneering work. His efforts quickly produced results. Tourists flooded into Lofthus, and soon the parish could not meet the demand. Another inn was needed, and the cornerstone of what is now Ullensvang Hotel was laid.

THE UTNE FAMILY AND ULLENSVANG HOTEL

At about the same time the brochures were sent out, a young man rowed across the fjord from Utne to Lofthus. His name was Hans Utne and he was 14 years old. The family plot was too small to support 15 children, so he had to go out into the world to seek his fortune. He was ambitious and willing to work hard. It wasn't long before he had bought land down by the water and began to build a boat shed. He could hardly miss the steadily increasing stream of tourists coming on steamships, and he soon became friends with the ships' captains. The ships stopped only at Utne and Odda, but Hans wanted them to stop at Lofthus. He became the first person in Hardanger to open a steamship office, in Lofthus, of course. Many tourists who visited the area arrived by steamship, and Hans felt that a hotel would be a useful addition to his business. The only thing he could offer was his own loft above the office, but it would have to do. That was Hans Utne's first venture into the coaching inn business, and within a year, he had doubled his capacity to two beds, with some help from Reverend Hertzberg. It was 1846 and 19-year-old Hans Utne had just founded Ullensvang Hotel.

Hans Utne was both a steamship office operator and a hotel owner, and later he became a businessman and post office manager. Meanwhile, tourists came in ever larger numbers. Hans needed to expand the hotel. Soon he had built a new and modern hotel with 20 beds right next to the water. He needed help to run the hotel, and Brita Aga entered the picture. She was the daughter of Johannes Aga, Norway's first farmer member of parliament and had grown up on the other side of the fjord. Brita and Hans got along well, so well that they married when Brita turned 17. Hans was 20 years her senior, but they had a happy marriage and reared 12 children together.

The hotel blossomed, and the building was expanded and modernized in 1875 and 1881. Lofthus and Hardanger became two of Norway's most popular tourist destinations and also attracted famous painters

who found inspiration in the scenery. It was here that Tidemann and Gude found the inspiration for their famous painting "Bridal Procession in Hardanger". The painting combines many local attractions, central of which is Ullensvang church, a gothic stone church built in 1250 on a promontory just outside of town. Brita and Hans became good friends with many of their customers, including composer Edvard Grieg and his wife Nina. Grieg composed some of his most famous works at Lofthus.

Hans Utne died in 1895. Brita continued running the hotel until 1919. Then her son Bjarne and his wife Brita took over the hotel. By that time, the hotel was dilapidated and in need of renovation. Bjarne started the renovations, and at the same time registered the hotel as a private company. It now had 50 rooms, and they decided to run it year-round.

They expanded again in 1933. The old boathouse was torn down and replaced with a modern annex which cost NOK 40 000 and took a year to build. With 35 new bedrooms and hot and cold running water in all the rooms, Ullensvang Hotel marketed itself as the most modern hotel in Hardanger. Four years later, the old building was demolished and replaced with a modern one. But then the war came and with it, German occupation. Ullensvang Hotel served as a retirement home throughout the war. The occupation forces had confiscated all the retirement homes in Bergen, so the inhabitants had to be rehoused within the local community.

Bjarne's mother Brita died in 1941. She had spent most of her 94 years at the hotel. After the war ended, the hotel was reopened. Bjarne looked after the finances and kept old traditions alive, while Brita was the decision maker, and tried to keep the hotel up to modern comfort standards. They had a good partnership, but it didn't last long. Bjarne died in 1947 leaving Brita alone with the hotel, but her son Hans and daughter-in-law Ellen helped out. Ellen Utne was from Haugesund but had lived at the hotel since 1939. She ran the hotel, reared four children, and earned a degree in hotel management in 1950, the first in the family to do so.

Brita died in 1962, and Hans and Ellen became the third generation to run the hotel. The first thing they did was make a market survey of potential Norwegian and foreign customers. They then used this survey to make a five year plan, becoming the first Norwegian hotel to schedule renovation work according to a survey. The hotel was refurbished according to modern standards. While only 5 out of 100 rooms had a private

bath in 1962, 96 rooms had private facilities in 1972.

Hans Utne died suddenly in 1966, leaving Ellen responsible for the hotel. She continued with her plans and in 1967 presented a hotel that could compete with any other in Norway.

ULLENSVANG HOTEL TODAY

1969 saw the appearance of the fourth generation Edmund Harris Utne and his wife Ina, and they've run the hotel with Ellen ever since. And there have been many changes. New buildings have replaced the 1934 annex and 1939 old wing. New additions, conversions, renovations, and modernizations have happened continuously, making Ullensvang Hotel a completely modern hotel.

Today, the hotel houses 157 rooms, a dining room that seats 550 guests, modern conference facilities, display rooms, a cafe, a bar, a disco, and a souvenir shop. Many activities are also offered. There's an indoor swimming pool, a tennis court, a sauna, a hot tub, a squash court, a bowling alley, a golf simulator, billiard and tennis tables and a playroom for children. There are also many outdoor activities. There are beautiful mountain paths, there is the fjord to swim in, rowboats, a sun terrace, paddleboats, bicycles for rent, and aerial sightseeing. A lot has changed since Hans Utne rented out his bed in the loft. Ullensvang hotel is a thoroughly modern hotel, but the Utne family has sought to retain four generations worth of style, atmosphere, and traditions. The menu still includes regional specialties, and the hotel is

Hotel Ullensvang lies perfectly situated in the middle of Hardanger's orchard. From the terrace, there's a breathtaking view over the Sorfjord, an arm of the famous Hardangerfjord, the powerful mountains, and Folgefonn glacier.

filled with local antiques collected over generations. They tell the story of a family, a hotel, and the development of local tourism.

Hospitality is an important concept at this family-run hotel. The buildings may have changed, but the view is still the same – the glittering blue green fjord, and Folgefonn glacier and the mighty mountains.

The hotel is filled with beautiful antiques collected over many generations. They are combined with beautiful new furniture and exciting textiles to create a unique setting.

Cider-marinated salmon from Hardanger

300 g (10 1/2 oz) skinless, boneless salmon fillet
1 teaspoon chopped parsley
1 teaspoon chopped chives
1 teaspoon chopped dill
1 teaspoon chopped tarragon
1 dl (1/2 cup) apple cider
salt, sugar
freshly ground pepper
1 dl (1/2 cup) sour cream

Cut the salmon into thin slices and arrange them on a large dish with a raised edge. Place the herbs and cider in a food processor and process until smooth. Sprinkle a little salt, a little more sugar and pepper over the salmon. Drizzle the herb-cider mixture over the fish. Cover with plastic wrap and refrigerate for 3 hours before serving.

Combine the sour cream with some of the brine from the fish and serve as dressing.

Arrange with mixed greens and garnish with Norwegian caviar, if desired. Enough for 4 appetizer servings.

Potato dumplings with salt lamb, sausages, rutabaga and bacon

800 g (1 3/4 lb) salted lamb shoulder, in slices

750 g (1 2/3 lb) peeled raw potato
250 g (9 oz) peeled boiled potato
3/4 dl (1/3 cup) barley flour
3/4 dl (1/3 cup) all-purpose flour
1 teaspoon salt

1 rutabaga
600 g (1 1/3 lb) cooked lamb or pork sausage (preferably coarsely ground)
250 g (9 oz) fatty slab bacon

Place the lamb in a stockpot and add water to cover. Simmer until tender, about 1 1/2 hours.

Grate the raw potatoes and dice the boiled potatoes. Combine and add both flours and salt. Knead well either by hand or with an electric mixer. Form into 8 balls and simmer lightly salted water or cooking liquid from the lamb for about 25 minutes.

Peel and cut the rutabaga into 1 cm (1/2") dice. Cook in lightly salted water for 20 to 25 minutes. Heat the sausage in water until just hot. Dice the bacon and fry in its own fat. Do not drain.

Serve the dumplings with the lamb, sausage, rutabaga and bacon in its own fat. This is very salty food, so don't use too much salt in the dumplings.

Edvard Grieg, the famous Norwegian composer, wrote some of his best-known works at Lofthus in Hardanger. His old composer's hut stands in the garden at Hotel Ullensvang.

Nostalgia and gingerbread along the Hardangerfjord

Sandven Hotel, Norheimsund

Potato dumplings and lamb and cabbage stew. Roast rack of lamb, young goat in cream sauce and ocean perch. Sour cream porridge, trout and horsemeat. Sour cream waffles, cloudberries and veiled country lass (applesauce pudding) from Hardanger. Sandven Hotel serves an exciting combination of traditional country cooking and more refined dishes made from first class local ingredients at its new restaurant, Privaten. In the old wing, built in neoclassical style in 1920 and locally known as "Privaten", because it used to be the living quarters of the hotel owner and his family, Tron Bach has transformed four rooms into a unique and intimate restaurant with a charming blend of old and new. When he took over the historic Sandven Hotel in Norheimsund in April, 1994, it was shabby and worn. He began to rehabilitate the hotel in close collaboration with the regional historical office. He had to build a completely new kitchen to conform with fire regulations. This was done in record time, and by May 12, 1994, the old chalet-style hotel was ready to open its doors once again. Now this unique hotel on the Hardangerfjord is completely renovated and is just as majestic as it was in its heyday.

The old warehouse on the edge of the water has been fixed up and now houses the charming arts and crafts shop, Nova. In the old Tingstova, a courtroom has been made ready for the rural magistrate, just as King Oscar I required, when he granted a license to the place in 1857. On the floor below is an exhibition of historical transport. In its first year of operation, the hotel owner was granted a license from the local official at Søndre Bergenshus (today, this would be the district governor) to provide local transportation. The hotel had a permit for up to 100 horse and carriages, as well as a snazzy 7-seater Cadillac convertible from 1927!

In the festive hotel building, there is a high-ceilinged dining room, sitting rooms and guest bedrooms, all in the old elegant style. Some of the rooms even have their own saunas. Sandven Hotel is just as magnificent today as it was in its heyday, and Tron Bach loves to tell about the long, interesting history of the hotel. A history that started when Isak Bonde bought "all of Norheimsund" in 1324 and established the large farm called Sandvin.

FARMER AND PEDDLER
Both tenant farms on the property belonged to the Oppitun Sandven farm. One was at the site of the hotel today – that's where it all started. Young, ambitious Nils Sjursen Skutlaberg settled there, and as was custom in those days, he took the name of the farm as his own, Sandven. But Nils was not satisfied with just farming. He had learned to sail as a lad, and he rented a boat. He loaded it with butter, meat and skins produced by the farmers in the area and sailed to Bergen. He came home with a boatload of goods from the city. Trade boomed, and Nils could sell the contents of a fully-loaded ship in one day.

Until 1842, carrying on trade was considered an urban privilege, and Nils had problems obtaining an official trading license. The local authorities were afraid that people would use all their money on unnecessary things that would "contribute to their

The large, high-ceilinged dining room is one of Norway's best preserved turn of the century interiors. It is more richly decorated than was the norm, with woodcarving and stencils on the walls.

own downfall". But the trade laws were changed and Nils got his royal license, and it was signed by six cabinet ministers! He was obligated to hold court sessions, be the postal steamship clerk, to "keep the place adequately supplied with the necessary wares that everyone needs" and to provide travelers with "the necessities and good lodging".

The tax collector had recommended that Nils be granted a license. He and the rural magistrate had been dissatisfied with the old arrangement in which the parsonage was used for a courtroom and lodging. For that reason, Nils was aware of what was needed with regard to comfort and service. He realized that he had to build a new house to serve as the inn.

Tones from a violin and the whistles of steamships

The industrious trader immediately started work on the building, and in 1858, a new two-story inn was finished on the site of the old tenant farm. Nils build a courtroom alongside and added another floor to the old general store from 1845 and connected it with the warehouse from 1851. The latter is still standing today.

Word spread of the new inn at Norheimsund, and guests came from all over – business men and civil servants on official business, as well as tourists. Some returned year after year, including the famous violinist and composer Ole Bull. He often stood on the steps and played for the guests and the people of the area. Other times, he climbed up to Grautaberg and stood there and played, sending the beautiful tones from his violin out over the small settlement, so that "many eyes filled with tears".

During that time, a courthouse and a coaching station went together, and now the parsonage also lost its coaching traffic to Nils Sandven. Those using this service were mainly civil servants. It soon gave way to steamship traffic. In 1846, the first steamship was seen on the Hardangerfjord, and in 1854, the "Patriot" began scheduled traffic, but it was not until the 90-foot-long paddle steamer "Vøring" came into service that there was regularly scheduled traffic on Norheimsund. During the first years, the ships were not allowed to dock at the quay because of the fire hazard. They had to drop anchor out in the fjord, and

Above: The hotel facade facing Hardangerfjorden is stunning, no matter when you arrive.

Left: Sandven Hotel still has many of its original details.

Right: The largest sitting room, "The Ladies' Salon", is one of the hotel's best preserved old interiors and is decorated with antiques and older furniture.

Nils Sandven rowed out, fetched and returned both passengers and freight. Eventually, a larger boat, the "Hardanger" was put into traffic, and it could pull right up to the quay. Then people could go right on land and walk the few meters to the hotel, which led to a considerable increase in tourist traffic.

Like father like son

Busy years followed for Nils Sandven. Running a hotel back then was hard work. In Sandven Hotel 100 Years, Frithjof Sælen gives an idea of some of the problems involved: "Before a waterworks was built to supply water from Krokavatn lake in 1899, water had to be fetched from an underground spring. Food storage wasn't easy, either. Sandven organized a kind of cold storage in the old courtroom. He sawed ice from Movatn lake during the winter and had many people helping him. He piled the blocks of ice, closed the windows tightly and sealed around them. Two solid doors served as an airlock."

And Nils Sandven was not just in the hotel business. He also had a store and a steamship office to run! In addition, he was one of the founders of Vikøy Savings Bank, where he worked as cashier for 22 years. When Norheimsund got its own post office, the postmaster was, of course, Nils Sandven.

In 1875, his son Nils Nilson Sandven, took over the properties. The number of tourists was constantly increasing, and he realized that he needed additional guestrooms, and these had to be of a higher standard. He then built the present hotel. At the same time, he filled the beach below the hotel and created a small but beautiful garden with weeping birch and other exotic plants – with tables and benches where guests could sit and enjoy the beautiful view over the fjord, the mountain and the mighty Folgefonn glacier. Eventually, he also built a large floating wharf for the rowboats that guests could use, and for the barges that carried people to the shore from the large tourist ships. Many tourists who visited Norheimsund at that time came to see what had fascinated Kaiser Wilhelm, the Øvsthus waterfall, later called the Steindal falls. Nils Nilson Sandven soon realized there was money to be made here. He bought the entire falls and built a booth in the dragon style alongside. There he sat and collected 10 øre from everyone who wanted to visit the café for refreshments.

Like his father, young Nils was an industrious fellow. He liked new inventions and created his own electric company to light the hotel long before the power plant was built at Kaldestad in 1914. He also had the first car in the area. In 1890, he established the Vikør telephone company, and the central was located at Sandven until 1934.

tearing down the building, but the locals loved the old hotel that had been the center of the village for more than a century. It was now taken over by a foundation "Sandven Cultural Hotel", owned by some of the villagers. From 1991 to 1993, everyone in the village joined in to refurbish the hotel. Parts were fixed up, and the foundation tried to keep the business going, but in August, 1993, bankruptcy was declared. The administrators wanted to split up the property and sell off the buildings separately, but fortunately, the regional historical office prohibited this. At the end of 1993, the entire property was sold to the local council.

They, in turn, offered the property to hotelier Tron Bach. He had lived in Finse for many years, first as a glacier guide, then he purchased Hotel Finse 1222. He restored and ran the hotel for many years and he was also active in establishing the Rallar Museum (about the building of the Bergen railway) at Finse. He accepted the offer, and since then, he has managed to recreate the style and atmosphere of bygone days at the fairy tale castle on the Hardangerfjord.

Sandven Hotel serves an exciting combination of traditional country-style food and well prepared dishes made from the best local ingredients.

In the beginning of the 1920s, Nils' nephew, Nils Oleson Sandven, took over. The years during and after World War I had been difficult, and the tourists had stayed away. But now traffic was increasing rapidly, and in 1925, Nils had to expand the hotel. Roads were improved and extended, and more and more tourists found their way to the beautiful settlement along the Hardangerfjord. Even though there was increased competition from cruise ships, there was still enough to do. The passengers had to go on land, and they were taken to the falls by horse and buggy.

The years passed, and generation followed generation at Sandven Hotel. In 1951, Nils Oleson Sandven passed the historic hotel to the fourth generation, Ola N. Sandven. He ran the hotel, not always successfully, until 1990.

RESCUED BY THE LOCALS, THE REGIONAL HISTORICAL OFFICE, KVAM HERAD AND TRON BACH

Over the years, the proud old wooden building became down at heels and it could no longer satisfy the needs of modern tourists. There was discussion about

Sandven soup

500 g (1 1/2 lb) salted and smoked lamb
4 carrots
1/2 onion
1/2 small rutabaga
4 potatoes
1/2 leek
1 tablespoon minced celeriac
1 teaspoon bouillon granules

Place the meat in a stockpot and add water to cover. Heat to boiling, skimming well. Simmer about one hour, until the meat is tender. Wash, clean and cut the vegetables into large cubes. Remove the meat from the soup and cut into medium pieces. Add the vegetables and celeriac to the stock and let simmer until the vegetables are tender, about 15 minutes. Return the meat to the pot and season with bouillon granules. Serve with fresh whole grain bread or flatbread.

Lemon Bavarian cream

5 gelatin sheets
3 eggs
1 1/2 dl sugar
juice and grated zest of 1 lemon
water

Soak the gelatin in cold water to soften, about 5 minutes. Beat the eggs and sugar until light, thick and lemon-colored. Combine the lemon juice and zest and add water to make 2 1/2 dl (1 cup) liquid. Stir into the egg mixture. Squeeze to remove excess water and melt the gelatin in a water bath. Whisk the gelatin into the egg mixture in a thin stream. Stir until it begins to set. Pour into individual dishes and refrigerate for at least 3 hours. Serve with a red berry sauce.

The Pride of the town

Grand Hotel Terminus, Bergen

Above: One of Bergen's best restaurants, Ambrosia, is at Grand Hotel Terminus.

Below: Grand Hotel Terminus lies in the heart of Bergen, just 20 meters from the railway station.

Right: The grand hall, with its original interior, has a very special ambience and is an excellent example of the Bergen craft tradition.

The Grand Hotel Terminus first opened on April 20, 1928. The architects, Arnesen and Darre Kaarbø, were well-traveled and had created a beautiful building, so beautiful that they received the A. H. Houen prize for excellent architecture the following year. Its continental style and elegant ambience made it Bergen's first luxury hotel. Few hotels of the period could offer four bathrooms per floor and wash basins in most rooms. And that wasn't all! Two maids were assigned to each floor to look after the needs of the guests. If a female guest required assistance in the bathroom, she rang for a maid. Each night, someone went around and polished all the shoes left outside the bedrooms, so that they shined along with the floor, which was scoured clean every night – by a Dane with steel wool attached to the soles of his shoes!

The elegant dining room offered a new menu every day, as well as elegant waiters in white uniforms. And if a guest should have a special request, such as oysters, caviar, or lobster, it was granted in record time. The beer hall, with its musicians on the balcony entertaining the guests, was probably livelier than the dining room.

The location is perfect - on a quiet, cobblestone street next to the main train station. Just a short walk to the wharf or center of town, it became the hotel of choice in Bergen. Summers were especially hectic, with many American tourists and other boat passengers.

As the years passed, the hotel became more and more popular, and it kept its good reputation. This was one reason why the German occupational forces used it as its headquarters and officer base during World War II.

After the war ended, things returned to normal and remained so until 1959, when the hotel was sold to a group of missionary organizations. Thus began 33 years as Bergen's missionary hotel. No more Champagne and caviar here! The day to day operations of the hotel changed, and it was simplified both in style and interior. All the accoutrements that had made it

Bergen's first luxury hotel were removed.

THE RETURN TO GRANDEUR

Businessman Magne Hisdal bought the hotel in 1992. He wanted to restore its former glory and make it financially viable. The first thing he did was to renovate it. He and his wife, textile artist Solveig Hisdal, who designed the popular Oleana jackets, and their daughter Trude worked actively to return the hotel to its 1928 grandeur. The unique attention to detail and extravagant splendor that had characterized the hotel slowly returned. After intense searching both in and outside Norway, they managed to obtain some of the original interior. The refurbishment has cost NOK 40 million to date, but it was money well spent.

The elegant 1930s ambience greets everyone at the door. The style is immediately visible. The colonnaded foyer has a richly decorated ceiling and Persian carpets. The great hall is the heart of the hotel. The glow from the giant fireplace illuminates the sitting room where polar explorer Roald Amundsen once lectured. The sitting room retained the original interior with its solid wainscoting, richly carved oak doors, and comfortable sofas. You can enjoy a cup of coffee or a drink here, or you can attend one of the literary or music evenings held here during the winter. Next to the sitting room is the old breakfast room. It was completely renovated and now houses Ambrosia, one of Bergen's best restaurants. The pale green walls, gold moldings and crystal chandeliers make a stylish interior which compliments the French-inspired international menu.

The old beer hall, which was closed during its days as a missionary hotel, now houses the Terminus Cafe and Restaurant. The cafe serves hearty Norwegian fare, and their sandwiches and cakes are much sought after. It too has been restored to its former glory, so time typical that you expect to hear music from the orchestra balcony at any time. And…who knows? Maybe that's one of the few things missing. But it seems that all of Magne Hisdal's dreams for the Grand

Hotel Terminus have come true. The Grand Hotel Terminus is once again the pride of the town.

Below: The old beer hall has now been replaced by the popular Terminus Café and Restaurant, which serves Norwegian cuisine made with top quality ingredients and a modern touch.

Right: They don't build hotels like this anymore! The architects Arnesen and Darre Kaarbo brought home impulses from study trips on the Continent and used them to create a richly detailed hotel.

Gratinéed chevre salad with nut vinaigrette

1 liter (quart)
mixed salad greens

Preheat the grill or preheat the oven to 220°C (400°F). Wash and tear the lettuce into bite-size pieces and place in a bowl. Combine all ingredients for the vinaigrette in a jar with a lid. Shake, then pour most of the dressing over the greens. Toss.

Nut vinaigrette
1 dl (scant 1/2 cup)
3 tablespoons balsamic vinegar
1 tablespoon sugar
2 tablespoons finely chopped walnuts
salt, pepper

Remove the crusts from the bread. Halve four slices, cube the rest and sauté all the bread in butter until golden. Top the half-slices with chevre and place under the grill until melted, about 1 minute.

6 slices white bread
3 tablespoons butter
300 g (10 oz) chevre
chives or fresh herbs

Arrange the lettuce on individual plates. Arrange chevre and croutons on the salad. Drizzle the remaining dressing around the edge of the plate. Garnish with chives or fresh herbs.

The hotel's old breakfast room is now the gourmet restaurant Ambrosia. The elegant interior has pale green walls, gold trim and crystal chandeliers.

Salt-baked cod with forestiere potatoes and avocado sauce

4 asparagus stalks
4 spring onions
1 carrot
100 g (4 oz) celeriac
1 small leek
2 dl (3/4 cup) water
1 tablespoon butter
1/2 teaspoon salt

4 boneless cod fillets, skin on,
about 170-180 g (6 oz) each
2 tablespoons butter
4 ss (1/4 cup) coarse sea salt

Forestiere potatoes
4 large baking potatoes
2 dl (3/4 cup) whipping cream
4 egg yolks
2 tablespoons minced onion
1 garlic clove, minced
salt, pepper

Avocado sauce
2 tablespoons minced onion
1 garlic clove
1 tablespoon butter
1/2 dl (3 1/2 tablespoons)
white wine
1 dl (1/2 cup) whipping cream
1 avocado
1 tablespoon lemon juice
2 tablespoons butter
salt, pepper

Trim the asparagus and spring onions. Peel the asparagus stalks and split lengthwise. Boil in lightly salted water for 2 minutes.

Wash and peel the carrot, and celeriac, clean the leek. Cut the vegetables into 3-4 cm long, thin sticks. Heat the water, butter and salt to boiling. Add the carrot and celeriac and boil 1 minute. Add the leek and boil one more minute.

Preheat the oven to 190°C (375°F). Fry the cod, skin side down, in butter until crisp and golden. Turn and transfer to a baking sheet, skin side up. Sprinkle with salt. Bake 10 to 12 minutes (with the potatoes).

Forestiere potatoes
Preheat the oven to 160°C (320°F). Peel and grate the potatoes. Drain any liquid that accumulates. Whisk the cream and egg yolks with the onion and garlic. Season with salt and pepper. Arrange the potatoes in an ovenproof dish or in individual casseroles. Pour over the egg mixture. Bake for 20 to 25 minutes.

Avocado sauce
Sauté the onion and garlic in butter in a small saucepan until shiny. Add the wine and cream and boil 3 minutes. Peel and pit the avocado. Chop the flesh and add with the lemon juice. Puree with an immersion blender. Just before serving, beat in the butter. Season with salt and pepper.

Gooseberry soup with strawberry parfait

Gooseberry soup
300 g (3 cups) gooseberries
150 g (3/4 cup) sugar
1 dl (1/2 cup) water
1 tablespoon lemon juice
3 tablespoons white wine
1/2 vanilla bean

Strawberry parfait
100 g (1 cup) frozen strawberries
30 g (2 1/2 tablespoons) sugar
1/2 vanilla bean
50 g (1/4 cup) sugar
2 tablespoons water
2 egg yolks
2 dl (3/4 cup) whipping cream

Place all the ingredients in a saucepan and simmer for 5 minutes. Remove the vanilla bean and puree the rest with an immersion blender. Refrigerate for at least 1 hour before serving.

Simmer the strawberries, sugar and vanilla bean for 3 minutes. Remove the vanilla bean and puree the berries with an immersion blender. Heat the sugar and water to boiling. Lightly beat the egg yolks and whisk them into the sugar syrup, beating until room temperature. Lightly whip the cream. Fold the egg yolk mixture into the cream and add the strawberries. Pour into a mold or into individual molds and freeze. To serve, ladle the soup into bowls. Place parfait in the center. Garnish with berries and mint.

Four old houses and a lot of drive

Solstrand Fjord Hotel, Os

"When the fjords are as blue as the violets in the
field and the glaciers glisten in the light of the sun,
When the lily of the valley by the chokecherry trees
spreads its beautiful scent toward the rock wall,
While the elf behind the alder bush dances wildly
and the thrush from the spruce-covered landscape
sings along, then it touches my heart.
Yes it touches my heart, and all I can do is whisper,
God bless you, Norway, my beautiful homeland."
(Alfred Danielsen 1849-1936)

This is how the picturesque landscape along the
Bjørnefjord is described in one of Norway's national
hymns. And this is where we find Solstrand Fjord
Hotel, in Os, just 30 kilometers from Bergen. The
yellow buildings are light and airy, and the surrounding gardens are filled with fruit trees, rhododendron
bushes, and a large expanse of green lawn stretching
all the way down to the fjord. The view is
overwhelming. The idyllic fjord with its tiny islands
and skerries, and in the distance, Tysnes, Folgefonn
glacier, and the powerful Kvinnherad mountains.
This peaceful idyll, punctuated only by the sound of
waves and gulls, is the reason why the hotel was built.
This was what the "landlubbers" wanted. They were
mostly Bergen bourgeoisie, who liked to spend the
summer months in the country with their families.
These summer holidays became increasingly popular
after 1850, as transportation to these remote spots
improved. The Bjørneselskapet steamship company
was established in 1866 with two steamships providing scheduled traffic beween the Bjørnefjord area and
the city. These ships brought many of the first

"landlubbers" to Os. The railway between Nesttun
and Os was opened in July, 1894, and although it was
only a narrow-gauge railroad, it still made the trip
from Bergen to the countryside much easier. The
speed and comfort of the railway weren't impressive,
but the trip was still an adventure, as O.W. Fasting
tells us. This is how he describes a journey to
Solstrand Hotel and Spa in Os at the beginning of
the 20th century.

"I should probably start by telling you how I arrived at
Solstrand. The hotel lies alongside the Bjørnefjord,
near Os railway station. One takes the train from
Bergen to Nesttun, where a change of trains is in order. The beautiful and comfortable carriages of the
Bergen-Voss line are traded in for a small cardboard
box, where every second there is the fear of going
through the wall and falling onto the railway tracks.
If you are in a hurry, just jump off the train and run.
But don't let the conductor see you after insulting his
railway so – in the mean time. All things considered,
the Os railroad is a nice little piece of track, and it is
useful. The speed isn't too bad. It takes almost one
and a half hours to go 30 kilometers, a speed that is
comfortably midway between an earthworm and a
flash of lightning."

But the "little piece of track" did its job, and until it
was replaced by cheaper bus service and retired in
1935, there is no doubt that the railroad, as well as
the steamships, laid the foundation for the tourist
trade in Os. And the improved communications and
steadily increasing tourist traffic at the end of the

19th century inspired the young shipowner Christian Michelsen to build a hotel alongside the beautiful Bjørnefjord.

SHIP OWNER, HOTEL OWNER, AND GOVERNMENT MINISTER

In January, 1895, he bought Haugstræ, an outlying field on Hauge farm. It had originally been one of over 200 farms along the west coast of Norway that had belonged to the powerful Lyse Abbey. This Cistercian monastery on the banks of the Lysefjord was founded by Bishop Sigurd of Bergen in 1146 and was under Fountains Abbey in York, England. This monastery soon became one of the richest in the country, but it was stripped of all its land and farms during the Reformation. Senior royal officials administered the property during the 17th century, but in 1722, Hans Henriksøn Formann took over the estate and settled at Lysekloster Manor. For centuries, the estate had been run as one farm, and the individual farmers were tenants of the squire. When the last owner of the estate, Henrik Formann, died without heirs in 1871, the tenants were given the option of purchasing their farms. That was how Ola Johannesson Heggland bought Haugestræ in 1873 for 120 *spesidaler*. In 1875, he sold the property to a local Os merchant, Hans Nikolai Hansen. He in turn left the property to his niece, Inger Sofie Hansen, and in 1895 Christian Michelsen purchased it for his hotel. Michelsen was already an established ship owner, and in 1905, he would become Norway's first prime minister, but in the meantime, he needed some extra capital to buy Haugstræ, or Solstrand as he called it. He asked his wealthy father-in-law, merchant Rasmus Wallendahl, to co-sign a loan, and then he started to build his dream hotel – a summer hotel with all the modern conveniences, where landlubbers could enjoy healthy fresh air and bathe in the cold waters of the sea. Solstrand Hotel og Bad was ready for guests in 1896. O.W Fasting described the hotel as it looked back then:

"It is a large establishment, with grand corridors, magical staircases, a spacious vestibule complete with fireplace, a dining room that seats 150, a smoking room with a fireplace, an elegant salon, large guest bedrooms with wide beds and verandas outside - room for 80 guests, and all windows facing the Bjørnefjord and Folkefonn glacier.

You can play lawn tennis, croquet, row and sail – Bjørnefjord is the best place for those who enjoy sailing. And you can bathe in the sea or in mud, pine needles or even in a tub.

There's a large garden filled with the most divine roses. And all around the hotel are villas owned by wealthy Bergeners. There's everything your heart could desire. But the best things here are the secluded walking paths, where you can forget the world and all your troubles, and there are so many of them that you never have to take the same path twice."

Christian Michelsen had created a fancy hotel. The hotel itself was built in a restrained chalet style, with a moderate amount of gingerbread but with large roof extensions and characteristic gable decoration. The "Annex Villa Trouville", which Michelsen had moved down from Sunnmøre, was a typical chalet-style building with two verandas and a small corner tower. There was also a barn, a long and narrow bath-house on the beach, and a smaller bathhouse out toward the fjord.

THE FIRST FEW YEARS

It wasn't long before this fashionable hotel, with its ideal location, beautiful garden and peaceful surroundings became a popular summer destination. Wealthy Bergen merchants brought their families to Solstrand for the summer, while they visited on the weekends. Then the children and their nannies moved into "Annex Villa Trouville", while the adults stayed in the main building. The hotel also marketed itself internationally, primarily attracting English tourists. Norwegian fjords and mountains were a popular des-tination at the end of the 19th century. Solstrand eventually gained a solid reputation in England. More and more English tourists found their way to Solstrand, and the hotel soon earned the nickname "Little England".

But it wasn't always easy to find enough guests to make the hotel profitable – and this is probably why it changed owners several times during the first few years. The hotel was run as a personal company for the first few years, but in 1903, Lutlaget Solstrand Spa and Hotel was established, with Christian Michelsen as chairman. The new company bought the title to the property for NOK 60 000 on the writ-ten condition that the building should always be run as a hotel. It was sold to Torstein Bårson Lunde from Voss, a former manager at Solstrand, in 1908. He and his wife, who was chef at the hotel, ran it until 1917, when Lutlaget Solstrand Spa and Hotel bought it back. It changed hands again in 1926. This time, Jens Blomqvist, director of Hotel Norge in Bergen, took it over and ran it almost as a branch of that well-known metropolitan hotel for the next three years. In 1929, the hotel was purchased by restaurateur Ludvig Larsen from Halden and his wife Marie Schau. The hotel is still owned by the Schau-Larsen family today.

A NEW ERA, A NEW NAME, AND COURSES

Ludvig Larsen died in 1931, leaving his wife in charge of the hotel. It wasn't an easy task. Marie and Ludvig had lost three of their four children, and now she had lost her husband as well. But life went on, and the hotel continued its seasonal trade. Solstrand remain-ed open even during World War II, but the hotel was required to keep a few rooms available for the occupa-tional forces. The hotel changed its name to Solstrand Fjord Hotel just after the war. This was done primarily to fulfill the local authorities' licens-ing requirements.

Their son Sverre soon began to show an interest in the hotel. Sverre Schau-Larsen was a far-sighted and efficient hotel manager, and he and his wife Astrid began renovating and adding onto the hotel. In 1950, he started Vestlandet Hotel Management School, a boarding school at Solstrand that offered an eight-month course in hotel studies, languages, and economics. Sverre Schau-Larsen was also a well-respected figure in the Norwegian tourism industry. He was chairman of the Norwegian Tourist Hotel Organization, president of the Norwegian Hotel and

Restaurant Association, and chairman of the board of the Norwegian Hotel Management School.

But a letter to the editor written by Rolf Waaler, a teacher at the Norwegian School of Business Administration in the early 1950s would change the face of Solstrand forever. Waaler asked for a course in leadership and administration for business executives and public officials. Sverre Schau-Larsen liked the idea and felt that Solstrand would be the perfect place to hold courses such as this. Things moved quickly. Rolf Waaler founded the Norwegian Administrative Research Fund in 1952 to deal with leadership development and education and administrative problems. The first course in administration was held at Solstrand on April 13, 1953. It was so popular that more followed, giving the hotel an important, stable source of income. These courses are still popular, although contents, length and price have changed over the years. The program is still run according to the same principle: "the participants shall learn from one another and with one another."

CONCRETE AND INSULATED WINDOWS

The gradual transition from summer hotel to year-round course and conference center required large investments and structural changes. The beautiful old main building was remodeled. The facade was stripped of its gingerbread ornamentation. The nooks and crannies were removed, and the large old windows were replaced with modern insulated glass. A new concrete wing housing an indoor swimming pool, a conference room, and guestrooms was built. When Sverre's health began to fail in 1976, his son Erik and wife Børrea took over the hotel. Erik Schau-Larsen was well prepared for the job. He was a trained chef and had studied hotel management in Stavanger and Lucerne, as well as hotel administration at Cornell University in New York. In addition to working at Solstrand, he had also gained experience with several international hotel chains and aboard a cruise ship. After Sverre died in 1980, Erik took over and began renovating and expanding the hotel. A new guest wing was added in 1986, and the swimming hall was rebuilt to include a fitness center complete with squash courts, a gym, saunas, and a whirlpool bath. That same year saw the addition of Solstrand Leadership Development Center with 600 square meters of conference facilities to host the ever popular leadership courses run by the Norwegian Administrative Research Fund.

BACK TO THE OLD GLORY

Sadly, Erik Schau-Larsen died in 1992 at the age of 45, leaving Børrea and her three young daughters. Børrea had been running the hotel before Erik's death, but she was still unsure of herself. The old building needed a complete renovation in connection with the installation of a sprinkler system. Could she really cope with this enormous responsibility – or should she sell? After many long discussions, Børrea and her daughters decided to keep the hotel.

Børrea Schau-Larsen soon proved herself worthy of the task. Today she is one of the most respected figures in the Norwegian hotel business, and Solstrand Fjord Hotel is considered one of the best run hotels in Norway. She has given the hotel a facelift, both inside and out, bringing back the romance and nostalgia that was once such a vital part of this fine old hotel. She has recreated the gingerbread façade, adding gables, old-fashioned windows and elaborate carvings. The concrete addition from 1964 is now hidden behind a bright yellow wooden facade with white window frames.

Solstrand is a course and conference center in the winter and a tourist hotel in the summer. Whether guests come for courses or for pleasure, they are all received with a hearty welcome. This closeness and consideration has been the hallmark of Solstrand for generations, and Børrea Schau-Larsen continues that tradition.

Left: A detail on one of the terrace doors leading to the promenade down to the sea. This was the main entrance in the days when most guests arrived by boat.

Right: The old garden pavilion is surrounded by blossoming fruit trees, burgeoning rhododendron bushes, and green lawns that stretch all the way down to the fjord.

Scallops in filo pastry with saffron sauce

Chicken stock
1 small carrot
100 g (4 oz) celeriac
1 medium onion
1 small leek
2 garlic cloves
bones and trimmings
from 1 chicken
1 liter (quart) water

Scallops in filo pastry
1 medium carrot
1 small leek
100 g (4 oz) celeriac
4 large scallops
4 filo sheets
chopped fresh parsley
salt, pepper

Saffron sauce
5 dl (2 cups) chicken stock
2 dl (3/4 cup) whipping cream
100 g (3 1/2 oz)
cold unsalted butter
1 g (1/4 teaspoon) saffron

Prepare the chicken stock first
Coarsely chop the vegetables and place in a stockpot with the chicken. Add the water and heat to boiling. Skim well. Simmer 45 minutes, skimming often. Strain into a clean saucepan. Reduce to 5 dl (2 cups).

Scallops in filo pastry
Preheat the oven to 180°C (350°F). Peel and cut the vegetables into thin strips. Remove 4 to 8 strips of leek and blanch quickly in boiling water. Set aside. Clean the scallops and place each scallop in the center of a filo sheet with 1/4 of the vegetables, parsley, salt and pepper. Form into a "bag" and tie with a leek strip. Place on an oven tray and bake for 10 minutes.

Saffron sauce
Reduce the chicken stock by half. Add the cream and reduce to 2 dl (3/4 cup). Beat in the butter in pats. Stir in the saffron.

Make a mirror of sauce on each plate. Place the scallop bag in the center.

Poached halibut with beet sauce, cider-glazed carrots and curried mussels

200 g (8 oz) fresh beets
2 shallots
1/2 dl (3 1/2 tablespoons) olive oil
5 dl (2 cups) fish stock
5 dl (2 cups) apple juice
salt, pepper
50 g (3 1/2 tablespoons) butter

4 boneless halibut fillets, about 160 g (5-6 oz) each

4 mussels
3/4 teaspoon curry powder

400 g (14 oz) carrots
butter
2 dl (3/4 cup) apple cider

You will need fish stock for this recipe. Follow the previous recipe for chicken stock, but use bones and trimmings from white fish, such as cod or haddock, instead of chicken.

Wash, peel and cube the beets and shallots. Sauté lightly in oil. Add the stock and juice. Simmer 30 minutes. Pour into a food processor and puree until smooth. Season with salt and pepper and beat in the butter in pats.

Heat water in a large stockpot to boiling. Add the fish, lower the heat and simmer at just below the boiling point for 10 minutes.

Place the mussels and curry powder in a small saucepan. Cover and dry-steam until they open, about 2 minutes.

Wash, peel and grate the carrots. Sauté in a little butter. Add the cider and cook until tender.

Make a mirror of sauce on individual plates. Top with a mound of carrots, then the fish. Garnish with a mussel.

Fruit tartlets with vanilla cream

Pastry
300 g (2 cups) all-purpose flour
100 g (1 cup) confectioner's sugar
200 g (7 oz) butter
1 egg

Vanilla cream
1 vanilla bean
5 dl (2 cups) milk
90 g (1/2 cup) sugar
40 g (1/3 cup) cornstarch
2 eggs

Pastry
Preheat the oven to 200°C (400°F). Place all the ingredients in a food processor and pulse until they begin to stick together. Do not overprocess. Press into tartlet shells. Bake about 10 minutes.

Vanilla cream
Split the vanilla bean lengthwise and scrape out the seeds. Scald the seeds, milk and sugar. Stir the sugar and cornstarch together, then whisk in the eggs. Add the hot milk. Return the mixture to the saucepan and heat to boiling, stirring constantly.

Spoon the vanilla cream into the tartlet shells and garnish with berries or fruit. Brush with jelly, if desired.

From a farm to a hotel
Bjørnefjorden Gjestetun, Os

Bjørnefjorden Gjestetun lies on a hill above the center of Os, just a 30-minute drive from Bergen and Flesland Airport. The Bjerke family has run the farm, with its beautiful view of the Bjørnefjord, Folgefonn glacier, Rosendal valley, and the mighty Tysnes mountains, since 1655, and Synnøve Bjørke is the 18th generation to manage the farm. It used to be called Hauge farm and was originally a part of Lyse Abbey. The monastery was founded in 1146 by Bishop Sigurd of Bergen as a subsidiary of Fountains Abbey in York, England, and was the first Cistercian monastery in Norway. It soon became rich and powerful, with its own subsidiary monastery in Tautra in Trøndelag, and over 200 farms along the Norwegian west coast. The monks had a great influence on the crops cultivated on these farms, and they decided to concentrate on fruit production, which is still one of the most important crops grown along the fjord. Salmon fishing was another important source of income, and when the managers of Hauge farm were given the option of buying the farm after the Reformation, they had to pay just as much for the fishing rights in the Os river and the sea, as for the land. In 1990, after many hundreds of years of traditional farming, Synnøve, or Synni as her friends call her, and her parents, Synnøve and Samson Bjørke, decided to try some tourism in addition to traditional farming. Soon sheep and cows, tractors and reapers had to yield to tourists, and now Hauge farm is Bjørnefjorden Gjestetun, a cozy, unique bed and breakfast in the heart of fjord Norway. The old cowshed from 1655 was renovated and now houses theme rooms, all with their own names like: "the stall", "the virgin room", "the farmhand room", and a conference room. Some of the other old houses on the estate, such as "the dowager house", "the carriage house", and "Stølsheimen", can be rented on their own. Many of these houses have three bedrooms with two beds in each. The new main building, built in 1997 to match the style of the old buildings, houses the reception area, a lounge, a restaurant, a conference room, and bedrooms.

FISHING, SPORTS, AND CULTURE ALL IN ONE PLACE

Bjørnefjorden Gjestetun also offers a wide range of activities and experiences – both on the farm and in the surrounding areas. Evidence of habitation as early as 300 AD have been found on Hauge farm. A king lies buried in a mound from the migration period in the farmyard, and the site is marked by a giant oak tree and a magnificent view over the fjord and mountains. The grave was opened at the end of the 19th century and contained swords, arrow heads, and pottery shards, which are now on display at the Historical Museum in Bergen. Near the mound is a rune stone. This three and a half meter tall stone monument was originally erected as a shipwreck memorial in the early Viking era. Wandering around and among all these archaeological sites are rabbits, cats, ducks, chickens, and turkeys. They belong here, much to the delight of the children who visit the farm.

Old-fashioned herbs and plants are grown in the historical garden, just as they were in the past, and the farm shop sells homemade products like smoked fish, firehouse smoked sausage, jam, and honey, all made in the good old-fashioned way.

Bjørnefjorden Gjestetun is a paradise for fishermen. All kinds of fish can be found in the Bjørnefjord, while the Os river is rich in salmon and trout. Guests can even clean and pack their own catch in the slaughterhouse. They can also smoke eel, salmon, and trout in the old-fashioned smokehouse.

The property also contains a nine-hole training golf course, and the guesthouse is the perfect starting point for exploring western Norway's breathtaking

landscape. Summertime offers many activities: There are many marked walking trails, and there's canoeing, riding, and swimming in the Bjørnefjord. Foglefonna ski center offers year-round skiing, while Eikedal ski center is open only in winter.

And, while you're in the area, why not visit some of the many local cultural attractions? The ruins of Lyse Abbey and Lysøen, the summer house of violinist Ole Bull, built in 1872-3. Galleri Solbakkstuen, where Bente Bratland Mæland and Arne Mæland, an artist couple, exhibit picture, reliefs, and sculptures. Vargavågen, with its rock carvings dating back to 4000 BC, is well worth a visit. So is the idyllic old

officer's estate, Engevik Gård by the Sævareid fjord, which dates from the 18th Century. And if you have some time left over, why not visit Bergen, it's only 28 kilometers away.

Left: There's a fantastic view of the Bjørnefjord and the wild western Norwegian landscape from the dining room.

Spiced herring roulade

4 spiced herring fillets
2 hardcooked eggs
2 tablespoons minced parsley

Pickled red onions

1 large red onion
1 dl (1/2 cup) red wine vinegar
2 dl (1 cup) water
4 tablespoons (1/4 cup) brown sugar
1 clove
8 rose peppercorns
1 bay leaf

Herbed new potatoes

4 large new potatoes
1 dl (1/2 cup) oil
1 tablespoon minced chives
1 tablespoon minced thyme
1 teaspoon salt
freshly ground pepper

Marinated greens

2 teaspoons minced shallot
1/2 teaspoon Dijon mustard
2 tablespoons white wine vinegar
1 tablespoon water
1/2 teaspoon sugar
pinch salt
freshly ground white pepper
1 teaspoon minced parsley
1 teaspoon minced chervil
1 teaspoon finely chopped chives
1 dl (1/2 cup) olive oil
3 kinds of lettuce
cress
1 spring onion, sliced

Spiced herring roulade with herbed new potatoes, marinated greens and pickled red onions

Soak the herring in cold water about 6 hours. Dry well with paper towels and arrange on a plate. Press the eggs through a sieve and mix with parsley. Spread the egg mixture over the herring and roll up. Fasten with a satay stick, if desired.

Pickled red onions

Peel the onion and cut into thin rings. In a large saucepan, heat the remaining ingredients to boiling and cook until the sugar is dissolved. Remove from the heat and add the onion rings. Mix to coat. Store in the refrigerator.

Herbed new potatoes

Preheat the oven to 200°C (400°F). Scrub the potatoes well, then cut into 1/2 cm (1/4") slices. Combine the remaining ingredients. Coat the potatoes with the herbed oil and arrange on an oven tray. Drizzle the remaining oil over the potatoes and bake about 15 minutes, until tender.

Marinated greens

Combine the first 10 ingredients in a bowl. Gradually whisk in the oil in a thin stream. Season with sugar and salt.

Rinse the lettuce well and tear into large pieces. Place in a bowl with the cress and onion. Pour over 2/3 of the marinade. Toss well.

Arrange potato slices, lettuce, pickled onion and herring roulades on flat plates. Drizzle the remaining marinade all around.

Mussels and baked fish with tomato-herb bouillon and julienne vegetables

150 g (5 oz) monkfish fillet
150 g (5 oz) boneless trout fillet
olive oil
juice of 1/2 lemon
1 teaspoon salt
freshly ground pepper

2 kilos (4 1/2 lb) fresh mussels
oil
3 garlic cloves, pressed
1 shallot, minced
1 tablespoon minced parsley
1 tablespoon minced fresh thyme
1 teaspoon minced fresh rosemary
5 dl (2 cups) dry white wine
5 dl (2 cups) water
1 can (400g/14 oz)
chopped tomatoes
1 tablespoon tomato paste
1/2 teaspoon salt
pepper, sugar

200 g (7 oz) snow peas
2 carrots
200 g (7 oz) celeriac

Preheat the oven to 160°C (325°F). Remove any bones from the fish. Cut into 1 cm (1/2") thick strips. Place on a large sheet of aluminum foil. Drizzle with oil and lemon juice and sprinkle with salt and pepper. Fold and seal. Bake about 15 minutes.

Scrub the mussels. Discard any that are not tightly closed. Heat a little oil in a stockpot. Sauté the garlic, shallot and fresh herbs for a few seconds. Add the mussels, wine, water, tomatoes and tomato paste. Cover and steam the mussels until they open, 1 to 2 minutes. Transfer the mussels with a slotted spoon to a bowl. Cover with aluminum foil. Strain the cooking liquid into a smaller saucepan and season with salt, pepper and sugar.

Clean, peel and julienne the vegetables. Simmer in the cooking liquid about 3 minutes. Arrange the mussels in large, deep bowls. Top with fish. Pour over the stock and top with vegetables. Garnish with fresh herbs. Serve with homemade bread and butter.

Hazelnut snaps with fresh berries and vanilla cream

Hazelnut snaps
150 g (5 oz) unsalted butter,
softened
100 g (1/2 cup) sugar
5 egg whites
50 g (1/3 cup) all-purpose flour
100 g (4 oz) hazelnuts, chopped
in a food processor

Vanilla cream
1 vanilla bean
3 dl (1 1/4 cups) full fat milk
3 dl (1 1/4 cups) whipping cream
125 g (2/3 cup) sugar
5 egg yolks
2 tablespoons cornstarch
3 gelatin sheets

Preheat the oven to 180°C (350°F). Beat the butter and sugar until light and fluffy. Beat the egg whites until they form soft peaks, then fold into the butter mixture. Stir in the flour and nuts. Line an oven sheet with baking parchment. Brush a spoonful of batter into a 4 cm (1 1/2") circle. Bake until golden, 6-8 minutes. Cool on a rack. Makes about 40 cookies.

Vanilla cream
Split the vanilla bean lengthwise and scrape out the seeds. Place in a saucepan with the milk, cream and sugar and heat to boiling. Whisk the egg yolks and cornstarch together in a small bowl. Whisk about 2 dl (3/4 cup) of the hot milk mixtures into the eggs, then return to the saucepan. Return to boiling, whisking constantly. Soak the gelatin in cold water for about 2 minutes. Squeeze to remove excess water, then melt in the hot vanilla cream, stirring often. Refrigerate.

Fresh berries
Use seasonal berries, such as strawberries, raspberries, boysenberries, blueberries and red currants. Wash and clean.

Spoon vanilla cream into a pastry bag and pipe onto individual plates. Top with fresh berries and a hazelnut snap. Repeat for as many layers as desired. Garnish with berry coulis, mint leaves and a sprinkling of cocoa. 8 servings.

A inn with neither electricity nor a road

Kubbervik, Uggdal

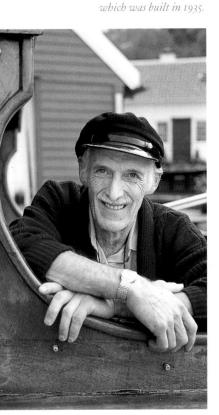

It's dawn. Morning is breaking and the water is shining like a mirror. We draw in our fishing net as seagulls comment on the quality of our catch. They follow us to the dock, and after a few tasty morsels, they fly off into the horizon with full stomachs. Kubbervik is quiet once again.

The first thing one notices is how still everything is. It is a deafening silence, broken only occasionally by the waves, by the wind blowing through the trees, by the flapping wings of the mighty grey sea eagle, and by a single deer walking through the brush in the forest. Bergen is not far away, but everyday life seems very remote in a place like this. It's as if time has stood still in this peaceful bay deep in the fjord. You almost feel like Christopher Columbus as you arrive at Kubbervik for the first time. But Kubbervik's quiet harbor was actually discovered many thousand years ago. Archeologists have found remains dating back to the late stone age, around 2500 BC. Kubbervik had its heyday at the beginning of the 17th century, when the Hanseatic League was exporting dried fish from Bergen. At the same time, the Scottish trade was booming. Ships came from the western isles to buy timber in Bårdsund. Kubbervik was the commercial center for a business that would last about 100 years, until around 1720. Then came an economic downturn, and the tenants on the farm had to find other means of support. Fishing, a couple of cows, and a few chickens weren't enough to support a growing family, so new tenants came, toiled hard and then left. But there were permanent settlements at Kubbervik until the 1930's, and legend tells tales of bootleg liquor, barter and other such things.

FROM A COUNTRY HOUSE TO AN INN

Today, you can once again enjoy an alcoholic beverage at Kubbervik, and it is legal! This old trading post is now an inn with a liquor license. After a long succession of different owners, Ingeborg Marie and Eystein Michalsen, a Bergen architect, bought it for NOK 25 000 in 1957 and used it as their summer house until 1998. At that time, Berit Michalsen, the present owner of the main buildings at Kubbervik, turned it over to her son Eystein and his partner Nina Havn, so they could follow their dream and turn Kubbervik into an inn.

Eystein is a trained chef and has also studied economics and hotel management, while Nina worked in advertising. Both wanted to leave the city and head for the countryside. Kubbervik was the perfect place. They wanted to preserve the historical and cultural value of Kubbervik on the idyllic island of Tysnes, but they also realized they had a lot of work ahead of them before they could accept paying guests. The following months were filled with digging, construction, and lots of carrying. The lack of road connections meant that everything had to be transported by boat and then carried up to the house. But all their hard work paid off, and now the old trading center is worth a special journey. All the buildings have new roofs made of Dutch bricks salvaged from an old demolished house in Oslo. The "new" windows are from an old herring factory and were carefully scraped and repainted. The red boathouse at the edge of the quay, with its collection of old fishing equipment adorning the walls, can seat up to 50 guests on long antique wooden tables. A shower and toilet have been installed in the old outhouse. The water comes from Kubbervik's own well. Electricity for the pump is supplied by a submarine battery. An addition which houses the kitchen and dining room has been built onto the main house from the 17th century. In order to obtain a restaurant licence, the house needed a dishwasher, so a generator was installed. Gas is still used to heat water, and to run the stove, refrigerator, and freezer. All modernization was done with care, and most of the white wooden buildings seem unchanged, with their crooked floors, tiny windows, crackling fires, candles and paraffin lamps.

MOTOR YACHT OR KETCH

The hosts at Kubbervik believe that food is very important. Together they create exciting and delicious dishes made from raw materials found on the grounds of the hotel. That includes blackberries, wild raspberries, wild strawberries, lingonberries, chanterelles, and herbs gathered from the 122 acres that belong to the house. They also have their own small flock of sheep, goats, and chickens, and they buy game from local hunters. There are loads of trout in lakes on the property and plenty of salmon, monkfish, ocean catfish, cod, herring, and mackerel in the nearby sea, as well as delicacies like lobster, crab, oysters, mussels,

Nina Havn and Eystein Michalsen turned the old cabin at Kubbervik into a unique, peaceful guesthouse. The hosts are joined by their mascot, Blackfoot the goat.

and scallops. The guests often help set out fishing nets and traps at night, and they get up early to experience the excitement of drawing in a net full of fish. Fishing, crabbing and digging for mussels are all popular activities, but so are boating and swimming. After all, a stay at Kubbervik begins with a boat ride. It's still the most natural way to get there. Guests fly into Bergen and are met at Flesland dock by the beautiful and very fast, motor yacht M/Y Storm. It was designed by Furuholmen and built in 1935 and has been restored to its former glory. The journey from Flesland to Kubbervik takes about an hour. If you go there by car, you are picked up at Os center and can expect a 40-minute boat ride. Bigger groups are transported on the sailing ship "Loyal" built in 1877. This newly restored ketch has been sailing the seven seas for 120 years. Everything has been restored down to the smallest detail, and there are many comfortable cabins below deck. If there are more guests than the inn can accommodate, they can sleep aboard the "Loyal" when it is docked in the calm seas of Kubbervik harbor. If there's room in the heart, there's room in the house. That's the motto of Nina Havn and Eystein Michalsen, hosts at this unique and peaceful inn.

Above: It's a good idea to bring an extra pair of wool socks for chilly nights. Sylvia Slettebakken of Salhus knits the original Kubbervik socks.

Left: A brand new addition houses the dining room. The log wall is the old outer wall. The chairs are handmade from Norheimsund birch and pine and joined without screws or nails. The Kubbervik symbol is carved into the backs of the chairs.

Right: The sitting room staircase leads up to the second floor guest bedrooms.

Kubbervik scallops

12 large scallops
3 tablespoons butter
3 dl (1 1/4 cups) dry white wine

Fish stock
bones and trimmings from 1
white fish
1/4 celeriac
1 carrot
1/4 leek
salt, pepper
juice of 1/2 lemon

Sauce
scallop stock
3 dl (1 1/4 cups)
whipping cream
2 tablespoons fish stock
1 tablespoon lemon juice
1/2 teaspoon saffron
4 tablespoons (1/4 cup) finely
chopped chives

Open the scallops. Remove everything except the muscle and coral. Melt the butter in a wide, deep pan and sauté the scallops for about a minute per side. Add the wine and simmer for 30 seconds. Transfer the scallops to a platter and reserve. Reserve the stock for the sauce.

Fish stock
Rinse the bones and trimmings in cold running water. Wash, peel and coarsely chop the vegetables. Place the bones, trimmings and vegetables in a stockpot. Add cold water to cover. Heat to boiling, then skim well. Lower the heat and simmer for 20 minutes. Strain, then reduce by half. Season with salt, pepper and lemon juice.

Sauce
Combine the first five ingredients in a saucepan and reduce to a full-bodied sauce. If it becomes too thick, dilute with white wine or cream. Add the scallops and gently reheat. Just before serving, stir in the chives.

Arrange the scallops and sauce on individual plates. Serve with buttered asparagus and garnish with rose pepper and chives.

Gratinéed lobster with chanterelles

2 large lobsters

In a large stockpot, heat salted water to boiling, add the lobsters and simmer for 20 minutes. Remove the lobsters from the pot, cool and halve lengthwise. Remove the sac behind the head and the black intestinal cord. Crack the claws, but leave them attached to the body. Remove the meat from the shell, but not from the claws. Cut the meat into 2 cm (3/4") dice.

Sauce
7 1/2 dl (3 cups) fresh chanterelles
50 g (3 tablespoons) unsalted butter
3 tablespoons all-purpose flour
2 dl (3/4 cup) fish stock (see previous recipe)
1/2 dl (3 1/2 tablespoons) dry white wine
1 dl (1/2 cup) whipping cream
1/2 teaspoon fine sea salt
1/4 teaspoon white pepper
pinch chile pepper
2 tablespoons minced parsley
1 tablespoon finely chopped dill
1 teaspoon finely chopped lovage

1 1/4 dl (1/2 cup) grated Jarlsberg cheese

Clean and cut the chanterelles into bitesize pieces. Melt the butter in a large saucepan and sprinkle over the flour. Whisk in the stock, wine and cream. Simmer 3 minutes, stirring constantly. Add the seasonings and the chanterelles and simmer 1 minute more. The sauce should be relatively thick.

Preheat the oven to 225°C (425°F). Arrange the lobsters on a baking sheet. Place 5 tablespoons (scant 1/3 cup) sauce in each lobster shell. Top with lobster meat. Sprinkle with cheese. Bake 8 to 10 minutes, until the cheese is melted and golden and the lobsters are hot.

Garnish with dill and a few fresh chanterelles. Serve with a green salad and good light bread.

Raw oysters

24 oysters
crushed ice
4 limes, in wedges
coarsely ground pepper

Shuck the oysters, keeping as much juice as possible in the shells. Arrange crushed ice on a platter and place the oysters on the ice. Serve with lime wedges and pepper.

Scandinavia's smallest castle

The Barony Rosendal, Rosendal

Below: The Barony Rosendal lies in the shadow of the powerful mountains, surrounded by fjords, snowdrifts, and waterfalls.

Right: The grand staircase leads up to the second floor.

"…The Barony Rosendal lies there like a strange, ancient memory;
in Norway's history only as a whiff of lavender in an old spinster's drawer.
Or like a cotillion sash from a long-ago ball.
It does not pretend to be more than it is:
A memory of the "Danish times"
Hans E Kinck

The Barony Rosendal, Scandinavia's smallest castle, in Sunnhordaland on Norway's western coast, lies in the shadow of the 889-meter-high Malmangernuten, surrounded by a beautiful landscape with fjord, snowdrifts, mountains, and waterfalls. Its history stretches all the way back to 1658, when Norway's richest heiress, Karen Mowatt married Ludvig Rozenkrantz, a Danish nobleman.

A RICH AND POWERFUL BRIDE

Karen Mowatt came from a powerful Scottish noble family that came to Kvinnherad sometime during the 16th century. There were many Scots in the area because of the trade routes to Hordaland and Rogaland. They came to Norway to buy timber and tar and brought with them everything from flour and salt to liquor and cloth. They were well-liked and many settled in Norway, where they often married into rich and powerful families. Karen's grandfather was a naval officer, Anders Mowatt, who had acquired large properties in Kvinnherad through lucrative marriages. As a widower, he married Else Rustung, who had been married twice previously, and through these marriages had acquired a number of large properties. Karen's father, Axel Mowatt, married Karen Bildt, a Bergen heiress. He was a good businessman and soon became one of Norway's largest property owners. He managed to combine Mel, Hatteberg, and Seim, three of the noblest farms in the area, through inheritance and purchase. He also owned Hovland, his father's farm at Tysnes, which was where he lived. He was so powerful that his daughter Karen was considered Norway's richest heiress.

A POOR, BUT PROUD BRIDEGROOM

Ludvig Rozenkrantz was not rich at all, but he was descended from one of Denmark's oldest noble families, with roots way back to the 14th century. His grandfather, Chamberlain Frederik Rosenkrantz of Rosenvold and Stjerneholm, had caused a terrible scandal at the Danish court in his youth. He had happily returned to Denmark from abroad, and "at an age in which one needs to feed one's desires, he had had improper relations with Rigborg Brockenhuus, one of the Queens ladies-in-waiting." It was to have serious consequences. Not only did Rigmor get pregnant and give birth to a son Holger, her father was so furious that he beseeched the king to uphold the law and punish the young parents. Rigborg never experienced the joys of motherhood. Instead, she was forced to spend many years languishing in a dungeon at Egeskov, her father's castle. Frederik got off more easily. He was a man, so the king required him to win back his honor on the battlefield. He lost his title but was awarded custody of Holger in 1624.

Ludvig Rosenkrantz was Holger's son, and when he came of age he wanted to help rehabilitate the family name and position. The king sent him abroad to train to become an officer. He was appointed to the Norwegian Nordenfjells commission in 1658 and participated in the recapturing of Trondheim, which had been forfeited to the Swedes in the Peace of Roskilde earlier that year.

THE BARONY ROSENDAL

No one knows where or when Karen Mowatt and Ludvig Rosendal met for the first time, but they did, and they married. The bride's father, Axel Mowatt, gave the newlyweds Hatteberg farm in Kvinnherad as a wedding gift. The main house on the estate was a log building. Ludvig wasn't impressed. He felt that people of a certain station should live in brick buildings. When his father-in-law died suddenly in 1661, he became one of Norway's richest men and immediately started to build a grand brick house. The Renaissance castle, comprising a main building with two side wings, a courtyard, and a richly decorated stone entrance complete with the family arms, was completed in 1665. The castle became the natural seat of the enormous estate he now presided over.

Squire Rosenkrantz had many irons in the fire. In 1673, he was appointed general war commissioner of Norway and was a district official. Honorable appointments to be sure, but the icing on the cake came in a royal letter dated January 14, 1678, in which the

*Above: One of the second
floor bedrooms.*

*Right: The Pompeiian
Room, probably decorated
by a Dane named Holm in
1856.*

Christian, all held the title for short periods before they died on European battlefields, while the youngest, Axel Rosenkrantz, inherited the title in 1691 and spent most of his life at Rosendal.

He married Anna Godtzen, daughter of a Stavanger clergyman, but unfortunately she bore no sons, and none of their daughters survived childhood. So the Rosendal branch of the Rosenkrantz family died out when Baron Axel died in 1723.

FROM A BARONY TO HEREDITARY PROPERTY TO AN ESTATE

The lack of male heir meant that ownership of the estate passed to the king. He quickly sold Rosendal to Ditlev Wibe, governor of Norway. Wibe was an engaged owner, but he spent little time at Rosendal, and the estate passed to his Danish relatives, the Lerche family who were already landed property owners, after his death in 1731. At the same time, Edvard Londemann, a titular bishop, was living in Stavanger. Through a few advantageous appointments and two marriages, he had managed to amass several valuable properties. The ambitious Londemann was soon eyeing up Rosendal. He bombarded the Lerches with letters, and finally, in 1745, the family gave up and sold him the estate. Londemann then turned Rosendal into an entailed estate. That meant that the estate would follow the bloodline, first through the men, and then the women. He even managed to get elevated to the nobility. After that he changed his name to the more impressive Rosencrone.

One week later, on September 16, 1749, Edvard Londemann de Rosencrone died. The estate passed to his favorite son, Marcus Gerhard Londemann de Rosencrone. He spent his entire adult life in Denmark, where he was both foreign minister and prime minister, as well as being made a baron, and later a count. The running of Rosendal was left to a manager, and the estate did not regain its status as a barony until 1779. But it was only a "titular" barony and would remain so as long as it stayed in the family of Chamberlain Rosencrantz and his descendants.

When Count Marcus died in 1811, the estate passed to the children of Chamberlain Londemann's next eldest daughter. Marie Margrethe was married to a Bohemian nobleman, Lieutenant Colonel Hoff, and their grandson inherited the estate in 1812, elevating him from Major Hoff to Baron Christian Hendrich Hoff de Rosencrone. The new baron moved to Rosendal and spent his years there maintaining and improving the house. Among other things, he added blue glazed tiles to the roof. His death in 1837 marked the end of the estate's classification as a barony. The new nobility law of 1821 eliminated any

estate was classified as a barony. It was Norway's only barony, and the newly appointed Baron Rosenkrantz decided to re-christen his estate Rosendal. The estate was actually too small to be classified as a barony, but Rosenkrantz sidestepped the rules by making a deal with the state. If the family produced no male heirs, then the estate would be turned over to the king.

The baron spent little time at Rosendal. After his wife died, he remarried, this time to Clara Catharina von Stickhausen, a former lady-in-waiting to the Queen, and now her mistress of the wardrobe. Baron Rosenkrantz was promoted to chief administrative officer of the Stavanger diocese in 1680. That meant that the baron and baroness lived most of the time at the royal residence in Stavanger, leaving little time for Rosendal. In 1684, the baron's administrative area was changed to Lister and Mandal, so the couple moved to Kristiansand. The Baron died the following year. Ludvig and Clara had no children together, but he had a whole flock of children with Karen Mowatt. Four of their sons in succession became barons of Rosendal. The three eldest, Holger, Frederik, and

The Barony Rosendal

privileges that went with the estate. Both his sons were born after 1821, so they could not claim their title and were considered normal Norwegian citizens.

The elder son, Marcus Gerhard Hoff Rosencrone, inherited the estate at age 14. He eventually became a lawyer, but he was also interested in foreign languages, art, and music. He turned the estate into a cultural center. He changed the C in Rosencrone to a K, and lived together with his brother and two sisters at Rosendal. Marcus was a bachelor and died childless. Herman, who died four years later, was also a bachelor. The estate passed to their sister Edvardine Reinholdine who was married to Hans Christian Weis, an Århus physician. Edvardine's eldest son, chief surgeon Christian Weiss, inherited the property on her death. He changed his name to Hans Christian Weiss Hoff Rosencrone and moved with his charming wife Dagmar to Rosendal. They were soon popular with the locals. The village finally had a doctor, and one who rarely accepted payment at that. Dagmar even managed to build a gymnasium in the town. During the years they lived on the estate, many of the tenant farmers were able to buy the land their families had been tending for centuries. The couple had no children, so Christian's brother Edward inherited the estate. He too settled at Rosendal and installed indoor plumbing at the castle. He died a bachelor in 1927, and the estate passed to his eldest sister Clara Gædeken, who was the last descendent to own Rosendal. She inherited the property on July 4, 1927 and five days later, she wrote a document giving the entire estate to the University of Oslo

MUSEUM AND CULTURAL CENTER

The Barony Rosendal is now owned by the Weis Rosenkrone Foundation, which is affiliated with the University of Oslo. It is run as a museum and cultural center. In summer, there are daily tours of the formal rooms and living quarters at Rosendal, which remain unchanged since the last owners left in 1927. You can wander through different stylistic periods – rooms that all bear the mark of the different owners over the last 250 years. Then take a walk through the 300-year-old Renaissance garden, with its rose labyrinth and the romantic landscape park designed in the 1850s. At that time, the high white wall surrounding the Renaissance garden was removed and replaced with a large park in the national romantic style to make the grounds more natural. There are regular art exhibitions in the palace wine cellar, concerts in the Yellow and Red Rooms, and theater performances in Borggården. The old Borgstova has been restored, and here you can watch carding, spinning and weaving. In the old kitchen, baking is still done in the fireplace as well as in the ovens. Homemade delicacies, such as milk biscuits, potato cakes and the Baroness' chocolate cake are served in the Thee & Caffe salon in the garden room. You can see a display of carriages used at the barony on special occasions, or go to Husmannsplassen Treo, dating from the 1840s, to see how the tenant farmers on the estate lived and worked. Once you are at Rosendal, you should visit nearby Kvinnherad church, one of Norway's most beautiful mediaeval churches. This stone church was built around 1250 and was once part of the Rosendal estate. The Rosenkrantz family is buried here.

You can also spend the night at the Barony Rosendal, in Rosendal Avlsgård & Fruehus. Marcus Gerhard Hoff-Rosencrone founded Rosendal Avlsgård in the 1850s. It was a model sheep and horse farm and influential in the development of local farming and agricultural methods. In 1875, Rosendal Upper School was founded in the main building on the farm. Classes were subsidized by the estate owner, who taught foreign languages, geography, history, and physics at the school.

Today, Rosendal Avlsgård & Fruehus houses 25 guest bedrooms, where you can spend the night in a unique milieu. The rooms are simply furnished, with iron beds and quaint old furniture. And breakfast, served in the large kitchen, with its open hearth fire and candles, is an experience in itself.

The table is set for a dinner in The Blue Hall, the second floor dining room.

❧ *The Barony Rosendal*

Left: One of the guest rooms in the main building at
Rosendal Avlsgård.

Above:Breakfast at Rosendal Avlsgård is served in the
main kitchen, accompanied by lit candles and a roaring fire.

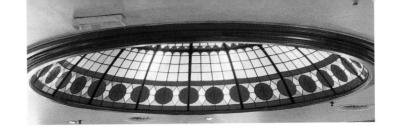

Stavanger's first luxury hotel

Victoria Hotel, Stavanger

The opening of Hotel Victoria
The "Skansen" corporation's hotel, which opened for the public today, was officially dedicated Saturday morning (July 14, 1900) in the presence of more than 100 invited guests, city and local officials, the press, foreign consuls and others.

After a tour through the elegant modern hotel, everyone gathered in the large tastefully decorated dining room for a Champagne toast. As mentioned earlier, all of the more than 70 rooms in the hotel are equipped with electric lights, central heating, an elevator and all modern conveniences as befitting a first-class hotel.

Alongside the dining room are three large salons. Both the large, grand chambers and the smaller ones on the fourth floor are stylishly furnished. The corporation has been able to engage a well-known hotel man, Mr. Patterson, to manage the hotel, so conditions have been made favorable for the success of the establishment.

The cafe on the first floor is unique to Stavanger and deserves a visit. The wall panels have been decorated with paintings by Julius Holck. It will be run by Hansa Cafe.

"Stavanger Amtstidende" newspaper, July 16, 1900

Finally Stavanger had its first luxury hotel! Now it could compete with Bergen and Kristiania for the steadily increasing flow of tourists. This was long before the oil boom, but Stavanger was still a rapidly growing city. Three optimistic men from Bergen were behind the "Skansen" corporation Johan Gustav Nielsen, a master bricklayer; Waldemar Stoud Platou, brewmaster at Christiania Brewery and a founder and director of Hansa Brewery in Bergen; and attorney Hans Bonnevie Angell. They had established "Skansen" to exploit the company's property in Stavanger. The property in question lay on the sound between Kuholmen and the mainland, between Bådegaten and Skansegaten. They had mortgaged six properties to borrow NOK 250 000 to build Stavanger's first luxury hotel. The contractor was Johan Gustav Nielsen, while Henrik Bucher, a Christiania architect, was hired to plan the new hotel. And it was a beauty. Victoia Hotel was the city's

largest brick building at the time, and it was definitely an eye-catcher.

INDUSTRY, TRADE, AND TOURISM
The area between Holmen and Østervåg welcomed anyone coming to Stavanger by sea, especially from nearby Ryfylke, but also increasingly from abroad. Skanse wharf was the center of the import-export trade, and steamships had come to stay.

So with a fantastic location and a routined and experienced hotel manager, Albert Patterson, a Swede, the hotel had to be a success. The target markets were business travelers and tourists.

Commerce flourished in Stavanger, and most of its inhabitants worked either in business or in the relatively new canning industry. Stavanger was becoming one of Norway's leading industrial cities, but it had lagged behind in tourism. Stavanger had established its own tourist association in 1887, which had arranged the first trips to the Lysefjord and coined the name "Prekestolen" (Pulpit Rock) for the cliff which was to become one of Rogaland's greatest tourist attractions. But in order to attract more tourists, the city needed a better quality hotel.

NEW OWNERS AND MORE TOURISTS
Many new owners, and even more hotel managers characterized the first decade at Victoria Hotel. Patterson didn't stay around long. In 1907, Ferdinand Runge bought the hotel, and that began a long stable period. The former owners had rented out the first floor to different businesses, and Runge did the same. It was a good source of guaranteed income. There was a cigar shop, a milk bar, and Victoria Cinema. But the most important tenant was Bennett's travel agency, with its entrance at quayside.

The first fifteen years of the new century saw a slow but steady rise in tourism. The end of the Swedish-Norwegian Union in 1905 followed by the coronation of King Haakon VII brought a marked increase in international tourists. The newly elected king was good publicity for Norway, and Danes were especially

eager to visit the country that had chosen one of their princes to be its king. Another important event that would affect tourism in Norway for years to come took place in 1912, when Stavanger County gave the green light for the trial run of "automobile routes", which the tourist association had been working on for years. The stretch between Sand, Osen, Nesflaten and Røldal was especially important in making Stavanger and Ryfylke more accessible and interesting to visitors. But then came World War I, and the tourism industry ground to a halt in the fall of 1914.

CHRISTIAN BJELLAND, THE CANNERY KING, AND AXEL LUND, THE HOTEL KING

The war may have stopped tourism, but it fueled other industries, including shipping and ship-building, and canning, where Christian Bjelland was king. The Bjelland group of companies consisted of eight canning factories in Stavanger, Skånevik, and Skudneshavn, as well as a sheet metal and paper printing press in Stavanger. In addition, there were warehouses, ice houses and quayside storehouses in Stavanger, a factory in Hamburg, and a fleet of steamships and motorized boats used for herring and sprat fishing. Christian Bjelland was also the city's largest property owner, and in 1916, he was ready to add Victoria Hotel to his property empire. He needed to gather the administration of his far-flung companies under one roof, so he bought the Hotel Victoria to provide them with prime office space. But what was he going to do about the hotel business? Wartime and rationing weren't the best conditions in which to run a profitable hotel, and in addition, the Stavanger city council had just decided to revoke the liquor licenses of every hotel in town.

Alternatives were considered. The Stavanger city council was given the option of renting the hotel, but they declined. Eventually, a consortium of Stavanger men, Torger Soma Iversen, Olaf Kvia, and Thormod Vaaland, took over the management of the hotel. Optimism and drive were no match for war and rationing, fuel shortages, prohibition, and few guests. They were soon forced to give up. Then followed a five-year period with ever-changing owners and management. No light appeared at the end of the tunnel until 1922. Axel Lund, the hotel king, came onto the scene, and that marked the beginning of 30 stable years at Victoria Hotel.

WAR AND PEACE

Danish-born Axel Rosenkrantz de Lassen Lund is now regarded as one of Norway's greatest hotel figures of all time. When he took over Hotel Victoria in 1922, he not only arrived at a bankrupt and dilapidated

Café Leopold serves both Norwegian and international dishes.

hotel, he also came to a city deep in crisis. The ship-building industry was in trouble, there was mass unemployment, social unrest, and prohibition. The fight for a liquor license soon became a nightmare that followed him throughout his time as hotel manager. By the end of the 1920s and well into the 1930s, tourist traffic increased. Norway won almost all the medals at the 1928 St. Moritz Winter Olympics, and that put the country permanently on the tourist map. That same year, the visa requirement between Norway, Finland, and Germany was removed. The tourism association was recognized as a public institution and received state funds, and it changed its name to the National Organization for Tourism in Norway. The Stavanger Tourist Traffic Committee was established 1930 in its wake. Improvements in public communications and the opening of Sola airport in 1938 meant that more and more tourists visited Stavanger. But another war was on the way. The German occupation of Norway in 1940 effectively halted all tourism. Victoria Hotel was requisitioned almost immediately to serve as living quarters for high-ranking German naval personnel.

But the war did bring about one good thing. The Germans completed the Southern railway link connecting Stavanger with Oslo. The post-war years saw rapid growth in the tourism industry in Stavanger, but by then Axel Lund was tired of running the hotel. He had been accused of being a traitor during the war, and even though his case was dismissed, it affected him deeply. There were also rumors that the hotel

would never get a liquor license as long as he was director. In 1952, he gave up and Viste Hotel A/S took over his lease with Christian Bjelland & Co. A/S to run the hotel part of the Victoria building.

RENOVATION AND MODERNIZATION

An extensive renovation and modernization program was immediately implemented. No expenses were spared in making sure that the modern interior harmonized with the Victorian exterior. It was a costly affair, and soon management heads began roll. But Victoria Hotel was an impressive place, and business picked up from the mid-50s. The number of guests increased, and soon many of the first floor tenants moved out, so there was more space for new hotel facilities. Christian W. Bjelland became majority shareholder in 1974. The remaining shares were held by several people, among them the relatively unknown Rudolf Hodne, who took over as board chairman after Christian W. Bjelland.

THE HODNE FAMILY AND VICTORIA HOTEL

Rudolf Hodne has administered the hotel ever since and has turned it into one of the most profitable businesses in Stavanger. He entered the hotel business at about the same time Stavanger entered the oil age. After oil was found at the Ecofisk field in 1969, there was almost a Klondyke atmosphere in the town. Thousands of people from around the world flocked to Stavanger over the next few years to work in the oil industry. This was the age of opportunity for hotel managers, and Rudolf Hodne knew just how to exploit it. He and his wife Ellen Margrethe Smedvig turned the "boarding house at the wharf" into an elegant hotel. They expanded and added more rooms, modernized the interiors and improved the restaurants. Today, Rudolf's son Rolf runs this historic hotel. With its unique location right in the heart of the city, close to the best shopping district and walking distance from the charming old part of town with its low wooden houses and narrow lanes, Victoria Hotel is still the oil city's most exciting hotel.

Mushroom soup

50 g (2 oz) shallots
1 garlic clove
200 g (8 oz)
mushrooms
15 g (1/2 oz)
dried morels
50 g (3 1/2 table-
spoons) unsalted butter
2 dl (1 cup) white wine
2 dl (1 cup) veal stock
1 tablespoon Port wine
1/2 dl (3 1/2 table-
spoons) cognac
1/2 bunch parsley
5 dl (2 cups) whipping
cream
lemon juice
salt, pepper
1/2 tablespoon unsalted
butter
1 tablespoon whipped
cream

Peel and mince the shallots and garlic. Wash the mushrooms and cut into matchstick pieces. Crush the morels. Sauté the shallots and mushrooms in the butter in a stockpot. Add the wine, stock, Port, cognac and parsley. Heat to boiling and simmer until reduced by half. Remove the mushrooms, onion and garlic with a slotted spoon and reserve. Discard the parsley.

Add the cream, heat to boiling and season with lemon juice, salt and pepper. If the soup is too thin, thicken with a little cornstarch stirred into cold water. Just before serving, return the mushrooms, onion and garlic to the stockpot and stir in the remaining butter and cream.

Grilled vegetables
1 red bell pepper
4 asparagus
4 shallots
4 cherry tomatoes
1 zucchini
1/2 eggplant
200 g (7 oz) pumpkin
4 garlic cloves
safflower oil

Garlic potatoes
600 g (1 1/3 lb) potatoes
3 garlic cloves
2 dl (3/4 cup) chopped parsley
salt, pepper
soybean oil

Soy jus
20 garlic cloves
10 shallots
50 g (3 tablespoons) butter
1 liter (quart) veal stock
2 dl (3/4 cup) sweet soy sauce
(ketjap manis) (regular soy
sauce cannot be used in this
dish)

Beef tenderloin
4 filets of beef,
about 180 g (6 oz) each

Victoria's beef tenderloin with grilled vegetables, garlic potatoes and soy jus

Grilled vegetables
Clean the vegetables. Cut the pepper into 8 strips, the asparagus and shallots in half. Halve the zucchini and eggplant lengthwise and slice the pumpkin. Brush a ridged grill pan with oil and grill the vegetables on one side only. Preheat the oven to 170°C (350°F). Transfer the vegetables to an oven tray, drizzle with oil and bake 25 minutes.

Garlic potatoes
Wash and peel the potatoes. Dice and blanch in boiling water. Strain. Peel and crush the garlic. Combine the potatoes, garlic and parsley and season with salt and pepper. Fry in oil until brown on all sides.

Soy jus
Clean, mince and sauté the garlic and shallots in the butter in a saucepan until golden. Add the stock and soy sauce and simmer about 30 minutes. If the jus is too thin, thicken with a little cornstarch stirred into cold water.

Beef tenderloin
Grill or pan-fry the filets about 3 minutes per side.

Crème brûlée with blueberry sorbet

1 vanilla bean
150 g (3/4 cup) sugar
3 dl (1 1/4 cups) full fat milk
3 dl (1 1/4 cups) whipping cream
6 egg yolks
demerara or light brown sugar

Preheat the oven to 90°C (195°F). Split the vanilla bean lengthwise and scrape out the seeds. Combine the sugar, milk, cream and vanilla seeds. Whisk in the egg yolks. Pour into 4 to 6 individual ovenproof dishes. Bake about 90 minutes. Just before serving, preheat the grill. Sprinkle a layer of demerara sugar over the custards and place under the grill until the sugar is bubbly and caramelized.

Blueberry sorbet

5 dl (2 cups) water
400 g (1 3/4 cups) sugar
500 g (1 lb) frozen blueberries
1 egg white

Heat the water and sugar in a saucepan to boiling. Simmer until the sugar is completely dissolved. Puree the berries in a food processor, gradually adding the syrup. Strain. Beat the egg white until stiff and fold into the blueberry mixture. Freeze in an ice cream machine.

A National sanctuary and a protected cultural heritage landscape

Utstein Kloster, Mosterøy

Utstein Kloster is one of Norway's best preserved medieval constructions still in its original setting. It is situated on the sea route between Stavanger and Karmsund.

Below: The colonnade facing east.

Utstein Abbey lies on the north side of Mosterøy island, at the entrance to the Ryfylke fjord system, just 30 minutes by car from Stavanger. Mosterøy, which belongs to a small group of islands in the Boknafjord, now part of Rennesøy county, has been an attractive dwelling place since the bronze age, about 1800 BC. There are remnants of farms dating back to the migration and Viking eras, and there are burial mounds all over the island. Its strategic location on the sea route between Stavanger and Karmsund meant that whoever controlled the island controlled all coastal traffic. Combined with its easily tilled soil and lush grazing pastures, it was the perfect seat for a ruling clan. Utstein is first mentioned in Torbjørn Hornklove's poem about the Battle of Hafrsfjord in 872 AD:

"They wanted to tempt the brave
he who taught them to flee
the chief of the men from the east
he who lives at Utstein. "

Utstein is also mention in <u>Snorre's</u> <u>Sagas</u> <u>of</u> <u>the</u> <u>Norse</u> <u>Kings</u>. He tells us that King Harald Hårfagre spent part of his old age at Utstein. We don't know how this royal residence looked, but it probably lay at the site of Utstein Abbey today. The construction of what was supposed to be a royal residence in stone, but instead became a monastery, was probably begun by Magnus Lagabøter, who was given Rygjafylke as a fiefdom in 1257 and crowned king shortly thereafter. In March, 1264, he received word that his father, Håkon Håkonsen, had died in the Orkney Islands, and therefore Magnus settled in the royal residence in

Bergen as the absolute monarch. He no longer had use for a royal residence at Utstein and therefore it is likely that he gave the property to the Augustinian monks at Olav Abbey in Stavanger. The monks finished the building and dedicated it to the popular Roman martyr, St. Laurentius.

MONASTERY LIFE

The first monks probably came from Great Britain, France, and Denmark, and at most, there were probably 20 or 30 monks at Utstein. There were twice as many lay brothers and servants. The Augustinians were the scholars of their day. There was strict discipline, and they were not allowed to partake in manual labor. Instead they looked after the spiritual and physical health of the local population. They functioned as doctors, and sick people were brought to the monastery, where they lived in a hospice. The Augustinian monks are credited with establishing the first fruit orchards in Norway. They imported fruit trees and herbs from other European monasteries. Daily life at the abbey was always the same. One-third of the day was spent working. The monks spread the word of God, studied, practiced medicine and copied manuscripts. The also cultivated medicinal herbs and plants used to make ink and dye for their colorful manuscripts. The lay brothers looked after the fruit, vegetable, hemp, and linen crops. Mass was held every three hours from 2 in the morning until 9 at night, so one-third of the day was spent in prayer, and the last third was used for resting. The monks did not suffer. Utstein was a wealthy monastery, and it has been estimated that Utstein's income could feed

250 people. The monastery owned 150 properties in Rogaland and Sunnhordland, and all of these paid a tithe in the form of either meat, grain, butter, or other products to Utstein. But the great plague at the end of the 14th century brought hard times for both the country and the church. A large proportion of the population died from the epidemics, and with fewer people, the abbey's income was also reduced.

In addition, Utstein was brutally plundered and twice destroyed by fire. In 1515, there was a bitter feud between the Stavanger Bishop Hoskold and Abbot Henrik at Utstein. The bishop's men forced their way into the monastery and the abbot was beaten, bound, and taken to Stavanger, where he languished in jail for 100 days. In the meantime, the bishop and his men returned to Utstein, where they abused the monks and plundered the monastery before setting it alight.

A ROYAL ESTATE AND A MANOR HOUSE WITH ITS OWN PERSONAL GHOST

After the Reformation in 1537, Utstein monastery was turned over to the Danish king. The number of monks was gradually reduced, and just two years later, in the spring of 1539, Christoffer Trondsson Rustung went to Utstein with 60 men, plundered the monastery and burned it to the ground once more. The buildings were left in ruins for a number of years before they were restored. During its time as a crowned estate, which lasted until 1665, Utstein was lent to nine lords in succession. Only a few of them actually visited Utstein, and only one, Erik Urne, actually left his mark there. At the beginning of the 17th century, he had the buildings repaired and he installed the lovely renaissance interior in the choir of the abbey church, part of which remains to this day.

In 1665, the estate was sold to five Danish noblemen, but none of them ever settled at Utstein. Instead, they hired managers and tenants to run the farm, and in 1700, they allowed Johan Frimann to take over the property. Now it was in Norwegian hands, and today, it is still in the same family. His daughter, Karen married a Bergen man, Johan Garmann. Their son Christopher moved to Utstein in 1749 and was appointed tax collector for Ryfylke in 1750, when he took over all the abbey property with the exception of the church which had been sold in 1724. A refined man and a good musician, he was an active and engaged squire and immediately began renovating and adding on to what eventually became the main building on the estate. He imported a special breed of sheep from Scotland to improve the local breeds and he established spinneries in Stavanger to process wool which earlier had been exported as raw material. He even published a pamphlet about improving wool-quality in sheep. When a syphilis epidemic raged over the area, Christopher Garmann organized nursing help.

He married three times, first to Wenche von der Lippe. When his second wife, Cecilia Catharina Widding was on her deathbed, she asked Christopher to vow never to remarry. Twenty years later, he broke that vow. On February 9, 1779, as he was standing before the altar in Stavanger Cathedral with 36-year-younger Helene Kamstrup, Cecilia appeared before him. He died eight days later. He was buried under the floor of the abbey church, and since that time, Cecilia Catharina Widding has wandered restlessly through the eastern wing in a long white shroud.

FROM A MANOR HOUSE TO A MUSEUM AND AN INN

At the time of Christopher Garmann's death, the estate was saddled with debt. It was sold at auction, but the family was able to buy much of it back. The buildings stood empty until his son Johan married the following year. When he died, his children were too young to inherit, so the farm was run by a manager until his son, also called Johan, could take over. When this Johan Garmann died in 1849, the farm was divided between his sons Christopher and Børre. Utstein was still a large farm with 113 cows, 300 sheep and 24 horses. After some years, Christopher sold his share to his brother. Børre ran the farm well, and like his great-grandfather, he was especially interested in sheep husbandry and became a leader in the field. In 1875, he adopted his aunt's grandson, 16-year-old Eilert Gerhard Schanche, and in 1885, Børre transferred ownership of the estate to him. Eilert Gerhard Schanche had studied at Aas Agricultural College and was an excellent farmer, who won many prizes at fairs and agricultural exhibitions. He was also a public figure, eventually becoming both mayor and a member of parliament. Eventually, he settled in Kristiania, and his sons Børre and Eilert ran the farm from 1910 to 1919, when Eilert bought out his brother's heirs and became sole owner. But there were financial problems. In 1933, he sold the abbey and the garden within its walls to Rennesøy Savings Bank. In 1935, the "Committee for the Preservation of Utstein Abbey" was allowed to purchase the bankrupt estate from the bank for NOK 37 500. The rest of the farm remained in family hands, and Eilert's grandson, another Eilert, later developed the land into a model farm. His daughter Elin now runs the farm.

The first archeological investigations of the abbey were made in 1859 by architect Chr. Christie on behalf of the Norwegian Association for the Preservation of Ancient Monuments. The church choir was restored just after the turn of the century, and

✤ *Utstein Kloster*

architect Gerhard Fischer's investigations in the 1930s were the basis for the large-scale restoration that began in the 1950s. Norway's only remaining monastery from the Middle Ages was reopened by King Olav in 1965.

Today the abbey is run by the "Utstein Abbey Foundation", which was established in 1953 to re-build and manage the monastery as national monu-ment. Utstein Abbey is a national sanctuary, and the land surrounding it is protected as a part of Norway's national heritage. The beautiful old abbey church is used for religious services, weddings, and concerts, and there are tours of the church and the rest of the abbey most of the year. The property is now run as a seminar and conference center for organizations, companies and institutions. Banquets are held in the refectory, the monks' dining hall, where a genuine medieval dinner is served. There are 19 pleasantly but spartanly furnished guest bedrooms, as is only ap-propriate in an old Augustinian monastery, where the monks lived their pious and simple lives.

Left: The monks at Utstein belonged to the Augustinian order. They gave the chapel its unique shape. The only similar church known is the original Augustinian church at Inchcolm Abbey near of Edinburgh.

Above: The dining room was formerly the monk's old refectory and sitting room in the western wing and dates from the 1630s.

Right: The main hall was the building's showpiece. The velour wallpaper is a late baroque copy. The table is a copy of a 17th-century English table, while the black baroque chairs date from around 1700 and are original inventory from Utstein. The portraits of Christopher Garmann (1720-79) and his second wife, Cecilie Widding (1734-59), were copied from originals owned by the Schanche family.

Medieval Menu

This medieval menu has been updated to include ingredients readily available at the supermarket, rather than the wild roots and herbs originally used.

Spring soup
(inspired by a recipe from 1746)

2 onions
2 parsnips
1 liter (quart) water
5 dl (2 cups) frozen peas
1 small iceberg lettuce
1 bunch arugula
1 bunch chervil
2 tablespoons chopped parsley
50 g (3 1/2 tablespoons) butter
1 tablespoon salt
2 egg yolks
4 teaspoons creme fraiche or
dairy sour cream

Peel and chop the onion and parsnips and simmer in the water until tender, about 20 minutes. Add the peas and simmer 10 minutes more. Puree the lettuce, arugula, chervil and parsley in a blender or food processor and add to the soup about 2 minutes before serving. Beat in the butter in pats with the salt. Whisk in the egg yolks just before serving. Do not allow the soup to boil after the egg yolks have been added. Beat until frothy with an immersion blender. Place a teaspoon of creme fraiche in each bowl. Pour over the soup and serve immediately.

Above: The courtyard at the abbey.

Hotpot

Boiled beef and chicken on a bed of root vegetable puree (after a recipe from 1668)

400 g (14 oz) bottom round of beef
1 stewing chicken
1 tablespoon salt
2 onions
3 carrots
8 potatoes
1 dl (1/2 cup) milk
2 tablespoons butter
1/2 teaspoon salt
1/2 teaspoon pepper
flat leaf parsley

Divide the beef into four pieces of equal size. Quarter the chicken. Place in a stockpot with the salt, add water to cover, and simmer 2 hours. Peel the onions, carrots and potatoes and cut into chunks. Cook with the meat for the last 30 minutes, until tender. Transfer the vegetables to another pot and mash, adding milk, butter, salt and pepper. Reduce the cooking liquid until about 3 dl (1 1/4 cups) remain.

Place a mound of vegetable puree in the middle of each plate. Top with chicken and beef. Serve with the concentrated cooking liquid.

Apple tart with nutmeg cream

(inspired by a recipe from 1770)

2 puff pastry sheets (about 8 oz), defrosted
1 orange
3 apples
6 tablespoons sugar
grated zest and juice of 1/2 lemon
1 teaspoon ground cloves
1 1/2 dl (2/3 cup) whipping cream
1 egg yolk
1/2 teaspoon ground nutmeg

Preheat the oven to 200°C (400°F). Halve each sheet of pastry, place on a baking sheet and bake 10 to 15 minutes.

Slice the orange and place in a saucepan with a little water, cover and simmer 10 minutes. Press as much juice as possible from the orange slices and strain. Peel, core and slice the apples. Place in a saucepan with the sugar, lemon zest and juice and cloves and simmer 5 to 10 minutes.

Whip the cream and stir in the egg yolk and nutmeg.

Divide the puff pastry squares in half and arrange on plates. Top with apple compote, whipped cream and the remaining pastry.

A monument to the history of a town

GamlaVærket Gjæstgiveri & Tracteringssted, Sandnes

It was the blue clay, or Sandnes clay as it was called, that laid the foundation for the brick and pottery factories in Sandnes. The clay, formed during the last ice-age, was everywhere. The creeks teemed with clay, forming steep slopes of blue clay, almost ready to mold.

It just lay there waiting to be used until the 1780s, when 10 local government officials and businessmen decided to back Lauritz Smith Pettersen's plans to build a brick factory. Smith Pettersen, born in April, 1742, felt that the blue clay was the perfect raw material for bricks. And there seemed to be an endless supply. The local powers felt that this was a good way to use local resources.

One official was 23-year-old Peter Ulrich Benzon of Copenhagen. He had just been appointed Stavanger County governor. Chamberman Benzon had good connections with the administration of King Christian VII and made sure that the application was reviewed. It was a long, but fruitful wait. "Exclusive privilege for Lauritz Smith Petersen of Stavanger to open a brick and tile works in Sandnes."

The letter was signed and dated Christiansborg Royal Residence, Copenhagen, April 28, 1782, and bore the seal and signature of the king. Smith Petersen designed the factory after a Danish model. Sandnes brick factory started production in 1783. "GamlaVærket" (the old factory), as it was called, was the first industrial business in the area. The largest share holder, the first chairman of the board, and the first accountant was Chamberlain Benzon.

Making bricks and roof tiles wasn't an easy job. The clay mill was horse-powered, while everything else was done manually.

It wasn't until 1852 that another factory was established in the area, the Gravaren brick factory in Sandnes. More soon followed: Altona in 1856, Ullendal in 1860, Nynæs and Ganns in 1873, and Lura brick works in 1900. There were seven brick and tile factories in all, producing bricks, cooking pans, drain pipes, and weights for fishing nets.

THE POTTERS ARRIVE IN SANDNES

In addition to the brick factories, Sandnes also had a couple of large and a number of small potteries. In 1794, "GamlaVærket" was expanded to include a pottery, with Swedish potter Christopher Zimmermann. This was the beginning of Sandnes' rich potting history. Zimmermann was an accomplished potter, and stoneware glazes were his specialty. But he kept his technique a secret, telling only his son, Hermann Christopher Zimmermann, who inherited the business from his father in 1812. For the next 10 years, Zimmermann ran the business together with Ole Pottemaker Idland, and they were later joined by Simon Pottemaker Haustveit from Hardanger. Simon set out on his own in 1842 and spent the next 80 years building the Simonsen concern with five pottery factories in Sandnes and one in Sweden.

Another important potter was "The Old Master" Jacob Lund of Trondheim. During his 40 years in Sandnes, he was a source of invaluable expertise and inspiration from the potting traditions of his native region. Sandnes' potting industry was blossoming. New factories were springing up all over the place, but Ganns Pottery and Brickworks, founded in 1873, and Graverens Pottery, established in 1926, were to be the most important. They produced a wide

assortment of inexpensive, yet high quality items. Brown clay dishes, chamber pots, spittoons, jugs and other simply decorated household items brought them international fame. Other potteries soon followed, producing thousands of different items.

Today, there's almost nothing left of the Sandnes potting industry, for many reasons: Increased competition from practical modern glass and plastic products. Modern food products, refrigerators, and freezers have eliminated the need for salting, pickling and juice-making, so people don't need stoneware jugs and containers. Last, but not least, it became increasingly difficult to compete with cheap imported ceramics from southern and eastern Europe.

The kilns were left to cool in the 1960s, but no one doubted that it was the clay-rich Sandnes earth that had transformed the town from a glorified wharf to one of the ten largest cities in Norway.

GamlaVærket Gjæstgiveri and Tracteringssted evolves

Anders Christensen, a Dane, was 29 when he arrived in Norway in 1986. After opening several popular bars, he started looking for premises in which to develop a new restaurant and hotel. That was in 1994. He was lucky enough to secure a really old building in the center of Sandnes, right by the railroad station and the main shopping street.

Now that he had the building, all he needed was a concept. He found that by reading the book Sandnæs History 1860-1910.

"There is great uncertainty among the local population of Sandnes as to when the first brick factory was established, and even less is known of when and why the potteries came." wrote M.A. Gude, a local historian.

Anders's curiosity was aroused, and he threw himself into studying the history of the old brick factories and potteries. The more he read, the more certain he became. This was an interesting and important topic that deserved to be rediscovered. Why not recreate the old "Gamla-Værket" on his premises? If he intended to do it, he would do it thoroughly and properly. He decided to gather as much information about old business and production methods as possible. That was no easy task! Little to nothing of the town's history regarding these industries had been recorded, and many of the old factories and potteries had been torn down and replaced with modern concrete buildings. Even the local museum had little to offer, and Anders soon understood that he had to go farther afield.

He took many study trips, concentrating on Sweden and Denmark. There were still some Danish brickworks from the end of the 19th century, and the buildings remained, even if production had ceased long ago. It was still possible to see their operating and production methods. Eventually, the concept started to take shape. He bought old machines and equipment, and soon Gamla-Værket started to rise once again.

An exciting hotel

GamlaVærket Gjæstegiveri and Tracteringssted is one of Norway's most exiting and unique hotels. It shows a cross section of Sandnes's local history, and the interiors have been recreated so realistically, that most guests assume that it really was once a functioning brick factory. Everything has been recreated down to the smallest detail. The hotel brochure is written in archaic Norwegian, using all the superlatives of the age.

All the hotel employees are "brickworkers", the waiters are "carriers", the chef is a "kiln master", the domestic staff are "fashioners", and Anders Christensen is the "factory manager". The different dishes on the menu are named after the people and families that founded the different factories. Dishes such as "Chamberlain and Governor Benzon's tempting delicacies", and "Mrs. Lauritz Smith Petersen's seductive delights."

The food at GamlaVærket Gjæstgiveri and Tracteringssted is an exciting experience in itself. Anders Christensen wanted the hotel and restaurant to be equal partners. He was one of the first to believe that national and regional food traditions should be preserved, and GamlaVærket's kitchen serves traditional local dishes with a contemporary urban touch.

The atmosphere at GamlaVærket is reminiscent of a Danish inn. That's not at all surprising, considering that a Dane started it all and is still the "factory manager". It's a success, at any rate, and Christensen's

most recent additions are an artisan bakery with in-house production and sales, and a traditional coffee house. There's lots of activity at the old Sandnes brick factory.

Left: GamlaVærket Gjæstgiveri and Tracteringssted is known for its excellent kitchen. You can even buy some of their products to take home.

Below: "The Pottery" was established in 1998 with the help of one of Sandnes' oldest and most skilled potters, Ingvar Lund. Today, it is a living workshop right in the middle of the hotel. Here potter Mette Jensen produces the original clay pieces that made Sandnes famous.

Ister

Ister
1 kilo (2 1/4 lb) suet
5 tablespoons salt
1 teaspoon pepper

Chop the suet into small pieces and place in a saucepan. Melt until golden. Strain and discard the rind. Season with salt and pepper. Store in the refrigerator. Ister tastes better than butter on coarse rye bread served with herring.

Coarse rye crispbread

Coarse rye crispbread
50 g fresh (1 3/4 oz) yeast
(2 packets US dry)
1 liter (quart) lukewarm water
4 teaspoons salt
5 teaspoons caraway seed
15 dl (6 1/4 cups) coarse
rye flour
15 dl (6 1/4 cups)
all-purpose flour

Dissolve the yeast in the water. Stir in the remaining ingredients, mixing well. Refrigerate one hour. Roll out to thin rectangular sheets. Preheat the oven to 180°C (350°F). Bake 15 minutes.

Sandnæs herring

Sandnæs herring
3 1/3 dl (1 1/3 cups) water
2 dl (3/4 cup) vinegar
325 g (1 2/3 cups) sugar
1 teaspoon pickling spice
1 kilo (2 1/4 lb) presoaked
herring fillets
1 medium red onion
2-3 bay leaves

Place the first four ingredients in a saucepan and heat to boiling. Cool. Cut the herring into bite-size pieces and thinly slice the onion. Add to the brine with the bay leaves. Pour into jars, close tightly, and store in the refrigerator.

Exotic curried herring

Exotic curried herring
70 g (1/2 cup) diced
cucumber
35 g (1/4 cup) diced
white radish
1 1/4 dl (1/2 cup) mayonnaise
3/4 dl (1/3 cup) vinegar
1 tablespoon curry powder
1 hard-cooked egg,
finely chopped
minced lovage or celeriac
1 kilo (2 1/4 lb) presoaked
herring fillets

Combine all the ingredients except the herring. Cut the herring into bite-size pieces and carefully fold into the mixture. Pour into jars, close tightly, and store in the refrigerator.

Dalsnuten herring

Dalsnuten herring
3 1/3 dl (1 1/3 cups) water
2 dl (3/4 cup) vinegar
325 g (1 2/3 cups) sugar
1 teaspoon pickling spice
1 small onion, minced
2 dried birch shoots
3-4 tablespoons lingonberries
(or chopped cranberries)
2-3 tablespoons blueberries
1 kilo (2 1/4 lb) presoaked
herring fillets

Place the first four ingredients in a large saucepan and heat to boiling. Cool. Add the remaining ingredients except the herring. Cut the herring into bite-size pieces and carefully fold into the brine. Pour into jars, close tightly, and store in the refrigerator.

"The Molding Room" Clay good such as bricks and roof tiles were produced here. Today, the room houses a cozy and intimate restaurant.

Lamb ribs – our specialty

*1 1/2 kilo (3 1/4 lb) smoked
and dried lamb ribs
1 garlic, divided into
cloves, unpeeled
Dijon mustard*

Cole slaw
*1/2 dl (1/4 cup) light sour cream
1/2 dl (1/4 cup) mayonnaise
2 tablespoons Dijon mustard
salt, pepper
500 g (1 lb) cabbage,
finely shredded
50 g (2 oz) red cabbage,
finely shredded
1 medium carrot,
finely shredded*

Divide the ribs into serving portions. Place on a rack with the garlic cloves in a large stockpot. Add water just up to the rack. It should not touch the meat. Heat to boiling, cover, lower the heat and steam the meat for 2 to 2 1/2 hours. Dry the meat in a 60°C (140°F) oven for 2 hours. Increase the oven temperature to 180°C (350°F) and roast the ribs about 12 minutes. Remove the meat from the oven and preheat the grill. Spread the meat with mustard. Place under the grill until the mustard bubbles and the ribs are crispy.

Cole slaw
Combine the first five ingredients. Stir in the cabbage and carrot. 6 servings.

Jær bitters

*– fortifying spirits from
Jæderen*

*3 bottles Hammer Vodka 40%
3 cinnamon sticks
5 tablespoons wormword
2 tablespoons St. John's wort
1 tablespoon black peppercorns
1 tablespoon bitter orange peel
1 star anise
4 whole cloves
1 1/2 dl (2/3 cup) sugar syrup
(made of equal parts
sugar and water)
2 dl (3/4 cup) water*

Combine the vodka with the spices in a large jar with a tight lid. Shake the mixture twice a day for four days. Taste, then adjust the flavor with sugar syrup and water. Strain through a coffee filter. Fill into bottles with tight lids.

Mrs. Tronæs' chocolate cake

1 liter (quart) orange juice
3 star anise
400 g (14 oz) semi-sweet chocolate
250 g (9 oz) unsalted butter
1 1/2 teaspoons instant coffee
8 eggs
300 g (1 1/2 cups) sugar
100 g (3/4 cup) all-purpose flour
110 g (1 cup) walnuts, coarsely chopped
90 g (3 oz) semi-sweet chocolate, chopped
grated zest of 1 orange

Combine the juice and star anise in a saucepan, heat to boiling and reduce to 1 dl (scant 1/2 cup). Preheat the oven to 160°C (325°F). Grease and flour a 26 cm (10") springform pan. Melt the chocolate, butter and coffee in the reduced orange juice. Beat the eggs and sugar until light, thick and lemon-colored. Add alternately with the flour to the chocolate mixture. Stir in the nuts, chocolate and orange zest. Pour into the prepared pan. Bake 30 minutes. Cool completely on a rack. Frost with chocolate ganache.

Chocolate ganache

5 dl (2 cups) orange juice
1 1/2 star anise
375 g (13 1/2 oz) semi-sweet chocolate
2 1/2 dl (1 cup) unsalted butter
Cointreau or other orange liqueur

Combine the juice and star anise in a saucepan, heat to boiling and reduce to 1/2 dl (scant 1/4 cup). Melt the chocolate, cream and butter in the reduced orange juice. Add Cointreau to taste. Spread over the cake.

Four old houses and a lot of drive

Sogndalstrand Kulturhotell, Sogndalstrand, Hauge in Dalane

The picturesque coastal village of Sogndalstrand lies just south of Egersund. Sogndalstrand used to be one of Norway's most important trading centers and had a customs office as early as 1645. The markets for fish, trade and shipping grew rapidly during the 16th century and Sogndalstrand was given special trade status in 1798. Sogndalstrand traded extensively in Europe, concentrating on fish, shellfish, herring, and timber.

Fish has always been an important commodity in coastal areas. Herring was the main catch, but it was rivaled by cod from the 1750s onward. 29 000 barrels of herring were caught in 1837, an all-time record. The 1850s and 60s saw the beginning of drift net fishing for mackerel, as well as the building of several ice huts. Lobster was exported to England and Germany. There was also the salmon- rich Sokna River, which entered the sea at Sogndalstrand. 763 salmon, with an average weight of 6 kilo, were caught in the river in 1886.

Sogndalstrand experienced its "age of greatness" during the 19th century and was awarded township status in 1848. Fishing was the most important industry, with shipping and trade following closely behind. In 1845, 20 local families owned a total of 17 small ships and sailing vessels, all with grand names, such as "The Test of Luck", "Hope", "Freedom", and "the 17th of May" (Norway's Constitution day). In the 1870s, Sogndalstrand was added as a stop on the Oslo-Trondheim steamship route. At that time, its population totaled 526, mainly sailors and fishermen, but also civil servants, craftsmen, and tradesmen. Trade blossomed and the township included 20 shops, 4 bakeries, 2 liquor stores, 4 pubs, a customs office, a sheriff, a doctor, a midwife, a post office, and a telegraph office.

But Sogndalstrand was not immune from modern changes and soon it experienced centralization, depopulation, industrialization, and modern transportation methods. In 1944, the township was expanded with surrounding areas to create a larger township – Sokndal Township with its seat in Hauge in Dalane.

SOGNDALSTRAND TODAY

Today Sogndalstrand has 80 inhabitants, and there is little in this sleepy idyllic village to remind us of its former glory. The Norwegian Central Office of Historic Monuments has temporarily declared the old town a national preservation area. Many of the whitewashed houses along the narrow streets now serve as summer homes, and some have been turned into nostalgic shops. Fru Hansen's Snurrepiperier is an antique shop selling everything from old records to paintings and furniture, while Gallery Rosengren offers art and unusual souvenirs. Kjelleren sells antiques and gift items, and Madame Kielland's Country Store sells almost everything – including coffee and homemade cakes. These unusual shops are popular with the tourists, and there are more and more of those in Sogndalstrand these days. Increasingly, people are discovering this idyllic, charming town, and Eli Laupstad Omdal's Sogndalstrand Culture Hotel has given them added incentive.

A HOTEL IS FOUNDED

It all started in 1993, when Eli and Jan Oddvar Omdal moved to France for a year. Both are Francophiles, and they rented a house in Angles on the Bay of Biscay. There they planned to spend the year enjoying the best France had to offer. While there, they noticed how good the French were at looking after, restoring and using their old houses, as well as upholding old traditions. Maybe they could do something with the old houses in Sogndalstrand. After she returned home, she started to discuss opening a summer cafe with some of her friends. They rented "Krambua", an old country store dating back to 1862, where they served cake and coffee, ice cream and soda, as well as fish chowder, during the summer of 1994. The latter, a traditional Norwegian fish soup Eli had composed to serve to French dinner guests, became the specialty of the house. The recipe is a well-kept secret.

When summer ended, none of Eli's friends wanted to continue the cafe. They all had regular jobs, even Eli, who was a sports and activities organizer for Egersund Township. But she still had faith in her cafe. If they could do so well in just one summer, surely they should continue the business. The Omdals decided to rent the same locale for a longer period and reopened the cafe on a permanent basis in December, 1994. In the beginning, it was open only on weekends, and at times it was difficult to make ends meet, but they did not give up. They wanted to prove that this could work.

As word of the cafe spread, business picked up. Occasionally people would ask about hotels in the area. When the old tailor's house, built in 1831, was put up for sale in 1995, Eli and Jon Oddvar bought it, and soon they could offer four hotel rooms. But four wasn't much. Demand far outstripped supply, so when the local town hall came up for sale, the couple jumped at the chance. It had been built in 1897, when Sogndalstrand was still an independent township and it was financed with taxes from liquor, among other things. Over the years, it had housed a library, bank, post office, prison, apartments, and a polling station. Eli and Jan Oddvar started fixing and restoring it to make it as authentic as possible. The building's age should show, but the rooms had to be modern and comfortable, with good beds and nice bathrooms. There was room for nine bedrooms as well as a conference center, and even a pub in the old cellar that was once the town jail. No criminals ever sat behind bars here, but it did house the local

Sogndalstrand was designated a coastal town (without urban status) in 1798. From about 1850 to 1900, it was a bustling place.

Sogndalstrand Culture Hotel can look toward a bright future. Eli and Jon Oddvar have managed to create the hotel they always wanted, a different hotel – a unique hotel, where guests are greeted on the steps – welcome to a very special hotel, one with soul, warmth, charm, and atmosphere.

Left: These charming guest bedrooms have a nostalgic ambience, but with all modern conveniences.

Below: The old trading atmosphere of bygone days has been recreated at Sogndalstrand. You can buy almost anything at Madam Kielland's Landhandel.

Right: "The General Store" is the hotel restaurant.

drunks, those who were brought in to sleep it off. Local girls used to bring food to the prisoners. This could lead to all sorts of different things, as this poem on one of the walls tells us:

"Oh my dear girl, don't say no
You know that I really love you
I love you like the sun
But in a week I'm off to Poland."

IF ONLY THESE WALLS COULD TALK, WHAT STORIES THEY COULD TELL

Eli and Jan Oddvar's next project is restoring the old bakery from 1923 to provide five more bedrooms. The demand for rooms still outstrips the supply, as more and more people discover Sogndalstrand. Some come to enjoy the peace and quiet of the surrounding area, some come for the unique setting, but more and more come to fish salmon in the Sokna river. The Sokna is rich in salmon thanks to the efforts of the local regional commissioner.

Dessert pancakes

1 teaspoon baking soda
5 dl (2 1/4 cups) buttermilk
4 eggs
2 1/2 dl (1 cup) sugar
4 3/4 dl (2 cups) all-purpose flour
butter

Stir the soda into the buttermilk. Add the remaining ingredients and let the batter rest at room temperature for 10 minutes. Fry the pancakes in butter on a griddle or in a frying pan. Turn the pancakes when the batter begins to bubble. Serve with sour cream and jam. 8 large pancakes.

A dream comes true

Skipperhuset Seng & Mat, Rasvåg, Hidra

"How beautiful you smile on a summer day
Flying seagulls, flag waving on high,
Butterflies dancing over a flowering meadow,
Birds singing their jubilant song;
Hidra. Hidra,
Rustling through windswept trees,
Inviting paths, green meadows
Holms and skerries"
From Hidra Song by Olav Omland

Every night as Leif Waage Larsen steered his ship
through exotic waters, he longed to go back to Hidra,
his childhood summer home. His roots were in a
white house at Rasvåg on the island of Hidra, where
his great-great-grandfather had lived, and where both
his father and grandfather had been born. He had
spent most of his life abroad, but he had told his sons
about the old house and the three generations of captains it had borne. But it wasn't just the story of a
house and a family. It was the story of tough
Norwegian sailors and adventurers, of French mademoiselles, of courage, love, and war. It was just like a
fairy tale, and Leif's thoughts again drifted back to
Hidra, to Norway, to where it all started.

There were once two brothers who lived in houses by
the sea on one of the smaller outer islands beyond
Hidra, the largest island in West Agder county in
southern Norway. It was a tough and lonely life, and
in the middle of the 19th century, they decided to
move to Hidra itself. They chose a quiet inlet at
Rasvåg. From here they could look out over their beloved sea. They moved the houses in 1850. The
brothers were Lars Andreas and Lars Christian
Larsen, Leif's great-great-grandfather, and it was thus

that both his grandfather and his father, Leif Joseph
Larsen were born in the house at Rasvåg.

While Leif Joseph was still a child, Nicolay Waage
from Våge in Rasvåg went to Copenhagen to study
business. After finishing his studies, he moved to
Paris to work in shipping. There he met his French
wife, Charlotte and they had a daughter, Raymonde
Georgette Waage.

Every summer the family vacationed on Hidra. Thus
Raymonde Georgette knew the island well and became good friends with Leif Josef. Time passed. Raymonde Georgette and her parents divided their time
between Paris, where the family shipping business
had its office, and Dunkirk, where her father was the
Norwegian consul. Meanwhile, Leif Josef had trained
as a ship's mate and sailed the seven seas. One day he
sailed into Dunkirk and there was Raymonde
Georgette. He was 35 and she was 23. Their childhood friendship quickly developed into an intense
romance and they were married in the Dunkirk
Norwegian Seamen's Church in 1935. Two years
later, they moved to Oslo. Leif Josef continued to sail
abroad leaving his young wife at home.

Then World War II broke out. Raymonde Georgette
was in Oslo, lonely and scared as the German troops
marched past her window. Her husband's ship was in
Bergen loading cargo when the war broke out. He
managed to steal away and set sail across the Atlantic
Ocean to the United States. Both Raymonde
Georgette and his employer, Øivind Lorentzen
Shipping, thought he was still in Bergen.

Right: What tastes better than newly cooked crab eaten outside on a beautiful summer evening?

Below: Grethe and Leif Waage Larsen turned the old family house by the dock into a unique guesthouse and restaurant.

They soon found out that he had escaped. Raymonde Georgette was ready to move heaven and earth to get out of occupied Norway, where she felt isolated and alone. Her parents were still in France, and her Norwegian wasn't good. She obtained false papers and managed to cross the border into Sweden, where she worked as a housemaid while she waited for the right opportunity. She needed to get to America. She knew that her husband had landed in New York, and that he was working as an underwriter for NOTRA SHIP, a shipping company created by a pool of Norwegian ship owners to run Norwegian shipping abroad for the duration of the war. Its headquarters was in New York, and its director was shipowner Øivind Lorentzen, Leif Josef's peacetime boss.

Late one night, Raymonde Georgette was awakened late and told to get dressed. She was taken to an airstrip outside of Stockholm, where an airplane was waiting. Then she and a high-ranking English officer were flown to England. Once there, she had wait for a ship that could take her to New York. Finally that opportunity came in the summer of 1943. She was thrilled to see her husband again, so thrilled that little Leif was born exactly nine months later.

The family remained in America until the end of the war, when they moved back to Oslo. But they still spent every summer with Leif's aunt in the old skipper's house at Rasvåg, where Leif had spent the happiest times of his life.

There was no use dwelling on old memories. It gets you nowhere. Maybe this was where the adventure would end, Leif thought as he looked out over the seas that he had sailed for so many years. Or maybe he could stop dreaming and actually move into the skipper's house and become the fourth generation to live there.

A WANDERING LIFE

Leif had always loved the sea. He wished to follow in his family's footsteps and went to sea at 16. He gradually ascended the ranks and finished as a first officer on a large cargo vessel servicing South America. He was in Norway taking his skipper's exam when he met the love of his life, Grethe Jensen, who was working at the shipping company's Oslo office. They were married in 1971 in Buenos Aires. A year later, Leif got a job as port captain representative for a Norwegian shipping line in the United States. First they lived in New York, then in Miami, where their first son Erik was born, and finally New Orleans where their second son Alex was born. When the shipping company went bankrupt in 1984, Leif lost his job. He

had been lucky enough to inherit the skipper's house on Hidra, so he moved Grethe and the boys there. He went out to sea again. He started working for Norwegian Cruise Lines as a mate and gradually rose through the ranks to staff captain. He grounded himself in 1989, when he accepted a job as director of maritime operations at Renaissance Cruises in Fort Lauderdale, where he stayed for two years. He then accepted a job with Willhelmsen Shipping in Saudi Arabia, and the whole family moved there in 1991.

THE SKIPPER'S HOUSE BECOMES A BED AND BREAKFAST

His term in Saudi Arabia ended in 1993, and Leif was once more without a job. He was beginning to tire of the nomadic life and felt that it was time to turn his dream into a reality. Leif and Grethe had been contemplating their retirement plans for some time. They had discussed moving back to Hidra and turning the old skipper's house into a bed and breakfast. But why wait until they were old? Why not do it now?

They gathered up all their belongings and moved back to Norway. They renovated the 150-year-old house, dock, and warehouse. They opened their bed and breakfast in March, 1994. They were a bit insecure, but gave the plan six months before they made any final decisions. At the end of the trial period, they realized that they loved running the bed and breakfast, and they loved working together. They carved out a routine and stuck with it. They both loved to cook, and each had special areas. Grethe was responsible for baked goods and desserts, while Leif took care of starters and main courses. Grethe, who had studied business, was in charge of buying supplies and keeping the books, as well all cleaning and setting the table. Leif was in charge of maintaining the buildings, garden, and boats, as well as ordering and collecting supplies. Gutting and cleaning fish was also his domain, as was the wine cellar.

Grethe and Leif love their work. Skipperhuset is one of Norway's most charming and intimate bed and breakfasts. The service is excellent, and the food, a mix of international and local dishes, is delicious. In keeping with their surroundings, they serve a lot of fish and shellfish, but these Norwegian ingredients are prepared with a French touch. Just like the interior of the house – an eclectic mix of French and Norwegian antiques. And if the walls could talk, they'd tell stories of tough Norwegian sailors, of adventures. Of brave French mademoiselles, of courage, love, and war.

Above: The many small rooms at Skipperhuset have been turned into private dining rooms. Here you can enjoy a romantic dinner for two while looking out over the spectacular view and the calm sea.

Right: The beautiful rooms have been decorated with furniture and antiques collected by generations of sea captains sailing the seven seas.

Skipperhuset's fish chowder

Fish stock

2 liters (quarts) water
green part of 1 leek
1 carrot
parsley stalks
a little peel or greens
from a celeriac
1 bay leaf
1 horseradish leaf (optional)
10 black peppercorns
2 kilo (4 1/2 lb) small coley
or other white fish

Vegetables

1 carrot
1 potatoes
1 small leek
1 1/2 kg (3 lb) haddock or cod
1 1/4 dl (1/2 cup) chopped chives

Soup

35 g (2 tablespoons) butter
35 g (1/4 cup) all-purpose flour
7 1/2 dl (3 cups) boiling fish stock
2 1/2 dl (1 cup) full-fat milk
1 dl (1/2 cup) whipping cream

The secret with this soup is the fish stock, butter, cream and fresh fish, plus lots of chives.

Place all ingredients except the fish in a stockpot and heat to boiling. Simmer while cleaning the fish.

Clean and scale the fish. Remove the eyes and gills. Use a fish brush along the backbone to remove any membrane and blood. This is important to keep the stock clear. Cut the fish into pieces and add to the vegetable stock. Lower the heat and cook at a slow simmer for 25 minutes. Strain.

Vegetables and fish

Wash and peel the vegetables. Dice the carrot and potatoes, slice the leek. Clean and fillet the fish. Cut into 4 pieces of equal size. Cook the vegetables and the fish separately in lightly salted water until just tender, about 5 minutes. Just before serving, stir the vegetables into the soup. To serve, pour soup into heated bowls. Top with fish. Sprinkle 2 tablespoons finely chopped chives over each bowl to form a green layer over the soup.

Soup

Melt the butter and stir in the flour. Let sizzle for 30 seconds, stirring constantly. Whisk in the liquid. Simmer for 15 minutes, stirring constantly.

Braised endive

4-6 large endive
2 tablespoons butter or meat juices
1 teaspoon salt
white pepper
1 tablespoon fine breadcrumbs

Preheat the oven to 200°C (400°F). Clean and rinse the endive. Blanch in boiling water 5 minutes. Grease an ovenproof dish and place the endive close together (do not drain after blanching). Dot with butter and sprinkle with salt and pepper. Bake 15 minutes, until tender. Spoon butter/meat juices over the endive. Increase the oven temperature to 250°C (475°F). Sprinkle with crumbs and bake until light brown, maximum 5 minutes. 4 to 6 servings. This dish is good with lamb.

French chocolate cake

250 g (9 oz) bittersweet chocolate
250 g (9 oz) unsalted butter
2 1/2 dl (1 cup) sugar
1 3/4 dl (3/4 cup) all-purpose flour
1 teaspoon vanilla sugar
(or 2 teaspoons vanilla essence)
2 tablespoons Cointreau or orange juice
grated zest of 1 orange
4 eggs, separated

Preheat the oven to 180°C (350°F). Grease a 24 cm (9") springform pan. Melt the chocolate with the butter. Add the sugar, flour, vanilla, Cointreau, orange zest and egg yolks, mixing well. Beat the egg whites into stiff peaks, then fold into the chocolate mixture. Pour into the prepared pan and bake 30 minutes. The cake should be completely cool before glazing

Chocolate glaze
125 g (4 1/2 oz) bittersweet chocolate
1 dl (scant 1/2 cup) whipping cream
peanuts

Melt the chocolate with the cream. Remove from the heat and let cool for about 5 minutes. Whisk the mixture lightly, then spread over the cake. Garnish with peanuts.

A different kind of vacation
Holmen Gård, Gjerstad

Courses in making teddy bears, traditional regional costumes and knives. Courses in Hardanger embroidery, patchwork, felt, coloring cloth with natural dyes, restoration of rustic furniture, upholstery, spinning, traditional wood painting, kayak building, birch bark braiding….

These are just some of the innumerable course offered at traditional Holmen Gård (farm). This impressive old estate is owned by the Norwegian Art and Crafts Association, a nationwide interest group whose goal is to preserve Norwegian traditional arts and crafts and to teach us old techniques.

There are many activities at Holmen Farm. In addition to the numerous course, there are summer and Christmas craft fairs. The farm also houses Norway's largest permanent collection of knives, as well as ever changing arts and crafts exhibitions. They also host "hands-on vacations" with courses for both children and adults, as well as "theme weeks", such as "Celebrating a Traditional Christmas" where guests learn all about traditional Christmas food, decorations, and customs. Similar activities are arranged at Easter, along with trips to art galleries and other local attractions.

But you can stay at Holmen without taking any courses or participating in any activities. It is important cultural attraction all on its own, and its beautiful surroundings help make it the perfect holiday destination. The 200-year-old farm, which consists of several red buildings clustered around a central courtyard, is listed as a national historic monument. The whole scene is peaceful and pleasing, but if the walls could talk….

"AN IMPRESSIVE LOG DWELLING"

In the beginning of the 19th century, Trydal farm in Gjerstad township was divided between two brothers, Ola and Nils. Nils moved a couple of hundred meters up the stream from the main farm to Holmen. Local farmers let their pigs roam freely in the marshy landscape over the summer, so the place became known as Svineholmen. It was here that Nils Gislesen Trydal founded what is now Holmen Gård. He built a grand house, which the local parish log describes as "an impressive log dwelling." The two- story-high building has a wide hallway connecting the two rooms in the eastern with the two in the western wings. The second story also houses two rooms in the eastern wing, but there was only one large room in the western wing, known as the hall. It contains several beds lined with curtains to ensure complete privacy and darkness. The house itself was built of logs clad in wood paneling, and painted red. Nils also built a storage house, a cow shed, stables and a barn.

CONSULS, FORESTERS, AND WHOLESALERS

The Trydal family owned Holmen Gård until 1885, when it was sold to Consul J.W.P. Prebensen from Risør. For many years, he owned the largest business

in Risør, and he also dealt in timber and shipping. In 1884, he had bought many small forest holdings around Gjerstad. Holmen Gård became the seat of Consul Prebensen's real estate holdings, and it was here his family spent the summer months. He respected the old building traditions and changed very little, but he did buy local antiques and old furniture for the main building. He was very interested in the farm and initiated the first large scale timber planting in the area, over 22 acres. He also drained 12 acres of marsh for crops, and added new outbuildings.

In 1911, the farm was sold to Consul Axel Heiberg, who gave it to his daughter Ingeborg Fearnley and her husband, Nils Young Fearnley, in 1915. In 1918, they built a two-story manager's house, and during WWI, Ingeborg brought the old Bjorvasstova from Bjorvatn in Vegårdshei. This building, dating from 1720 and richly decorated by Salve Torjussen Flaten, was moved to Holmen in 1920-1 and reconstructed as an addition to the original main building on the farm.

In 1932, Holmen was sold to Henrik Harboe, and wholesalers Emil Steen and Nicolai Eger. Now the farm covered 20 000 acres in Gjerstad and 12 500 acres in Treungen townships. A the same time, the new owners bought Søndeled yard in order to gain access to a seaport from which to ship timber. To make transportation easier, they built a log slide of impregnated wood stretching from Vinterstø to Lundevann, a stretch of 1800 meters. It was opened in 1933. They also built a saw mill at Vallemoen, which employed 30 laborers during the summer season.

THE GOVERNMENT TAKES OVER
In 1956, the owners wished to sell the estate to an interested party, but the government demanded the right to preempt the sale. The land was leased, the main house stood empty, and the farm buildings soon began to decay.

Fifteen years later, the Aust-Agder County Museum was notified that they could take over Bjorvasstua. The other building was to be demolished and the land sold off. But the county curator did not feel that Bjorvasstua could survive another move, and halted those plans. But something had to be done. Bjorvasstua and the main building were definitely worth preserving, but the buildings were deteriorating so fast that something had to be done.

In 1973 the Norwegian Arts and Crafts Association received an offer from the Directorate of State Forests. For the sum of NOK 1600, they could purchase Holmen Gård, the immediate surrounding land, and its historical contents. The price was low, but they were still skeptical. Would they be able to -

restore the buildings properly? Could they afford to do the job? They set up a commission to evaluate the need for a course and conference center for arts and crafts enthusiasts, and after careful consideration, they decided to go ahead with the plan. They accepted the offer on June 28, 1976, and started renovating immediately.

HOLMEN GÅRD TODAY
The following weeks were hectic. The local inhabitants formed the society "Friends of Holmen Gård", and started cleaning the farm with the help of members of the Norwegian Arts and Crafts Association. Things with no value were removed, the houses were washed and painted, and basic repairs were done. The main house, the servants' quarters, the manager's house, and the storehouse were listed as heritage buildings. The barn was also designated as "worthy of preservation", but it was so neglected that it had to be partially rebuilt. The Central Office of Historic Monuments, the Norwegian Cultural Council, Aust-Agder county, and Gjerstad township have all helped to restore Holmen farm to its former glory. Little has changed in the main building and Bjorvasstua. The beautiful sitting rooms and unique guest bedrooms have changed little since 1921. The manager's house also contains comfortable and unique guest bedrooms, while the barn houses a smithy, a crafts center, a textile and wood workshop, as well as a show room, a shop, and a cozy restaurant that serves traditional cuisine based on local recipes. Now the Holmen Gård Foundation runs the hotel and welcomes people here to enjoy a different type of vacation.

Holmen farm is now owned by the Norwegian Home Crafts Association and is run by the Holmen Gård Foundation. It is filled with beautiful antiques and examples of Norway's rich arts and crafts heritage, which is brought alive in exhibitions and courses, where you can see, experience, and learn.

Holmen Gård's Christmas platter

Pork ribs
1 1/2 kilo (3 lb)
fresh bacon on the bone,
with the rind
salt, pepper
3-4 dl (1 1/2 cups)
water

Pork sausage
800 g (1 3/4 lb) finely-
ground pork ring sausage
1 liter /quart) water
4-5 peppercorns
1 bay leaf

Sausage patties
500 g (1 1/4 lb)
ground pork
1 1/4 tablespoons potato
starch or cornstarch
1 1/2 teaspoons salt
1/2 teaspoons pepper
1/2 teaspoons ginger
2 – 2 1/2 dl (up to 1
cup) full-fat milk
margarine

Pickled cabbage
1 kilo (2 1/4 lb) cabbage
2 teaspoons
caraway seed
1 1/2 teaspoons vinegar
2 teaspoons sugar
4-5 dl (1 1/2-2 cups)
water
2 teaspoons salt
2-3 tablespoons butter

Lingonberry compote
1 kilo (2 1/4 lb)
lingonberries
6-7 dl (2 1/2 cups) sugar
vanilla sugar (optional)

Preheat the oven to 200°C (400°F). Score the rind and rub with salt and pepper. (This can be done several days before roasting, so that the flavor will penetrate the meat). Place the meat in an oven tray, rind side down, add 1/2 dl (1/4 cup) water and cover with aluminum foil. Place the pan on the floor of the oven and let it steam for 20 to 25 minutes. Reduce the heat to 175°C (350°F). Remove the foil and transfer the meat, rind side up, to a rack over the oven tray. Roast in the lower part of the oven about 1 1/2 hours, adding water as necessary. For crispy rind, turn on the oven grill and place the meat just under the grill with the door slightly open for the last 10 to 15 minutes of the roasting time. Do not allow the rind to burn. Let the meat rest a few minutes before serving.

Pork sausage
Rinse the sausage. Bring the water and seasonings to a boil. Add the sausage, cover and simmer over low heat about 20 minutes. Do not allow the water to boil or the sausage might burst.

Sausage patties
Stir the meat a little, then add starch and seasonings. Gradually add the milk, kneading the mixture well. Make a small "trial" patty and fry. Adjust the seasoning. Form into patties and fry in margarine over medium heat until well-done.

Pickled cabbage
Clean and rinse the cabbage. Cut into quarters and remove the core. Shred and layer with the caraway seed in a stockpot. Combine the vinegar, sugar and water and pour over the cabbage, then add the salt and butter. Bring to a boil, cover and simmer over low heat for 1 to 2 hours. Red cabbage can also be used in this recipe. Use 800 g (1 3/4 lb) red cabbage and increase the sugar to 1 tablespoon.

Lingonberry compote
Clean and rinse the berries. Mix with sugar (and vanilla sugar) in an electric mixer until light and frothy. This fresh berry compote doesn't keep as well as a cooked compote, but it tastes so much better.

Rice cream with red sauce

5 dl (2 cups) rice porridge
2 dl (3/4 cup) whipping cream
2-3 tablespoons sugar
2 teaspoons vanilla sugar or 1 teaspoon vanilla extract

Most people make rice porridge for the holidays and leftover porridge can be made into this dessert. Whip the cream with the sugar and vanilla sugar. Fold into the porridge. Rice cream is not supposed to be too thick. Serve with red berry sauce and chopped almonds or walnuts.

Red berry sauce
4 dl (1 1/3 cups) raspberry juice
(or a cranberry juice blend)
2 teaspoons potato starch or cornstarch
stirred into 1 tablespoon cold water

Bring the juice to a boil. Stir in the starch mixture and cook until thickened.

Room in the heart....

LifjellStua, Bø in Telemark

Clear sunny days, expanses of white and long ski afternoons followed by crispy waffles and hot chocolate at LifjellStua…These are some of Per Ove Bakke's favorite childhood memories. They lingered on long after he grew up and moved to the capital. He often thought about the idyllic mountain lodge, 800 meters above sea level, at the top of Lifjell in Bø in Telemark. What if he could buy it….

His dream came true in March, 1996, when Per Ove and his wife Anemone Wille Våge bought the old yellow mountain lodge built by Skien Grenland Tourist Association in 1957. For the first 15 to 20 years, it was run as a tourist lodge, later as a hotel. Now it was dilapidated and in dire need of rehabilitation, both inside and outside.

Anemone and Per Ove agreed that they wanted to create a cozy hotel where people could relax and enjoy themselves. They did not want to turn the old lodge into an ordinary hotel. They wanted their guests to feel like they were visiting friends. They wanted to create an intimate atmosphere with a unique interior, and with that in mind, they went to work. Their budget was limited, so Amemone's background in interior design came to good use. The exterior was stripped of its yellow paint, then stained brown. They added a turf roof, painted the windowsills red and the shutters, with their decoratively carved hearts, were painted white. They also built a 60 square meter terrace and installed a whirlpool bath where guests can enjoy a cognac after dinner, or just loosen stiff muscles after a long day on skis.

Inside they wanted to create a unique interior while preserving some of the simplicity of a Norwegian mountain lodge. The sanded the wooden floors and stained them dark brown. They left the walls in the sitting areas as they were, with only the patina of age, while they painted the walls in the corridors and guest rooms. The furniture is a wonderful combination of rustic farm antiques, comfortable European furniture, and the occasional Indian piece.

But the details give LifjellStua its special character. Countless candles. Masses of fresh flowers. Aromatic potpourri in jars and bowls. Tired old teddybears, with the odd new bear mixed in. Delicate textiles, soft pillows, and large, cozy blankets. Meter upon meter of books. Shelves and tables piled with travel, food, and interior magazines. Beautiful porcelain and rustic stoneware, old and new harmonizing together. Hearts in all shapes and sizes, from the heart-shaped candies in the bowl on the front desk to the hearty welcome that greets you as you arrive at LifjellStua – a different kind of lodge decorated in the English country style in the middle of the Norwegian mountains.

ACTIVITIES AND EXPERIENCES

There are all kinds of activities year-round at LifjellStua. The adventurous can try gorge walking, camping, rafting, canoeing, waterfall ab-sailing, mountain climbing, snow rafting, and ice climbing. How about a beaver safari, dog sledding, ice-fishing, or sleigh riding? The mountains are just outside the door, waiting to be explored on foot or on skis. It's easy to reach 1300 meters, and there is a simple cabin for spending the night only a two-and-a-half-hour walk from LifjellStua. There is an alpine center with a range of activities for adults and children near the hotel. Hunting and fishing trips can also be arranged.

If you want to stay in shape, you can visit Gullbring Cultural Center, just 20 kilometers from the hotel, where there's a swimming pool, a climbing wall, and a gym.

Bø Sommarland, Norway's largest water and entertainment park with more than 100 different activities, is only 10 kilometers away. You'll never be bored here.

A culture tour on the Telemark Canal aboard MS "Viktoria" is a must. When the Telemark Canal, also called the "fast route" between Norway's eastern and western coasts was opened in 1892, it was heralded as the "eighth wonder". It took 500 men five years to blast through the mountains. It had 18 locks over the 105-kilometer route between Skien and Dalen, with a difference in height of 72 meters.

And after a long and active day, there is nothing better than to return to LifjellStua – to hot chocolate and Grandmother Anne's hot dessert pancakes.

Above: This cozy hallway leads to the bedrooms.

Right: The owners' friendly dogs, Emma and Murdoch, will gladly keep you company.

Right page: From the moment you enter, you know this is no ordinary mountain lodge. Anemone Wille Våge has used her keen eye for detail to create a highly personal and homey atmosphere at Lifjellstua.

Following page: The sitting room is filled with comfortable furnishings.

274　　　🌿 Lifjellstua

Juniper and aquavit marinated salmon with Thai dressing

Juniper and aquavit marinated salmon

1 large whole fillet of salmon, skin on
6 tablespoons salt
4 tablespoons (1/4 cup) sugar
10-12 juniper berries, crushed
1 dl (1/2 cup) aquavit
2-3 rosemary branches

Remove any small bones from the salmon. Place the fish in a glass dish, skin side down. Combine the salt, sugar and juniper and sprinkle over the salmon. Drizzle with aquavit. Chop the rosemary and sprinkle over the salmon. Cover with plastic wrap and refrigerate 72 hours, turning the salmon daily.

Thai dressing

1 large garlic clove
chunk of fresh ginger the same size as the garlic
1 1/4 dl (1/2 cup) soy sauce
1 1/4 dl (1/2 cup) oyster sauce
1 1/4 dl (1/2 cup) sweet soy sauce (kecap manis)
(regular soy sauce does not work in this recipe)

Peel and mince the garlic and ginger. Combine with the remaining ingredients.

lime juice
salt, pepper
shredded lettuce

Thinly slice the salmon and arrange the pieces to cover each plate in a single thin layer. Combine the lime juice, salt and pepper and brush on the salmon. Top with lettuce and drizzle a tablespoon of dressing all around. 12 servings.

Grandmother Anna's pancakes

2 eggs
4 dl (1 1/2 cups) cultured buttermilk
5 dl (2 cups) sifted all-purpose flour
2 dl (3/4 cup) sugar
1/2 teaspoon baking soda
1 1/2 teaspoons baking powder
butter

Whisk the eggs and buttermilk together. Whisk in all the remaining ingredients except the butter and let the batter rest about 30 minutes. Fry small pancakes in a little butter on a warm griddle or non-stick frying pan. Serve with butter and cheese or sour cream and jam.

Breast of ptarmigan with barley risotto, potato-celeriac puree, mushroom sauce and snow peas

Mushroom sauce
This sauce can be prepared a day in advance.
100 g (3 1/2 oz) dried porcini mushrooms
butter
1 1/2 dl (2/3 cup) ptarmigan stock
5 dl (2 cups) whipping cream
salt, pepper
1/2 teaspoon cornstarch dissolved in
1 teaspoon cold water

Soak the mushrooms in a generous amount of water overnight. Rinse under cold running water until completely free of sand. It is important to rinse the mushrooms by hand to remove sand and other impurities. Sauté the mushrooms in a little butter in a saucepan. Add the stock and cream and reduce by half. Season with salt and pepper and thicken with cornstarch, if necessary.

Ptarmigan breasts
Preheat the oven to 180°C (350°F). Sprinkle the ptarmigan breasts with salt and pepper and brown them quickly in oil. Transfer to a roasting pan and add ptarmigan stock until the breasts are completely covered. Roast for 6 to 8 minutes. Remove and wrap in foil. Let rest 5 minutes before slicing.

Snow peas
5 dl (2 cups) water
1 tablespoon butter
2 teaspoons salt
200 g (8 oz) snow peas

Heat the water, butter and salt to boiling. Add the peas and boil about 20 seconds.

Make a mound of potato-celeriac puree in the middle of each plate. Top with snow peas and barley risotto. Ladle the mushroom sauce all around. Slice the ptarmigan breasts lengthwise and lean them against the risotto. 6 servings.

Read the entire recipe carefully before beginning

6 ptarmigan
50 g (2 oz) chunk celeriac
1 onion
2 carrots
oil
salt, pepper

Carve out the breasts of the ptarmigans, pack in plastic wrap and refrigerate until later. Use the carcasses for stock. Peel and cut the vegetables into chunks. Brown the carcasses and vegetables in a little oil in a large stockpot. Add water to 3 cm (1 1/4") over the bones. Heat to boiling and skim well.

Reduce the heat and simmer 30 minutes. Skim frequently for a clearer stock. Partially remove the pot from the heat and simmer the stock for 3 hours. Strain, then return to the heat and reduce to slightly less than half the original amount. Do not reduce too much or it will be bitter.

Barley risotto
200 g (1 cup) pearl barley
olive oil
5 dl (2 cups) chicken stock

Barley risotto
Sauté the barley in a little warm olive oil in a saucepan. Gradually add the stock and boil for 22 minutes.

Potato-celeriac puree
200 g (8 oz) almond potatoes or other waxy potatoes
200 g (8 oz) celeriac
1/2 dl (1/4 cup) whipping cream
2 tablespoons butter
salt, pepper

Potato-celeriac puree
Peel the potatoes and celeriac. Cut both into chunks and boil in separate saucepans until tender. Drain, then return the saucepans to the heat so any remaining water can evaporate. Mash each well, then combine. Add the cream and butter, using an electric mixer, if desired, for a fine puree. Season with salt and pepper.

French apple cake with cardamom cream

French apple cake
2 dl (3/4 cup) sugar
2 tablespoons butter
8 tart apples, such as Granny Smith
1 puff pastry sheet (about 100 g/4 oz)

Preheat the oven to 150°C (300°F). Caramelize half the sugar in a deep non-stick ovenproof frying pan around 20 cm (8") in diameter until golden. Remove the pan from the heat. Peel, core and halve the apples. Cut each half into three wedges of equal size. Place the apple wedges in the pan. Begin at the edge, pressing the broad side of the wedges against the edge. Repeat until the bottom of the pan is completely covered with apple. Place the apple wedges close together, because they shrink while baking. Return the pan to the heat until the apples are caramelized on the bottom. Add the remaining sugar and dot with butter. Bake 15 minutes, but drain off accumulated juices   several times. Roll out the puff pastry to a thin sheet. Remove the pan from the oven and top with puff pastry. Press down the edges. Prick with a fork. Return to the oven and bake 8 to 10 more minutes.

Cardamom cream
1 1/2 dl (2/3 cup) whipping cream
3 tablespoons sugar
1 teaspoon crushed green cardamom seeds
1 dl (1/2 cup) creme fraiche
(or full-fat natural sour cream)

Place the cream, sugar and cardamom in a saucepan and heat to boiling. Reduce the heat and let simmer for a few minutes. Strain off the seeds and let cool. Whip the cream fraiche until almost stiff. Fold into the cream.

Serve the cake warm with cardamom cream alongside.

Telemark's best kept secret

Austbø Hotel, Rauland

Above: There's a fantastic view of Tansvatn lake, forest-covered hills, open countryside, and powerful mountain peaks from Austbø Hotel.

Below: Tone Helgetveit and Geir Midtbø run an untraditional mountain hotel in one of Norway's most traditional areas, Rauland in Telemark. The couple are interested in art and are passionate collectors of modern art.

Right: The interior of Austbø Hotel is simple and classic. The light and airy rooms are filled with sleek furniture, beautiful antiques, and modern art.

The mountain village of Rauland is known for its beauty. Located by the Hardanger plateau and surrounded by mountains and lakes, it is nature at its most wild and rugged, with high peaks more than 1400 meters above sea level, rambling terrain, and thick forests. Rauland, in Vinje township, is known for its cultural heritage, art, and literature. The impressive scenery has supported the community throughout the ages and inspired many local traditions. Few places in Norway can boast as many protected and culturally important buildings as Rauland, where innumerable farms and buildings date back to the Middle Ages. The locals are proud of their village, and rightly so. They work at keeping local building styles, crafts, and folk art alive.

Rauland is also a popular year-round tourist destination. A stable inland climate and large quantities of snow make it a favorite with skiers. There are miles of marked cross-country ski tracks, as well as many downhill slopes with different degrees of difficulty. There's as much to do in summer as in winter. There are walking trails, handicraft courses, day trips, boat and canoe rental, museum and gallery visits, riding, hunting, fishing, and mushroom and berry picking, to name just a few.

Austbø hotel is just outside Rauland, between Kongsberg and Åmot. At first glance, it is not at all impressive - an anonymous brown wooden building with a discreet brass plaque by the door. That's the outside. The inside soon reveals that the journey was worth it! It doesn't take long to realize that this is an unusual hotel.

Owners Tone and Geir Midtbø are on hand to greet you. The reception area, dining room, and sitting rooms are large and airy. The interior is classic and

spare. Most of the furniture was designed by the renowned designer Alf Sture especially for Austbø Hotel. Sture also helped select the colors, which form a quiet and harmonious background for the hotel's unique art collection. It includes many famous names such as Per Barclay, Olav Christopher Jenssen, Inger Sitter, Jan Groth, Anne Kathrine Dolven, Bård Breivik, Ian McKeever, Richard Artschwager, Jon Anton Risan, and Hedy Lothringen. Modern art is the Midtbø family passion. Their interest in art was nurtured by one of their former guests. The now deceased Ingeleiv Rugstad owned several galleries around Norway. Whenever she moved her exhibition from eastern to western Norway she spent the night at Austbø hotel. After all the other guests had retired for the night, she brought her pictures in for the Midtbøs to admire and study. Tone and Geir appreciated this and soon became interested enough in modern art to acquire some of their own.

There are no old landscape paintings at Austbø hotel, nor are there any other local scenes. They don't feel the need for them. Just look out the panoramic window if you want to see nature at its finest. The view will take your breath away. There's Transvatn Lake, forest clad hills, broad meadows and mighty mountain peaks, the best nature has to offer.

Inside you'll find an antique table piled high with art books and magazines, and the antique cupboards are filled with vintage Norwegian decorative arts. It's an eclectic mix of classic designer furniture, modern art, and rural antiques, which, along with the roaring fire and the glow of a multitude of candles, creates a cozy, homey atmosphere. The hotel reflects the personal taste of Tone and Geir Midtbø, and the way they feel a hotel should be run.

Above: This beautiful shelf holds the hosts' collection of Norwegian stoneware and faience.

SMALL IS GOOD

Knut and Aslak Svalastog built Austbø hotel in 1939. It was called Rauland Mountain Lodge and was run as a traditional mountain lodge until 1969, when a new wing was built. It now houses most of the guest bedrooms. This new wing changed the hotel's status. Ensuite bathrooms had transformed the lodge into a hotel.

The Svalastog brothers ran the lodge until the middle of the 1950s. Then there was a succession of new owners until Tove and Geir Midtbø took it over in 1977. Tove had spent most summers in Rauland as a child, and this was the fulfillment of a childhood dream. But she was no amateur - she had a Swiss degree in hotel and restaurant management. Geir, who also had a degree in hotel and restaurant management, hailed from Oslo. It took little to convince him of the hotel's potential, and soon a complete renovation was underway. The hotel was run down, and it needed new electrical, water, and sewage systems. They also had grand expansion plans. They wanted to build a wing with 30 new bedrooms, but these plans were soon scrapped. The guests seemed to appreciate a small hotel, and why should they go with the flow? So they decided to improve what they already had instead of expanding. They wanted to run a cozy and atmospheric hotel, a hotel that was just as enjoyable for them to run as it was for the guests to visit. So while other hotels were building indoor swimming pools, hot tubs and discos, Tone bought knitting needles and crochet hooks just in case the guests lost theirs.

It was a conscious choice. Tone and Geir are both extroverts. They love to interact with their guests, and they love to look after them. This is evident throughout the hotel, but especially in the food. Eating at Austbø is an experience in itself. They have managed to give their dishes an identity to match the distinctiveness of the hotel. They combine traditional Norwegian ingredients with a touch of French elegance. Dinner always consists of four courses, and in summer there is the added treat of a cold table with fresh salads, exciting cheeses and fresh bread.

One visit to Austbø hotel and you're hooked. You'll keep on coming back just like all their regular guests. Austbø hotel is definitely worth a visit. The only thing you'll wonder is why you didn't visit it sooner.

You can enjoy French-inspired international dishes made with the best Norwegian ingredients in the hotel dining room.

Baked turbot with spinach sauce and sautéed vegetables

1 turbot (1 1/4 kg – 2 1/2 lb)
2 tablespoons butter

Sautéed vegetables
50 g (2 oz) carrot
50 g (2 oz) zucchini
50 g (2 oz) leek
50 g (2 oz) broccoli
50 g (2 oz) cauliflower
50 g (2 oz) red bell pepper
50 g (2 oz) red onion
3 tablespoons olive oil
3 tablespoons water
salt, pepper

Potatoes
600 g (1 1/3 lb) almond or
other small waxy potatoes

Spinach sauce
2 shallots
1 tablespoon olive oil
100 g (4 oz) fresh
spinach leaves (no stalks)
1/2 dl (1/4 cup) dry
white wine
1/2 dl (1/4 cup) fish stock
1 1/2 dl (2/3 cup)
whipping cream
50 g (3 tablespoons) soft
unsalted butter
salt, pepper
4 lemon wedges

Preheat the oven to 180°C (350°F). Clean the fish. Cut off the head, tail and fins for stock. Cut the fish into triangular serving pieces and brown them in butter on both sides. Bake for 15 minutes, dark side up.

Sautéed vegetables
Clean and cut the vegetables into small chunks. Sauté in olive oil for one minute. Add the water, cover and steam for 2 minutes, until the vegetables are crisp-tender. Sprinkle with salt and pepper.

Potatoes
Peel and cook the potatoes in lightly salted water for 15-18 minutes, depending upon the size.

Spinach sauce
Mince and sauté the shallot in the oil in a saucepan. Rinse and chop the spinach. Sauté with the shallot for 1 minute. Add the wine and stock and reduce by 2/3. Add the cream and reduce by half. Pour into a blender along with the butter and blend until smooth. Return to the saucepan, heat carefully and season with salt and pepper. Just before serving, beat with an immersion blender until frothy.

To serve, arrange the vegetables in the center of each plate. Top with fish, dark side up. Arrange the potatoes behind the fish and spoon spinach sauce on the rest of the plate. Garnish with a lemon wedge and fresh herbs.

Variation: Other kinds of fish can be used in this dish, either in slices or fillets, both poached and fried. Another variation, which is especially beautiful, is to use fresh beets instead of spinach in the sauce.

Potato soup with foie gras

4 medium potatoes
2 shallots
1 leek
2 tablespoons olive oil
6 dl (2 1/2 cups) chicken or
vegetable stock
1 dl (1/2 cup) whipping cream
salt, pepper
4 slices duck or goose foie gras

Peel and dice the potatoes and shallots. Rinse and slice the leek. Heat the oil in a stockpot and sauté the potatoes, shallots and leek until shiny. Add the stock and simmer until the potatoes are tender. Pour into a blender and puree until smooth. Return to the stockpot, whisk in the cream and season with salt and pepper.

To serve, place a slice of paté in each heated soup bowl. Beat the soup with an immersion blender until frothy and carefully pour it around the paté. The soup should not cover the paté. It should just reach up to the edges. Garnish with fresh herbs.

Note: The starch content in potatoes can vary. Add additional stock if the soup is too thick. If the soup is too thin, boil another potato and puree it with the soup before adding the cream. It is also possible to serve the soup without the foie gras. Garnish with a spoonful of sour cream instead.

Rice pudding with raspberry coulis and vanilla cream

Rice pudding
7 1/2 dl (3 cups) full-fat milk
75 g (1 dl, scant 1/2 cup) round-grain rice
40 g (3-4 tablespoons) sugar
1 teaspoon vanilla sugar
or 1/2 teaspoon vanilla extract
1/2 teaspoon cinnamon
pinch salt

Raspberry coulis
150 g (5 oz) fresh or frozen raspberries
50 g (1/4 cup) sugar
1-2 teaspoons Cointreau (if desired)

Vanilla cream
1/2 vanilla bean
1 1/2 dl (2/3 cup) whipping cream
50 g (1/4 cup) sugar

Rice pudding
Preheat the oven to 140°C (275°F). Scald the milk and cool completely. Combine all ingredients and pour into a greased 1-1 1/2 liter ovenproof dish. Bake 2 1/2 hours.

Raspberry coulis
Place the berries and sugar in a food processor and puree until smooth. Sieve. Just before serving, whisk until frothy.

Vanilla cream
Split the vanilla bean lengthwise and scrape out the seeds. Whip the cream with the sugar and vanilla.

Serve the pudding warm in the serving dish with a pitcher of coulis and a bowl of cream. Just before serving, sift a little confectioner's sugar over the pudding.

From a sanitarium to a mountain hotel

Tuddal Høyfjellshotell, Tuddal

From the middle of the 19th century, many sanitariums were built in Norwegian mountains and valleys. The big city bourgeoisie experienced a sudden wave of health awareness and nature-worshipping and outdoor living reached almost cult status. But Norwegians weren't alone in visiting these institutions. Typhus epidemics raged over Europe, and many Germans and Englishmen chose to visit clean and untouched Norwegian sanitariums instead of those in central and southern Europe. There was also a wide-spread fear of tuberculosis among a population that had previously felt well- protected against the disease. People were convinced that fresh and clean air at high altitudes could cure tuberculosis, which made Norwegian sanitariums very appealing.

But the sanitariums weren't medical establishments. Most of them were vacation hotels, much like Swiss alpine hotels and German spas.

At the end of the 1880s, people from Sauland and Tuddal toyed with the idea of building a combined sanitarium and tourist hotel in Kovstulheia, 850 meters above sea level – in the heart of Telemark. Members of the Skien-Thelemark Tourist Society visited the area to check out locations. In spring of the following year, invitations were sent out to prospective shareholders in the planned establishment. NOK 20 000 was needed, and one of the driving forces was Heiberg Lexow, the local vicar. Unfortunately, there was little interest, and the idea was scrapped. But it didn't take long for new plans to appear. Now the driving force was a lawyer, Emil Roll, one of Norway's foremost ski enthusiasts and as head of the "Society to Promote Skiing", the man behind the Holmenkollen Medal. Roll was one of

many who left the big city and settled in the country at the end of the 19th century. One day on his way over the mountain from Tinn, he was completely captivated by the view over Kovstulheia. This was the perfect site for his sanitarium, surrounded by glittering mountain lakes, scattered evergreen forest, and majestic mountains.

He met Heiberg Lexow on the way down and told him all about his plans. The vicar was very enthusiastic. He hadn't been scared off by the unsuccessful attempt to raise capital a few years earlier, and he gladly joined Roll in his plans.

CELEBRITY SHAREHOLDERS

In 1892, the lawyer and the vicar bought three mountain farms comprising nine buildings at Kovstulheia and several thousand acres of mountain terrain. This time they were more realistic and detailed in their plans, and in 1893, they invited people to invest in a "sanitarium at Kovstulheien". They estimated capital needs at NOK 100 000, because building a 25-room hotel high up in the mountains without a road connection was not easy. First they had to build a five-kilometer-long road up from Tuddal town center, and they needed to lay a telephone line from Saudal, 27 kilometers away. But finding investors proved no easier this time than last time. But they did manage to attract some investors with the promise of enticing views and a seven-month season. By March 2, 1894, Tuddal Mountain Sanitarium Company was a reality. They had faith in their project, even though they hadn't managed to reach their minimum capital level of NOK 60 000. There were 82 stockholders in total, and many were local businessmen and large-scale

Tuddal has its own fire truck in case of emergency.

farmers. The lawyer and the vicar each bought six shares. Most of the shareholders, however, were wealthy citizens of Christiania, and the largest shareholder was Conrad Langaard, owner of a tobacco company. Gunnar Knudsen, later Norway's' prime minister, was also a shareholder.

ITS OWN SMALL SOCIETY

The sanitarium welcomed its first guests on July 15, 1894. The road was finally finished, having been delayed for two weeks in May because of a snow storm. That probably should have served as a warning, because communications problems would make running the hotel very difficult for many years.

The telephone system was in order. Work on the main building was just starting, but a tourist cabin, a storage house with five bedrooms, and a mountain hut were already finished. There was even a fish hatchery. They had bought 12 cows and had hired a shepherd and shepherdess. The sanitarium was going to be self-sufficient in meat, fish, and milk. They hired Mathilde Pettersøn, an economist from Buskerud hospital with work experience from Scotland, to manage the establishment.

The first season was not a success. Rain and all the construction work scared the guests away. They earned NOK 429.17, and almost half of that came from the dairy. But the owners persevered. They built a bakery and a barn, and the main building was finished on June 15, 1895. But that year was also a fiasco, despite Roll's proclamation that Tuddal was "the" fashionable place for Christiania's population to relax. It rained almost all the time, and they broke even with a couple hundred crowns to spare.

But then came two good seasons. People discovered the sanitarium and another cabin with more beds was added. They also built an ice-house, a slaughterhouse and an office building. The sanitarium at Kovstulheia was its own small society, and in 1897, they even got their own post office.

STAGNATION AND BAD TIMES

But good times don't last forever. Although there were plenty of guests in high season, low season was a disaster, and they went from just scraping by to losing money hand over fist. Reaching the sanitarium in winter was almost impossible on the make-shift roads, but summer was better. The sanitarium board decided to open the hotel only during the summer. From the middle of June to the middle of August, business was good, so good that they often had to turn people away. Roll wanted to expand the building, but he couldn't find any backers for his plans. He had many ideas for making the sanitarium more attractive to guests. The sanitarium didn't have a staff doctor, so it

appealed mostly to tourists. He could hire a doctor, but he would have to add a wing onto the main building for convalescing guests. But with the current financial situation, he had to table the plans. Another of Roll's ideas was to continue building the road over the mountain to Rjukan, but the shareholders didn't go for that either. The bad times continued, and in 1902, the sanitarium was quietly sold for NOK 50 000 at a bankruptcy auction. A new company was formed with nine shareholders. The original founders were still there and were joined by solid local farmers. The name was changed to A/S Tuddal Sanitarium, but little else changed, except that some land was sold off. The losses continued. In 1906, they decided to rent out the hotel, but this helped little, and by 1910, the sanitarium was up for sale again. This time, it wasn't easy to find a buyer, so the ever optimistic attorney Roll bought the sanitarium, its buildings, contents, and five shares in the East Telemark Automobile Club for NOK 43 000. He christened his new company A/S Tuddal Høifjells-Hotel (mountain hotel), and retained nine out of ten shares. The tenth was owned by I.M. Johannesen, a lawyer colleague.

Roll could have earned much more money if he had concentrated on his law practice in Oslo, rather than exhaust himself, year after year, at Kolstulheia, but he loved the place and refused to give up. Unfortunately, is spite of his undying belief in the project, multiple name changes and new corporations, his life work was never any success. Alone he fought against creditors, the weather gods and communications, and in the end, it got the better of him. Emil Roll died on September 1, 1934, and a 40-year epoch in the history of Tuddal was over.

WAR AND BUNK BEDS

Once again the hotel was sold at a bankruptcy auction. This time, it was bought by the Norwegian Central Bank and immediately sold to a company called A/S Tuddal for NOK 80 000. The company's board consisted of four people from Oslo. The chairman was Olaf Bjerke, and the others were Zakæus Gurholt, Magnhild Simonsen, and Karl August Haraldsen, the father of Norway's present Queen Sonja.

Magnhild Simonsen ran the hotel for the first few years and modernized the main building. She installed sinks with hot and cold running water in all the rooms, a bathtub on each floor, and a toilet in every corridor. A generator was installed in 1938. This supplied the main house with electric light and put an end to the filling and cleaning of the 35 paraffin lamps used every day. This made running the hotel much easier, both for guests and staff. War broke out in 1940 and all the tourists left the hotel. Then the

German occupational forces came and insisted that bunk beds be placed into all the rooms. Work on the power line between Rjukan and Herøy had begun, and they needed housing for as many workers as possible. But Magnhild Simonsen wasn't interested in running that kind of a hotel, and she sold her shares to Zakæus Gurholt and his wife Gudrun.

A LOT OF ANTIQUES BUT VERY LITTLE MONEY

Zakæus was an Oslo stockbroker and real estate agent. He had had little to do with the daily running of the hotel, but now he and his wife moved to the mountains. Gudrun had run the Trio banquet rooms in Oslo, but when the Germans confiscated the locale, she took her large collection of antique furniture to Tuddal. Mrs. Gurholt was both an avid collector and a shopper on a grand scale. Through the years, she assembled a magnificent collection of furniture, textiles, decorative, and practical items, and everything is on display at Tuddal.

But life could be far from idyllic in the mountains of Telemark. Zakæus Gurholt was a member of the NS (the Norwegian Nazi party) during the war, and after liberation in 1945, he was arrested and served time in jail. Tuddal was then taken over by the Norwegian War Compensation Directorate and was used by the Red Cross for a short time. Then it was known as Tuddal Mountain Hotel, the Norwegian Red Cross Reconvalescent Home, and it was here that physically and mentally exhausted former prisoners of war came to regain their strength. Later, Tuddal was leased for a short while by the Norwegian Home Forces, who invited their Danish colleagues to a free vacation in the Norwegian mountains.

By 1948, Zakæus Gurholt had served his sentence and returned to his hotel. He wasn't at all pleased with the situation. There was just enough money to keep the hotel afloat, with nothing left over for modernization. Luckily, Tuddal had been electrified just after the war, so he didn't have to pay for the generator. The Norwegian Telephone Company took over the private telephone line and the local authorities assumed responsibility for the road from Tuddal center. But things started to slow down. Those who still vacationed at Tuddal were starting to demand higher standards, and the hotel just couldn't meet them. Neither Gudrun nor Zakæus was getting any younger, and Zakæus died in the summer of 1967. Gudrun continued running the hotel alone, but it wasn't easy keeping the hotel alive. When Gudrun Gurholt died in 1976, its glory days were far in the past.

NOSTALGIA AND CULINARY DELIGHTS

Tuddal was taken over by the Gurholts' grandson, Rune Gurholt Pedersen and his wife, Elsa Holst

The exterior is well-preserved with a few smaller additions at the far end.

destination. The town of Tuddal is the home of Buen Kulturverkstad, which hosts summer concerts. Tuddal Bygdetun, with its fine collection of old Telemark houses and antiques, is close by. You can also experience art and culture at the hotel during the summer months. There are regular sales exhibitions and handicraft displays in one of the buildings, and you can see artisans and artists in action.

Tuddal is paradise for hunting and fishing enthusiasts. The trout almost jump out of the many mountain lakes and on to your fishing hook, and the hotel has 15 000 acres of hunting grounds rich in hare, ptarmigan and grouse. But the main attraction is still 1883- meter-high Gausdaltoppen. You can look out over 1/6th of Norway from its peak, which can be reached on skis in winter and by foot in summer. Tuddal Mountain Hotel is really worth a visit, and Else and Rune are looking at an optimistic future. Their son Einar Zakæus trained as a chef at Le Canard in Oslo, and then at Thornton's in Dublin, while their daughter Borghild Cecilie is in Switzerland studying hotel management. The future of this traditional mountain hotel on the sunny side of Gausdaltoppen looks secure.

Left: The hotel has many charming guest bedrooms. All have been refurbished with tasteful baths, new windows and floors. The furniture and lamps are in the old style and harmonize well with the rest of the hotel.

Right: Two staircases lead from the hall to the guest bedrooms on the second and third floors.

Pedersen. They leased the hotel to a Danish foundation for several years, but they canceled the contract in 1993. They wanted to run the place themselves! All the antiques, furniture, and decorative objects were brought down from the attic. Everything that had been stored since Gudrun died was put back in place. They installed showers and bathrooms in each guest bedroom, but otherwise, they kept the hotel as old-fashioned and charming as they could. They restored the old hay loft and turned it into a banqueting hall, with a banqueting room, party rooms, a restaurant and a bar. Tuddal Mountain Hotel offers personal service, an old fashioned milieu, a nostalgic atmosphere, and last but not least, unforgettable culinary experiences. The hotel is well-known for its homemade, refined dishes, and many come just to enjoy a delicious meal made from first class local ingredients, such as ptarmigan, grouse, mountain trout, deer, moose, and reindeer. More and more people are finding their way to the hotel for both short and longer mountain holidays. Tuddal is now a year-round hotel. In winter, it is filled with skiers who want to enjoy a few days in the beautiful snowclad surroundings. In summer, Tuddal Mountain Hotel is the perfect starting point for mountain walks and car trips in the local area. The road now extends across the mountains to Rjukan, and the old industry town is a popular tourist

Pickled trout

Brine
1/2 teaspoon crushed pepper
1/2 teaspoon mustard seed
1 teaspoon cloves
1/2 teaspoon allspice
3 bay leaves
1/2 dl (3 1/2 tablespoons) sugar
1 1/2 teaspoons 35% vinegar concentrate
1 liter (quart) water

4 small trout, about 100 g (4 oz) each

shredded iceberg lettuce
cucumber slices
sour cream
dill
lemon slices or wedges

Combine all the ingredients in the brine in a stockpot and heat to boiling.

Clean and rinse the trout well. Place in the boiling brine. Remove from the heat and refrigerate overnight.

Arrange the fish "standing" on a bed of lettuce and cucumbers. Garnish with sour cream, dill and lemon.

Cloudberry ice cream in a cookie basket with warm sauce

Cookies
200 g (7 oz) soft butter
200 g (1 cup) sugar
5 eggs
200 g (1 1/4 cups) sifted all-purpose flour

Cloudberry ice cream
1 dl (1/2 cup) cloudberries
4 tablespoons (1/4 cup) sugar
2 eggs
2 dl (3/4 cup) whipping cream
1 teaspoon vanilla sugar

1 tablespoon Lakka cloudberry liqueur

whipped cream
cloudberries

Beat the butter and sugar until light and fluffy. Beat in the eggs alternately with the flour. Refrigerate the batter overnight. Heat a "krumkake" or pizzelle iron. Use about 2 teaspoons of batter per cookie. Bake until golden. Immediately form into a basket over a cup. Cool on a rack. 30-35 cookies.

In a small saucepan, heat the cloudberries with half the sugar to boiling. Lower the heat and simmer about 5 minutes. Cool. Beat the eggs with the remaining sugar until light, thick and lemon-colored. Whip the cream with the vanilla sugar until soft peaks form. Combine the cream, egg mixture and half the berries. Pour into a mold and freeze or freeze in an ice cream machine.

Just before serving, reheat the berries. Puree in a blender, then strain. Stir in the liqueur.

Place small scoops of ice cream in each cookie basket. Garnish with cream and berries. Spoon warm sauce all around.

Grouse a la "Gausta" with honey-glazed Brussels sprouts and potato nests filled with game salad

A wood grouse is usually enough for 6 to 8 people.

1 wood grouse
2 teaspoons spice blend for poultry and game (see recipe below)
6 bacon slices
1 carrot
1/4 celeriac
3 shallots
4 tablespoons (1/4 cup) olive oil
2 tablespoons butter
stock or water with 2 teaspoons bouillon powder
5 dl (2 cups) whipping cream
salt, pepper

Spice blend for poultry and game
1 teaspoon ground pepper
1 teaspoon rosemary
1 teaspoon juniper berries
1/2 teaspoon sage
1/2 teaspoon basil
1/2 teaspoon ground paprika
1 tablespoon salt

Honey-glazed Brussels sprouts
1/2 dl (3 1/2 tablespoons) chopped walnuts
3 tablespoons butter
3 tablespoons olive oil
1 teaspoon sugar
1 tablespoon honey
300 g (10 oz) Brussels sprouts

Potato nests
4 potatoes
oil

Game salad
1/2 iceberg lettuce
grouse meat from thighs
1 dl (1/2 cup) sour cream
1 dl (1/2 cup) mayonnaise
1 teaspoon spice blend (see above)

Flay the grouse. Refrigerate 2 days before cooking, if possible. Rub the spice blend into the bird. Drape the bacon over the breast and truss with cotton string. Peel and chop the vegetables. Brown the bird lightly on all sides in oil and butter in a cast iron with the vegetables. Add the hot stock or water and bouillon powder to cover. Simmer for about 90 minutes, turning the bird several times. Remove the bird from the cooking liquid and let rest. Add the cream to the cooking liquid and reduce by half. Strain and season with salt and pepper.

Preheat the oven to 180°C (350°F). Carve out the breasts and thighs. Just before serving, reheat in the oven about 5 minutes. Remove the remaining meat from the carcass and use in the salad.

Spice blend for poultry and game
Crush all ingredients together, blending well. This spice blend is good in many different dishes.

Honey-glazed Brussels sprouts
Sauté the walnuts in butter and oil over medium heat. Sprinkle with sugar, add the honey and Brussels sprouts. Cook over low heat for about 10 minutes, turning the sprouts often.

Potato nests
Wash and peel the potatoes. Cut into julienne (2x2 mm). Soak the shreds in water for 1 hour. Drain, then dry thoroughly. Preheat the oil in a deep fryer to 180°C (350°F). Place 1/4 of the potatoes in a "nest iron" and fry until golden. Repeat with the remaining potatoes. Cool. These keep for 2 to 3 weeks in the refrigerator.

Game salad
Shred the lettuce and dice the meat. Combine with the remaining ingredients and serve in the potato nests.

To serve, cut the grouse breasts into even slices and serve with the Brussels sprouts and potato nests with game salad. Garnish with lingonberries or a juniper twig. Serve with lingonberry compote or rowanberry jelly. 6-8 servings.

A culinary island idyll

Engø Gård Hotell and Restaurant, Tjøme

The five houses that comprise the exclusive restaurant Engø Gård lie just a few hundred meters from the sea, in the heart of Tjøme, Norway's summer paradise. The whole farm was renovated in the 1990s, and now the white manor house dating from 1845, the guesthouse from 1933, the farm workers' quarters from 1935, and the barn from 1905, where the remains of the cowshed have been converted into a fireplace room, are all completely restored. There is also a swimming pavilion built to resemble an English conservatory, and it contains a heated indoor swimming pool, a whirlpool bath, a sauna, and a massage studio. The restoration was gracefully done and there is still an old-fashioned ambience, despite the modern luxuries and comforts. There is an atmosphere of beauty and harmony, and it is reminiscent of the Swedish and Danish manor houses that now serve as hotels. These charming houses are surrounded by parks with well-tended lawns, shady oak trees, with ivy and Virginia creeper climbing up the walls. There is also a lush kitchen garden with herbs, spices, fruit, and vegetables. Down by the sea is a dock with space for 20 boats. In bygone days, members of the aristocracy came with their sailboats. They cast their anchors and spent the summer along this magical Vestfold coast between Magerø and Røssesundet. Traditional Engø Gård, with its timeless charm and beautiful surroundings, has fascinated national and international travelers since the 1920s.

PHIL'S GUESTHOUSE AT ENGØ

A family of boat owners and sea captains originally owned the farm, but in 1911, the Engø family decided to sell. The farm changed hands several times until Carl Pihl bought it in 1923 and gave it to his children, Daisy and Frithjof. The siblings quickly understood that the farm needed an additional income to stay afloat. They decided to rent out rooms to English

and Dutch family friends. That was how Pihl's guesthouse at Engø got started, and under the talented management of Mrs. Babs Pihl, it developed into an exclusive club. The guests were hand-picked and approved – a good mix of Norwegians and foreigners. Demand increased, so Frithjof Pihl fenced in the beautiful farmyard with the guesthouse and farm workers' quarters. In addition, he built a number of cabins on the property. The guests lived in these buildings, but festivities took place in the old manor house, in the dining room and in fireplace room of the new guesthouse building.

In the 1960s, the guesthouse was closed and the buildings sold off. Frithjof Pihl and his second wife, Mary Mackenzie Anderson, were still interested in preserving the area and the buildings, so they sold the property to Nina Felling, an art historian. and Harald Andersen, a construction engineer, in 1983. The new owners started working with the architect Hans Gabriel Finne in 1986 to develop the guesthouse and barn into a luxurious hotel with all the modern conveniences.

A JOY FOR THE SOUL AND PALATE

It was a long, painstaking process, but Engø Gård Hotell and Restaurant finally opened its doors on June 17, 2000. A Danish couple, Randi Schmidt and Per Hallundbæk, run this idyllic hotel. They worked together previously at Fakkelgården, a Danish Manor house on the German border known for its delicious food. Randi is in charge of the restaurant and the hotel, while Per, who is known as one of Denmark's best chefs, of course, is responsible for the kitchen and its culinary delights. He has broad experience from Spain, France, and Switzerland, and the menu at Engø is an eclectic combination of French and Italian-inspired dishes. But they only use local produce! Per buys fish from local fishermen, and the

vegetables that are not grown in Engø's own kitchen garden are bought from neighboring farms. He likes to serve seasonal dishes, and Engø is already famous for its kitchen. Guests come here to relax, and enjoy the food. Unforgettable food and wine experiences, idyllic buildings, romantic and nostalgic interiors, beautiful nature with lush meadows and naked rocks, birds chirping and the smell of sea air, sea fishing and swimming, golfing, sailing, or horseback riding; a morning shopping and sightseeing trip to Tønsberg; a walk in beautiful surroundings; or just a deck chair and a literary classic from the hotel library. You can do all these things at Engø Gård in Tjøme. Welcome to this coastal paradise!

Left: Engø Gård is both exclusive and cozy at the same time. Modern luxury is combined with nostalgia and romance.

Above: Engø Gård lies in lush green surroundings at Tjøme. Now it is an exclusive hotel and restaurant inspired by Swedish and Danish manor house hotels..

Mosaic of cauliflower mousse and marinated trout with lime cream

Marinated sea trout
200 g (7 oz) sea trout fillet
10 capers
5 tiny sweet pickles
juice of 1/2 lemon
chopped fresh dill
salt, pepper

Cauliflower mousse
1 small cauliflower
1 liter (quart) milk
7 gelatin sheets
4 dl (1 2/3 cups)
whipping cream
ground nutmeg
salt, pepper

Lime cream
2 dl (3/4 dl)
light sour cream
1/2 dl (3 tablespoons)
full-fat milk
grated zest and juice
of 1 lime
salt, pepper

It is a good idea to make this dish a day in advance.

Marinated sea trout
Finely chop the fish, capers and pickles. Season with lemon juice, dill, salt and pepper. Place on a sheet of plastic wrap and form into a "sausage". Roll tightly in the plastic and freeze.

Cauliflower mousse
Remove the green stalks from the cauliflower and divide into florets. Cook in the milk for about 30 minutes, until most of the milk has evaporated. Transfer to a blender or food processor and puree until smooth. Strain. Measure 600 g (1 1/3 lb) puree. Refrigerate. Soak the gelatin in cold water about 5 minutes to soften. Squeeze to remove excess water and melt in a little milk. Stir into the puree. Whip the cream and fold into the cauliflower puree. Season with nutmeg, salt and pepper

Mosaic
Line a terrine with plastic wrap. Fill with half the cauliflower mousse. Place the frozen trout "sausage" in the center. Top with the remaining mousse. Refrigerate overnight.

Lime cream
Combine all ingredients in a blender.

To serve, cut even slices of the mosaic and serve with lime cream. Garnish with cooked cauliflower florets, capers and boiled tiny onions which have been marinated in lemon juice. 8 servings.

Caramelized pineapple

2 pineapple
200 g (1 cup) unrefined sugar
1 vanilla bean
1 liter (quart) pineapple juice

Crispy pineapple

100 g (1/2 cup) sugar
1 dl (scant 1/2 cup) water
1/2 pineapple
(reserved from earlier)

Baba

150 g (1 cup) all-purpose flour
1/4 teaspoon salt
2 teaspoons sugar
7 1/2 g (1 tablespoon) dry yeast
3 eggs
60 g (2 oz) butter

Sugar syrup

125 g (2/3 cup) sugar
1 cinnamon stick
1 bay leaf
1 rosemary twig
1/2 vanilla bean
2 dl (3/4 cup) white wine
2 dl (3/4 cup) apple juice
grated zest of 1 lemon
1 dl (scant 1/2 cup) dark rum

Ice cream

Tonka nuts are difficult to obtain. Substitute 2 vanilla beans, split lengthwise, with seeds, for one tonka nut.

1 liter (quart) full-fat milk
250 g (1 1/4 cups) sugar
1 tonka nut, chopped
(or 2 vanilla beans)
10 egg yolks

Classic rum baba with caramelized pineapple and ice cream

Caramelized pineapple

Peel and cut 1 1/2 pineapples into 1 cm (1/2") slices. Set aside 1/2 pineapple. Cut out the core and quarter each slice. Caramelize the sugar in a large frying pan. Split the vanilla bean and add with the pineapple and juice. Simmer about 30 minutes. Remove the pineapple with a slotted spoon and set aside. Reduce the liquid to 2 dl (3/4 cup). Just before serving, dip the pineapple into this liquid.

Crispy pineapple

Bring the water and sugar to a boil. Cut the pineapple into thin slices with an electric meat slicer. Simmer in the syrup for a few minutes. Place on baking parchment. Preheat the oven to 80°C (175°F). Dry the pineapple slices until crispy, about 8 hours.

Baba

Combine the flour, salt, sugar and yeast. Add the eggs and mix well. Beat the butter until light and fluffy, then add the yeast mixture, mixing well. Cover and let rise until double. Punch down the dough. Butter and sugar 8 baba rings. Fill halfway with batter and let rise to the edge. Preheat the oven to 180°C (350°F). Bake about 12 minutes, until golden. Unmold onto a rack and let dry for 2 hours. Dip in sugar syrup for about 10 seconds before serving.

Sugar syrup

Combine all ingredients and heat to boiling. Just before serving, marinate the babas for about 10 seconds.

Ice cream

Bring the milk, sugar and tonka nut to a boil. Whisk the egg yolks together. Whisk in about 1 dl (scant 1/2 cup) of the milk and return everything to the saucepan. Stir over low heat about 3 minutes, until the mixture has thickened. It should not boil. Strain and refrigerate. Freeze in an ice machine.

Place a baba in the center with caramelized pineapple all around. Place a scoop of ice cream on the baba and garnish with crispy pineapple. Serve the sauce alongside. 8 servings.

Like a fairytale castle

Harahorn, Hemsedal

The poem, "Fanitullen" (The Devil's Tune), by Jørgen Moe, tells of a wedding in Hemsedal. As the fiddler went down to the cellar to get some beer, he heard the most fantastic music. At first he couldn't see who was playing, because it was so dark, but once his eyes had adjusted, he saw that it was the devil himself, playing a fiddle both upside down and backwards. Frightened at the sight, he ran back up the stairs as fast as he could. He then tried to duplicate the sounds, and that music has been handed down through the generations ever since. "Fanitullen" has become one of the most popular music pieces for the Hardanger fiddle. Poet-clergyman Jørgen Moe is best known for his collaboration with Peter Christen Asbjørnsen. About 150 years ago, they collected and published many of the Norwegian folktales which have become part of every child's experience.

Local inhabitants know that this famous legend of Fanitullen is set at Finset Farm in Hemsedal. They also know that the devil played the wedding music in the cellar of Finset house. Today, this typical 19th-century Halling-style dwelling sits at Harahorn together with its contemporary, Flågstugu, and 18 other buildings. Harahorn lies like a fairytale castle, nestled in the mountains of northern Hemsedal, one of Norway's most beautiful and pristine mountain areas. The mountain stretches south from Harahorn to Skogshorn, 1728 meters above sea level, and north to Ranastongi, 1900 meters above sea level. There are countless peaks, lakes, waterfalls, gorges, and broad open plains. You can reach all this from Harahorn. The mountain of the same name rises an impressive 1581 meters above sea level, and the view of southern Norway from its peak is breathtaking, as is the journey up and down its western side.

Harahorn is the perfect place to start exploring. It offers a wealth of opportunities, both in summer and winter. You can even ski right from your own doorstep. There are several mountain paths, three of which are marked, including a three-hour trail around Harahorn. Or you can slalom ski straight down to Solheisen ski center, on the sunny side of Grøndal valley. There are challenges for the whole family, and even a cozy restaurant. Hemsedal ski center, with 20 ski lifts, 40 kilometers of well-prepared trails, evening floodlighting, and several restaurants, is only a 20-minute ride away.

During the summer, you can hike in the mountains or go horseback riding, canoeing, and mountain biking in wild, untouched surroundings. Farther into the plateau, you can hunt for pheasant and hare, or you can try your luck fishing in Hemsila, one of Scandinavia's best fly-fishing rivers, or in one of many local lakes. Golfers can choose between two courses. The closest is Hemsedal golf course, which lies on the banks of the Grøndøla river, just three kilometers from Harahorn. This 9-hole course, in slightly hilly terrain, features many challenging water obstacles. And for those looking for greater challenges, there is also mountain climbing and paragliding. The Hemsedal area is rich in culture and tradition. Beautiful Huso Fjellgard farm consists of 11 old buildings, exhibitions, a troll cave, an elf workshop, and a wildlife park is well worth a visit. At Hemsedal Bygdatun, a farmyard dating from 1730, you can watch demonstrations of old handicraft techniques, and on the mountain you can experience life as it was on a mountain pasture. You can even try, or buy, traditional mountain food such as freshly churned butter, goat cheese, prim (soft, brown whey cheese) and sour cream.

Harahorn is also the perfect departure point place for day trips to western Norway and the Sognefjord. Borgund Stave church in Lærdal, the Norwegian wild salmon center, and charming Lærdalsøyri, with its beautiful old wooden houses, are all just over hour's drive away.

Above: Harahorn. Large and small houses around a courtyard. Constructed in wood, stone and turf, it is as if they grew out of the terrain, in keeping with the best Norwegian building tradition.

The interior at Harahorn is an example of the Norwegian rustic romantic style, with many beautiful antiques. The colors have been chosen carefully to fit the milieu. Paintings by Norwegian artists, including Kai Fjell and Fritz Thaulow, adorn the walls.

AN INFORMAL AND COZY ATMOSPHERE

Harahorn is located at 1100 meters above sea level – at the level where forest turns into naked rock. Harahorn opened for guests in 1992 and is part of "The Really Good Life" hotel chain, owned by Norwegian shipping magnate Knut Kloster Jr. Harahorn consists of old restored buildings and some new ones. A beautiful small courtyard, perfectly attuned to its surroundings was created with the help of traditional Norwegian building techniques, and local materials such as wood, stone, and turf. Here you can live in a cabin or storehouse, or in a cozy room in the main house. The cabins have from three to five bedrooms, two or three bathrooms, a sauna, and a large living room with a fireplace, TV, radio, and telephone. The kitchen is fully equipped for any occasion, with a dishwasher, freezer, refrigerator, and stove. You can prepare your own meals, or eat in the main dining room, or have dinner delivered to your cabin. The kitchen at Harahorn has gained a formidable reputation serving traditional food with a twist. The chef prefers to use local products and menus are based on seasonal ingredients.

Both the main house and the cabins are decorated in the Norwegian rustic style. The traditional peasant colors of yellow, red, and blue in different nuances appear again and again, but in a way that each room is unique. The furniture is an eclectic blend of Norwegian rustic antiques and classic, timeless new furniture, and paintings by famous Norwegian artists grace the walls. The ambience is cozy and informal. In 1996, Harahorn got its own chapel modeled on a traditional stave church, just like those that once stood on larger Hallingdal farms in the past. The church is constructed of rough, untreated logs, and the interior is decorated with stained glass, simple candlesticks, and a globe of candles as the only adornment. This room is surrounded by a gallery that seats 50. The church is a popular wedding chapel. But if the bride and groom hear the powerful tune of the devil late in the evening, we'll never know.

Left: Harahorn has an informal style and ambience. To come as a guest is to be invited to a home where everything is perfect.

Right: The pleasures of the table. The kitchen at Harahorn concentrates on Norwegian cuisine with a few touches from abroad. The wine cellar is excellent.

Grilled scallops in lemon-vanilla sauce

12 scallops
2 vanilla beans
1 onion
1 garlic clove
oil
1 1/2 dl (2/3 cup) dry white wine
3 dl (1 1/4 cups) fish stock (see next recipe)
1 dl (1/2 cup) whipping cream
3 sprigs lemon thyme
6 leaves lemon verbena
juice of 1 lime
juice of 1 lemon
60 g (2 oz) cold butter
freshly ground salt and pepper

2 dl (3/4 cup) balsamic vinegar

80 g (2 1/2 oz) puff pastry
1 egg yolk

1 garlic clove
1 chunk fresh ginger (same size as garlic)
2 large carrots
4 celery stalks
1 leek
1 zucchini
butter

Fish stock
1 leek
2 shallots
10 mushrooms
2 kilo (2 1/4 lb) fish bones and trimmings
4-5 dill stalks
6 white peppercorns
4 bay leaves

Open the scallops and remove the muscle and roe. Use the rest in the sauce.

Split the vanilla bean lengthwise and scrape out the seeds. Peel and mince the onion and garlic. Sauté in oil until shiny. Add the wine, stock, cream, thyme, verbena, lime and lemon juice, vanilla beans and seeds, and the rest of the scallops. Reduce to one-third of the original amount. Strain, then beat in the butter in pats. Season with salt and pepper.

In a small saucepan, reduce the balsamic vinegar until syrupy.

Preheat the oven to 190°C (375°F). Cut the puff pastry into four pieces of equal size, about 7 cm (3") square. Brush with egg yolk and bake 8 minutes. Cut each piece in half.

Wash, clean and shred the vegetables. Sauté in butter with the scallop roe just before serving.

Heat a dry grill pan or frying pan until very hot. Grill or sauté the scallops for about 30 seconds per side.

Sandwich the vegetables between the two layers of pastry. Serve with the scallops and sauce. Dot the sauce with the balsamic reduction.

Fish stock

Clean and coarsely chop the leek, shallots and mushrooms. In a stockpot, bring 1 liter (quart) water to a boil, add all the ingredients and simmer 20 minutes. Skim and simmer 20 more minutes. Strain and reduce to 3 dl (1 1/4 cups).

Raspberry-poached nectarines with chocolate mousse

Raspberry-poached nectarines
1 vanilla bean
200 g (1 3/4 cups) raspberries
100 g (1/2 cup) sugar
5 dl (2 cups) water
4 nectarines

Chocolate mousse
5 large egg yolks
4 dl (1 2/3 cups) whipping cream
50 g (1/2 cup) sugar
240 g (9 oz) semi-sweet chocolate

Split the vanilla bean lengthwise and scrape out the seeds. Place in a saucepan with the raspberries, sugar and water. Heat the mixture to boiling, then strain. Peel the nectarines and add them in the raspberry syrup. Heat to boiling, then remove the pan from the heat and let the nectarines steep in the syrup for 8 hours. Reheat just before serving.

Chocolate mousse

Whisk the egg yolks with 1/2 dl (1/4 cup) of the cream and the sugar over boiling water until light and thick. Melt the chocolate and fold into the egg yolk mixture. Cool to almost room temperature.

Lightly whip the remaining cream, then fold into the chocolate mixture. Pour into molds or into a glass bowl and refrigerate overnight.

To serve as illustrated, cut 4 strips of baking parchment and pipe melted chocolate over them. Form into cylinders, fasten with paperclips and freeze. Fill with mousse. Or just form eggs of the mousse with two tablespoons. Garnish the nectarines with pieces of vanilla bean to look like stalks and lemon verbena or mint leaves.

Stuffed filet of lamb with thyme potatoes and sun-dried tomato jus

Lamb stock
1 medium carrot
1 medium onion
100 g (4oz) celeriac
2 tablespoons tomato paste
1 kilo (2 1/4 ib) lamb bones
and trimmings
2 liters (quarts) water

Stuffed filet of lamb
100 g (4 oz) boneless lamb
salt
1 egg
2 dl (3/4 cup) whipping cream
1 garlic clove, peeled
15 sun-dried tomatoes
20 black olives
1/2 dl (1/4 cup) chopped parsley
pepper

600 g (1 1/3 lb) filet of lamb
100 g (4 oz) pork caul or
cotton thread
butter

Thyme potatoes
600 g (1 1/3 lb) almond potatoes
or other small waxy potatoes
4 shallots
4 bacon strips
2 1/2 tablespoons butter
2 tablespoons chopped
fresh thyme
salt, pepper

Vegetable layers
4 medium tomatoes
sugar, salt, pepper
1 red onion
1/2 eggplant
1/2 zucchini
oil

Sun-dried tomato jus
50 g (1/4 cup) sugar
1 dl (scant 1/2 cup) red
wine vinegar
3 dl (1 1/4 cups) red wine
1 liter (quart) lamb stock
10 black olives, minced
6 sun-dried tomatoes, minced
50 g (3 tablespoons) cold butter

Lamb stock
Preheat the oven to 200°C (400°F). Clean, peel and coarsely chop the vegetables. Place in an oven tray with the lamb bones, trimmings and tomato paste. Brown in the oven to a deep mahogany color, about 30 minutes. Transfer everything to a stockpot, add the water and simmer 3 to 4 hours. Skim often. Strain.

Stuffed filet of lamb
Place the lamb and salt in a food processor and pulse until coarsely chopped. With the motor running, add the remaining ingredients.

Preheat the oven to 190°C (375°F). Trim the filet, removing all membrane. Loosen the top layer of fat with a knife, but do not remove completely, as it will be used as a "lid" later. Cut a pocket into the entire filet and fill with the ground lamb mixture. Cover with the fat. Pack in caul or tie in several places with cotton string. Brown the meat in butter in a frying pan, then transfer to an oven rack and roast 8 minutes. Remove from the oven and let rest 8 minutes. Return to the oven for 6 more minutes. Remove from the oven and let rest 6 minutes before slicing.

Thyme potatoes
Scrub the potatoes, but do not peel. Cook until tender, then peel. Mash lightly with a fork. Peel and mince the shallots. Chop the bacon. Sauté in 2 teaspoons of the butter until shiny but not brown. Add the remaining butter and mix in the potatoes. Stir in the thyme and season with salt and pepper.

Vegetable layers
Preheat the oven to 90°C (195°F). Quarter the tomatoes, remove the seeds and sprinkle with sugar, salt and pepper. Place on an oven sheet and bake 3 hours. Peel the onion. Thinly slice the onion, eggplant and zucchini and brown in oil in a non-stick pan. Layer all the vegetables in four small round cylinders. Just before serving, unmold onto plates.

Sun-dried tomato jus
In a large saucepan, melt the sugar to a medium caramel. Add the vinegar and wine and reduce by half. Add the stock and reduce by half. Stir in the olives, tomatoes and butter in pats just before serving.

Arrange the thyme potatoes in a mound. Top with lamb. Serve with layered vegetables and sun-dried tomato jus.

In the land of fairy tales

Kleivstua, Krokleiva

The Queen's Road winds its way up from Sundvollen to Kleivstua. It passes through some of the most beautiful parts of eastern Norway on its way to Krokskogen – the real-life forest home of Norwegian fairy tale authors, Asbjørnsen and Moe. And Kleivstua is nestled in the middle of the forest like a fairy tale castle, looking out over the area of Ringerike and the Tyrifjord. In the olden days, the King's Road passed through Krokskogen on the way from Christiania (Oslo) to Ringerike. The name Krokskogen and the road date back to medieval times. We know that Magnus Lagabøte, King of Norway from 1263 to 1280, passed through a desolate area known as Krokskogen (Kroka forest) on his way to visit property in Ringerike and Hadeland. Until a new road was built in 1860, the road through Kroka forest was the only route from Oslo to Ringerike, and from around 1800, it was part of the King's Road between Oslo and Bergen.

The road brought people of all kinds to the area, including artists and writers. The Danish Court painter Erik Pauelsen, fellow Danes Johannes Flintoe and Martinius Rørbye, the Finnish painter W.M. Carpelan, and the Norwegian painters J.F.L. Dreier, J.C. Dahl, Thomas Fearnley, and J. F. Eckersberg were all inspired by the landscape there. And while the painters sought to render nature on canvas, the poets sought to do the same on paper. But it was first and foremost a local citizen Jørgen Moe and his poet friend, fairy tale collector, and natural historian Peter Christian Asbjørnsen, but also Henrik Anker Bjerregaard, Henrik Wergeland, and the Danish poet Adam Oehlenschlager, who described Krokskogen and Krokkleiva in folk tales, story, and poems.

All this attention led tourists to seek out this beautiful area known for its lush forest and fantastic views. The best viewpoints were named after visiting royals. "The Queen's view", close to the top of Krokkleiva, was named after Queen Desirée, wife of Karl III Johan, King of both Norway and Sweden, who visited the area in 1825. The famous "King's view", just over a kilometer west of Kleivstua was named after her husband paid a visit in 1832.

KROKKLEVENS HOTEL AND PENSION

There are two steep paths from Sundvollen to Krokskogen. The northern path was called Krokkleiva until 1805, when the road was changed to follow the southern route. The route changed, but the name remained the same.

The peak of Krokkleiva was a natural rest stop for travelers in both directions. Kleivstua was built at the top of the southern path after the road was moved in around 1807. Here the horses could rest, eat, or be replaced. Maybe the carriage needed fixed or the loads secured before heading down the treacherous path. The road between Sundvollen and Kleivstua was steep and rugged, and fraught with danger. A 1863 magazine article gives the following description:

"Krokkleiva is not long, but it is steep, and before the new road over Sollihøgda was built, it used to frighten travelers because of its extreme steepness. It is steepest at Kleivstua, where it seems to disappear into a dark abyss. The poor horses become exhausted trying to keep the carriage on the hill. It's a fine journey in summertime, but in winter or spring, it's terrible when the horses slip and slide on the slick ice-glazed hill, which is constantly being splashed with water from melting snow."

Thus the owners of Kleivstua were obligated to help travelers down the steep path. As the flow of tourist increased, so did the need for roadside coaching inns and restaurants along the way. Kleivstua, with its

Kleivstua also offers a rich assortment of outdoor experiences, as well as sports and cultural events. It's a fine departure point for cycling, walking or skiing. An illuminated ski trail starts right in the courtyard! And Tyrifjord Golf Club, one of Norway's best and most beautiful 18-hole golf courses is just a few minutes drive away. There's also historic Storøen Manor, with its art exhibitions at Galleri Dronning (Queen) Tyra. Hadeland Glassworks and Mo Gård, the childhood home of poet Jørgen Moe, are all close by.

But perhaps the best experience of all is a visit to Kleivstua's restaurant "Dronningens Utsikt" (the Queen's view), where you can enjoy an exquisite meal based on a combination of Norwegian traditions and the best from abroad. The restaurant has a spectacular view out over the Steinsfjord, Vikerfjell mountain, and the Tyrifjord up toward Norefjell. And you can think of the poetic lines from Jørgen Moe's famous song "The Light in the Forest," which describes the view from Krokskogen.

It was getting lighter in the forest, so I ran forward,
Soon I stood there, where the cliff abruptly stopped.
I looked out over the wide countryside, I saw my beloved home,
I saw where the far off hills turned blue.
I saw the wide fjords that cut coves into the mountains,
And I saw the river glisten as it snaked beautifully along –
I am drawn to the sunlit plains.

Above: The view over the Steinsfjord, Vikerfjell mountain and the Tyrifjord toward Norefjell mountain is fantastic.

Right: The guest rooms at Kleivstua are called forest suites and have names like Asbjørnsen, Moe and Kleiva.

spectacular view, soon became a popular tourist destination, with a reputation far beyond Norway's borders. More space was needed, and the result was Krokklevens Hotel and Pension, which could house over 100 guests. The hotel also offered guide service to the King's and Queen's views.

When the new road over Sollihøgda opened in 1860, few tourists traveled the old route over Kleivstua. The tourism industry got a boost with the building of a chair lift up to Krokkleiva in 1947-8. After 10 years, it was replaced with a barrel-lift, which was in use until 1978, when the Queen's Road was build from Sundvollen up to Kleivstua.

Kleivstua survived through good and bad times. It was finally closed down in 1993, after serving for a number of years as a vegetarian spa.

KLEIVSTUA TODAY

Shipowner Knut Kloster Jr. bought Kleivstua in 1996 and he commissioned architect Harald Melbye to redesign this venerable coaching inn. Toril Winger Johnsen and Kersti Melbye were in charge of the interior. Kleivstua reopened exactly one year later, in August, 1997, as a part of Kloster's "Really Good Life" chain of hotels. Considerable sums were invested in the restoration to satisfy the owner's demands. And Kleivstua, which consists of a main building, cabins, a storage building, and and outbuildings surrounding an idyllic courtyard, definitely fulfills his high standards. You can spend the night in the forest suites named after Asbjørnsen, Moe, and Kleiva in the main building, or Gyrihaugen or Bruløkka cabins, where you can enjoy a cozy fire and comfortable library, or simply enjoy the surroundings which have been lovingly restored and preserved. Soft, harmonizing colors, comfortable furniture, and beautiful antiques help to create a homey atmosphere.

Whitefish caviar in creme fraiche with tomato concassé and pesto

2 gelatin sheets
1 teaspoon
boiling water
2 dl (3/4 cup) creme
fraiche or dairy
sour cream
2 tablespoons
minced red onion
2 tablespoons whitefish
caviar or other
caviar (preferably
golden colored)
lemon juice
salt, pepper

Soak the gelatin in cold water to soften, about 5 minutes. Squeeze to remove excess water and melt in the boiling water. Beat the creme fraiche until it thickens. Stir in the gelatin, onion and caviar. Season with lemon juice, salt and pepper. Pour into a small mold and refrigerate.

Tomato concassé

2 plum tomatoes
4 tablespoons (1/4 cup)
minced onion
2 tablespoons
shredded basil
salt, pepper

Scald and peel the tomatoes. Halve and remove the seeds. Cut into strips and stir in the onion and basil. Season with salt and pepper.

Basil pesto

1 tablespoon pine nuts
1 garlic clove, peeled
2 tablesoons
shredded basil
1 tablespoon grated
Parmesan cheese
4 ss (1/4 cup) olive oil
salt, pepper

Place all the ingredients except salt and pepper in a food processor and puree until smooth. Season with salt and pepper.

Gastrix

1 tablespoon balsamic vinegar
2 tablespoons red wine
1 tablespoon sugar

Combine all the ingredients in a small saucepan and simmer until syrupy.

To serve, form 4 "eggs" of caviar cream with a warm tablespoon and place on individual plates. Topp with tomato concassé and serve with lettuce, pesto, Parmesan cheese and gastrix.

Rhubarb soup with vanilla ice cream

300 g (10 oz)
rhubarb
1 vanilla bean
1 liter (quart) water
200 g (1 cup) sugar

Peel the rhubarb. Split the vanilla bean lengthwise and scrape out the seeds. Place the peelings and trimmings in the water along with the vanilla seeds and sugar and simmer 30 minutes. Dice the peeled rhubarb and place in a bowl. Strain over the boiling rhubarb soup. Cool.

Vanilla ice cream

1 vanilla bean
7 egg yolks
200 g (1 cup) sugar
4 dl (1 2/3 cups)
whipping cream
1 dl (1/2 cup) creme
fraiche or dairy sour
cream

Split the vanilla bean lengthwise and scrape out the seeds. Beat the egg yolks, sugar and vanilla seeds until light, thick and lemon-colored. Whip the cream and fold with the creme fraiche into the egg yolk mixture. Freeze in an ice cream machine.

Serve the rhubarb soup in wide, low bowls with a large scoop of ice cream in the center. 6 servings.

Smoked duck breast with morel jus, potatoes in pastry, celeriac puree, spinach and red onion-plum compote

Smoked duck breast
2 duck breasts
salt, pepper
fresh juniper twigs

Morel jus
30 g (1 oz) dried morels
1 shallot
1/2 dl (1/4 cup) Port wine
5 dl (2 cups) concentrated
beef stock
salt, pepper
2 teaspoons cornstarch stirred
into 1 tablespoon cold water

Potatoes in puff pastry
200 g (8 oz) almond or
other waxy potatoes
1 egg yolk
50 g (3 tablespoons) butter
salt, pepper
1 sheet puff pastry
(85g, 3 oz)
beaten egg

Celeriac puree
200 g (8 oz) celeriac
2 tablespoons whipping cream
2 tablespoons butter
salt, pepper

Spinach
50 g (2 oz) cleaned
spinach leaves
1 tablespoon minced onion
pinch nutmeg
oil
salt, pepper

Red onion-plum compote
2 tablespoons sugar
2 red onions, in wedges
2 tablespoons balsamic vinegar
1 teaspoon freshly grated ginger
1 teaspoon minced garlic

Smoked duck breast
Cut a lattice pattern with a sharp knife in the skin of the duck breasts. Sprinkle with salt and pepper. Brown in a hot, dry pan, skin side down. Arrange the twigs over the bottom of a stockpot and top with a rack. Arrange the duck breasts on the rack. Cover and smoke over high heat for about 15 minutes. Cool.

Morel jus
Soak the morels in warm water for 30 minutes. Mince the shallot and brown lightly in a little duck fat. Add the Port and reduce until almost evaporated. Add the stock and reduce slightly. Season with salt and pepper. Thicken with the cornstarch mixture. Just before serving, add the morels and reheat.

Potatoes in puff pastry
Peel the potatoes. Boil until tender, then drain and dry. Press through a sieve or ricer. Beat in the egg yolk and butter. Season with salt and pepper. Cover with plastic wrap and refrigerate. Preheat the oven to 200°C (400°F). Roll out the pastry sheet. Form the potatoes into a "sausage" and place on the dough. Roll up, slice and place on a baking sheet. Pat down lightly. Brush with egg and bake 8 to 10 minutes.

Celeriac puree
Clean, peel and slice the celeriac. Boil in lightly salted water until tender. Drain. Add the cream and cook until almost evaporated. Transfer to a food processor, add the butter and puree until smooth. Season with salt and pepper.

Spinach
Sauté the spinach with the onion and nutmeg in a little oil. Season with salt and pepper.

Red onion-plum compote
Brown the sugar in a saucepan. Cut the onions into wedges and add with the remaining ingredients and simmer until tender.

Reheat the duck breasts. Slice on the diagonal and arrange on individual plates with the other ingredients. 2-4 servings.

Addresses

Balaklava Gjestgiveri
Postboks 1229
1631 Gamle Fredrikstad
Telephone: 69 32 30 40
Telefax: 69 32 29 40
E-mail: balaklav@online.no
Website: www.balaklava.no
13 rooms
28 beds

Bakkergården
Bakkergården, 1860 Trøgstad
Telephone: 69 82 55 50
Telefax: 69 82 51 31
E-mail: bakkergaarden@online.no
Website: www.bakkergaarden.no
9 rooms
23 beds
Restaurantcapacity: 60

Hotel Continental
Stortingsgaten 24/26
0161 Oslo
Postboks 1510, Vika
0117 Oslo
Telephone: 22 82 40 00
Telefax: 22 42 09 89
E-mail: booking@hotel-continental.no
Website: www.hotel-continental.no
145 rooms
18 suites
283 beds

Hotel Rica Grand
Karl Johans gate 31
0159 Oslo
Telephone: 23 21 20 00
Telefax: 23 21 21 00
E-mail: reservations-grand@rica.no
Website: www.rica.no
239 rooms
50 suites
500 beds

Hotel Rica Bygdøy alle
Bygdøy Allé53
0265 Oslo
Telephone: 23 08 58 00
Telefax: 23 08 58 08
E-mail: rica.hotel.bygdoey.alle@rica.no
Website: www.rica.hotels.no
57 rooms
99 beds

Bjørnsgard Oslo
Sørkedalen
0759 Oslo
Telephone 22 49 90 60
Telefax 22 49 90 83
E-mail: trond.skogvoll@os.telia.no
Website: www.bjornsgard.no
3 rooms
6 beds
By advance reservation only.

Holmenkollen Park Hotel Rica
Kongeveien 26
0787 Oslo
Telephone: 22 92 20 00
Telefax: 22 14 61 92
E-mail: holmenkollen.park.hotel@rica.no
Website: www.holmenkollenparkhotel.no
220 rooms
11 suites
353 beds

Losby Gods/Losby Manor
Losbyveien 270
1475 Finstadjoret
Telephone: 67 92 33 00
Telefax: 67 92 33 01
E-mail: reservations@losbygods.no
Website: www.losby.no
65 rooms
5 suites
140 beds

Restaurant Trugstad Gård
Trugstad Gård
2034 Holter
Telephone: 63 99 58 90
Telefax: 63 99 50 87
E-mail: restaurant@trugstad.no
Website: www.trugstad.no
1 room
2 beds

Bjerke Gård
Nordre Stranden
2608 Lillehammer
Telephone: 61 25 29 33
Telefax: 61 25 59 86
E-mail: post@bjerke-gaard.com
Website: www.bjerke-gaard.com
13 rooms
27 beds
By advance reservation only.

Kulturstua i Ro
Ruud Gård
2653 Vestre Gausdal
Telephone: 61 22 63 73
Mobil: 958 35 883
Telefax: 61 22 63 24
E-mail: kulturo@online.no
Website: www.gausdal.com/ro
www.gausdal.com/ro
1 room
8 beds
By advance reservation only.

GudbrandsGard Hotell
Postboks 203
2631 Ringebu
Telephone 61 28 48 00
Telefax: 61 28 48 01
E-mail: booking@gudbrandsgard.no
Website: www.gudbrandsgard.no
79 rooms
6 suites
180 beds

Kongsvold Fjeldstue
Dovrefjell
7340 Oppdal
Telephone: 72 40 43 40
Telefax: 72 40 43 41
E-mail: post@kongsvold.no
Website: www.kongsvold.no
32 rooms
74 beds

Uppigard Sulheim
2686 Lom
Telephone: 97025970
Telefax: 61 21 20 57
E-mail: post@sulheim.com
Website: www.sulheim.com
3 apartments
14 beds

Røisheim Hotel
2686 Lom
Telephone: 61 21 20 31
Telefax: 61 21 21 51
E-mail: r-drif-a@online.no
Website: www.roisheim.no
24 rooms
54 beds

Jotunheimen Fjellstue
2687 Bøverdalen
Telephone: 61 21 29 18
Telefax: 61 21 29 11
E-mail: mailto: info@jotunheimen-fjellstue.no
Website: www.jotunheimen-fjellstue.no
26 rooms
52 beds

Grotli Høyfjellshotel
2695 Grotli
telephone: 61 21 39 12
Telefax: 31 21 39 40
E-mail: post@grotli.no
Website: www.grotli.no
53 rooms
125 beds

Visnes Hotel
Prestestegen 3
6781 Stryn
Telephone: 57 87 10 87
Telefax: 57 87 20 75
E-mail: vibeke@visnes.no
Website: www.visnes.no
16 rooms
30 beds

Hotel Union Øye
6196 Norangsfjorden
Telephone: 70 06 21 00
Telefax: 70 06 21 1 6
E-mail: post@unionoye.no
Website: www.unionoye.no
26 rooms
52 beds

Gloppen Hotell
6823 Sandane
Telephone: 57 86 53 33
Telefax: 57 86 60 02
E-Mail: glopphot@vestdata.no
Website: www.gloppenhotel.no
40 rooms
75 beds

Selje Hotel & Spa Thalasso
6740 Selje
Telephone: 57 85 88 80
Telefax: 57 85 88 81
E-mail: post@seljehotel.no
Website: www.seljehotel.no
49 rooms
100 beds

Rica Sunnfjord Hotel
Storehagen 2
6800 Førde
Telephone: 57 83 40 00
Telefax: 57 83 40 01
E-mail: rica.sunnfjord.hotel@rica.no
Website: www.rica.no
153 rooms
4 suites
330 beds

Walaker Hotell
Gjestgivargarden
6879 Solvorn
Telephone: 57 68 20 80
Telefax: 57 68 20 81
E-mail: walaker.hotel.@.sf.telia.no
Website: www.dhh scandinavia.com
23 rooms
45 beds

Kvikne's Hotel
6898 Balestrand
Telephone: 57 69 42 00
Telefax: 57 69 42 01
E-mail: booking@kviknes.no
Website: www.kviknes.no
200 rooms
11 demi-suites
400 beds

Hardanger Gjestegard
Hardanger Gjestegard,
5778 Utne
Telephone: 53 66 67 10
Telefax: 53 66 66 66
E-mail: Hardg@online.no
2 rooms
6 apartments
24 beds

Hotel Ullensvang
5787 Lofthus i Hardanger
Telephone: 53 67 00 00
Telefax: 53 67 00 01
E-mail: ullensvang@hotel-ullensvang.no
Website: www.hotel-ullensvang.no
146 rooms
7 junior suites og 4 suites
312 beds

Sandven Hotel
Sandvenvegen 4
5600 Norheimsund
Sandven Hotel, Postboks 67,
5601 Norheimsund
Telephone: 56 55 20 88
Telefax: 56 55 26 88
E-mail: sandven@sandvenhotel.no
Website: www.sandvenhotel.no
29 rooms
6 suites
70 beds

Grand Hotel Terminus
Zander Kaaesgt. 6
Postboks 1100, Sentrum, 5809 Bergen
Telephone: 55 21 25 00
Telefax: 55 21 25 01
E-mail: booking@grand-hotel-terminus.no
Website: www. grand-hotel-terminus.no
131 rooms
5 suites
200 beds

Solstrand Fjord Hotel
5200 Os
Telephone: 56 57 11 00
Telefax: 56 57 11 20
Email: solstrand.fjord.hotell@online.no
Website: www.solstrand.com
90 rooms
45 junior suites and deluxe rooms
260 beds

Bjørnefjorden Gjestetun
5200 OS
Telephone: 56 30 40 00
Telefax: 56 30 04 01
e-mail: info@bjornefjordengjestetun.no
Website: www.bjornefjordengjestetun.no
40 rooms
90 beds

Kubbervik
5685 Uggdal
Telephone: 53 43 30 33
Mobile phone: 90677408
Telefax: 53 43 30 33
Email: mail@reddiken.no
Website: www.reddiken.no
6 rooms
25 beds
By advance reservation only.

Baroniet Rosendal
Postboks 235
5486 Rosendal
Telephone: 53 48 29 99
Telefax: 53 48 29 98
E-mail: info@baroniet.no
Website: www.baroniet.no
25 rooms
42 beds

Victoria Hotel
Skansegaten 1
P.O. Box 279
4001 Stavanger
Telephone: 51 86 70 00
Telefax: 51 86 70 00
E-mail: victoria@victoria-hotel.no
Website: www.victoria-hotel.no
104 rooms
3 suites
177 beds

Utstein Kloster
4156 Mosterøy
Telephone: 51 72 47 05
Telefax: 51 72 47 08
E-mail: utstein@online.no
Website: www.utstein-kloster.no
19 rooms
28 beds

GamlaVærket Gjæstgiveri og Tracteringssted
St. Olavsgate 38
4306 Sandnes
Telephone: 51 68 51 70
Telefax: 51 68 51 71
E-mail: post@gamlavaerket.no
Website: www.gamlavrk.no
27 rooms
1 suite
56 beds

Sogndalstrand Kulturhotell
Sogndalstrand
4380 Hauge i Dalane
Telephone: 51 47 72 550
Mobile phone: 41 43 77 44
Telefax: 51 47 62 52
E-mail: sogndalstrand@rl.telia.no
Website: www.sogndalstrand-kulturhotell.no
13 rooms
30 beds

Skipperhuset Seng & Mat
4432 Hidrasund
Telephone: 38 37 22 72
Telefax: 37 15 73 11/38 37 22 72
7 rooms
17 beds

Holmen Gård
4980 Gjerstad
Telephone: 37 15 70 20
Telefax: 37 15 73 11
E-mail: holmengaard@husflid.no
Website: www.husflid.no
18 rooms
33 beds

LifjellStua
3800 Bø i Telemark
Telephone: 35 95 33 80
Telefax: 35 95 33 67
E-mail: lifjellstua@lifjellstua.no
Website: www.lifjellstua.no
20 rooms
52 beds

Austbø Hotel
3864 Rauland
Telephone: 35 07 34 25
Telefax: 35 07 31 06
E-mail: austboh@online.no
Website: www.rauland.org/austbo
36 rooms
60 beds

Tuddal Høyfjellshotel
3697 Tuddal
Telephone: 35 02 88 88
Telefax: 35 02 88 89
E-mail: gurholt@tuddal.no
Website: www.tuddal.no
23 rooms
50 beds

Engø gård
Gamle Engø vei 25
3145 Tjøme
Telephone: 33 39 00 48
Telefax: 33 39 00 45
E-mail: betilling@engo.no
Website: www.engo.no
5 rooms
7 suites
24 beds

Harahorn
3650 Hemsedal
Telephone: 32 06 23 80
Telefax: 32 06 23 81
Email: booking@harahorn.no
Website: www.harahorn.no
31 rooms, 4 attic rooms
77 beds

Kleivstua
Dronningveien
3531 Krokkleiva
Telephone: 32 16 14 00
Telefax: 32 16 14 01
E-mail: booking@kleivstua.no
Website: www.kleivstua.no
23 rooms
50 beds

"The Really Good Life"
is a network of beautiful and unique places to spend
the night. This network is owned by Knut Kloster Jr.
and consists of the following places:

Balaklava in Fredrikstad Old Town
Kleivstua at Krokskogen
Bjørnsgard alongside Bogstad Lake in Oslo
Bøisheim Hotel in Bøverdalen
Harahorn in Hemsedal
Skagen Gård in Saltstraumen near Bodø
Stamsund Skjærbrygge in Lofoten
Nyvågar Rorbuanlegg in Lofoten
Kabelvåg Hotel in Lofoten
Henningsvær Bryggehotell in Lofoten

Each of these places is unique, but Kloster Jr. has also
made sure that they share the following:

-first class personal service
-an excellent kitchen and wine cellar
-beautiful and interesting setting
-built in an old, traditional style
-tasteful interiors
-a story to tell

Recipe Index

All recipes serve four unless otherwise indicated.
Follow the measurements either in metric or imperial: gram/deciliter or ounce/cup. Do not combine the two systems in the same recipe.